P9-BBO-258

TONIGHT WE BOMBED THE U.S. CAPITOL

The Explosive Story of M19, America's First Female Terrorist Group

WILLIAM ROSENAU

ATRIA BOOKS

NEW YORK · LONDON · TORONTO · SYDNEY · NEW DELHI

ATRIA
BOOKS

An Imprint of Simon & Schuster, Inc.
1230 Avenue of the Americas
New York, NY 10020

Copyright © 2019 by William Rosenau

All rights reserved, including the right to reproduce this book or portions thereof in any form whatsoever. For information, address Atria Books Subsidiary Rights Department, 1230 Avenue of the Americas, New York, NY 10020.

First Atria Books hardcover edition August 2019

ATRIA BOOKS and colophon are trademarks of Simon & Schuster, Inc.

All images courtesy the author except: Pages 28, 30, 124: AP Images; Page 41: Getty Images/Bettmann; Page 64: The Courtroom Sketches of Ida Libby Dengrove, University of Virginia Law School; Pages 71, 212, 240: Alan Berkman Papers, Archives & Special Collections, Columbia University Health Sciences Library; Page 244: Susan Rosenberg Papers, Sophia Smith Collection, Smith College, Northampton, MA

For information about special discounts for bulk purchases, please contact Simon & Schuster Special Sales at 1-866-506-1949 or business@simonandschuster.com.

The Simon & Schuster Speakers Bureau can bring authors to your live event. For more information or to book an event, contact the Simon & Schuster Speakers Bureau at 1-866-248-3049 or visit our website at www.simonspeakers.com.

Interior design by Dana Sloan

Manufactured in the United States of America

1 3 5 7 9 10 8 6 4 2

Library of Congress Cataloging-in-Publication Data

Names: Rosenau, William, author.
Title: Tonight we bombed the U.S. Capitol : the explosive story of M19, America's first female terrorist group / William Rosenau.
Description: New York : Atria Books, [2019] | Includes bibliographical references and index.
Identifiers: LCCN 2019014374 (print) | LCCN 2019016421 (ebook) | ISBN 9781501170140 (eBook) | ISBN 9781501170126 (hardcover) | ISBN 9781501170133 (pbk.)
Subjects: LCSH: May 19th Communist Organization. | Women terrorists—United States—History—20th century. | Domestic terrorism—United States—History—20th century.
Classification: LCC HV6432.5.M155 (ebook) | LCC HV6432.5.M155 R68 2019 (print) | DDC 363.325082/0973—dc23
LC record available at https://lccn.loc.gov/2019014374

ISBN 978-1-5011-7012-6
ISBN 978-1-5011-7014-0 (ebook)

For Annie and Hanes

El sueño de la razón

produce monstruos.

—Goya

CONTENTS

MAY 19TH MEMBERS AND ASSOCIATES

May 19th Communist Organization

Silvia Baraldini (born December 12, 1947), aka "Louise"

Alan Berkman (born September 4, 1945; died June 5, 2009), aka
"Leonard Cohen," "William Lunderman," "Kenneth Abrams,"
"David Levy"

Timothy Adolf Blunk (born May 21, 1957), aka "William Bassler,"
"William J. Hammond"

Donna Joan Borup (dates of birth used: August 5, 1952; March 5, 1947;
April 10, 1950), aka "Donna Austopchuk"

Marilyn Jean Buck (born December 13, 1947; died August 3, 2010), aka
"Delia Richards," "Louise Harmon," "Eve Mancuso," "Dee"

Judith Alice Clark (born November 23, 1949), aka "Alex"

Elizabeth "Betty Ann" Duke (born November 25, 1940), aka "Bess J.
Lunderman," "Loretta Polo," "Janice Adams"

Linda Sue Evans (born May 11, 1947), aka "Christine Porter," "Louise
Robinett," "Katherine Orloff," "Christine Johnson"

Susan Lisa Rosenberg (born October 5, 1955), aka "Elizabeth," "Barbara
Grodin," "Susan Knoll"

Laura Jane Whitehorn (born April 16, 1945), aka "Milagros Matese,"
"Anne Morrison"

"The Family"

Kuwasi Balagoon (formerly Donald Weems; born December 22, 1946;
died December 13, 1986), aka "Maroon"

Cecilio Ferguson (born November 16, 1946), aka "Chui"

Edward L. Joseph (born January 17, 1953), aka "Jamal Baltimore," "J.R."

Sekou Odinga (formerly Nathaniel Burns; born June 17, 1944), aka "Big Daddy"

Tyrone Q. Rison (born February 9, 1947), aka "Osedrick Lalupe," "Little Brother"

Mutulu Shakur (formerly Jeral Wayne Williams; born August 8, 1950), aka "Doc," "Donnell Jackson"

Mtayari Shabaka Sundiata (formerly Samuel Smith; born February 18, 1944; died October 23, 1981), aka "Sonny"

Others

Sundiata Acoli (formerly Clark Edward Squire; born January 14, 1937)

Kathy Boudin (born May 19, 1943)

David Gilbert (born October 6, 1944)

William Morales (born February 7, 1950), aka "Willie," "Guillermo"

Assata Shakur (formerly Joanne Deborah Chesimard; dates of birth used: July 16, 1947; August 19, 1952), aka "Sister Love," "Cleo"

PROLOGUE

WASHINGTON, DC, APRIL 26, 1983

The U.S. National War College occupies a chunk of riverside real estate at Fort Lesley J. McNair. Up-and-coming military officers, diplomats, and spies from all over the world compete for coveted slots at the school with its rich campus, complete with tennis courts, a bowling alley, and even a three-hole golf course. In 1982, it was also an open base. No mandatory ID checks, no X-ray scanners, no security waving wands across visiting backsides. Anyone who wasn't obviously deranged or disorderly could expect to stroll in, hassle free.

The young couple who walked onto campus the afternoon of April 26 didn't appear outwardly disturbed. Maybe the woman stepped a little gingerly, as though she were carrying something fragile in her bulky purse, but they set off no alarms among the military personnel who they most likely passed as they headed toward Roosevelt Hall, a hulking granite-and-brick building named after the twenty-sixth U.S. president.

The intentionally ordinary couple walked up to the front of the building. Their compatriots who had scoped out the place on a reconnaissance run had mentioned a large concrete planter just outside the front door. The planter was more than big enough for the bomb that was in the woman's purse.

The raw materials for the bomb were simple enough; the whole rig fit compactly in a purse.

The bomb had been built using stolen Hercules Unigel Tamptite dynamite, a Dupont blasting cap, and a Westclox pocket watch used as a timer that was set to detonate later that night.

At 9:45 p.m., a faint voice, probably prerecorded, called the Pentagon and United Press International, lashed out about events in Central America, the military, and U.S. imperialism, and warned that an explosion would be coming in fifteen minutes.

The blast blew out windows in Roosevelt Hall and sent Fort McNair into lockdown mode. Nobody was hurt, but no one was meant to be. Rather, the bomb was intended to deliver a thunderous message.

A group calling itself the Armed Resistance Unit, or ARU, took credit for the Roosevelt Hall attack. Shortly after the operation, the ARU issued "Communiqué No. 1," which announced that the bombing was carried out to support the liberation movements fighting U.S.-backed regimes in Guatemala and El Salvador. "El Salvador will win," the ARU predicted. "Guatemala will win, the people of Latin America and the Caribbean will be free, U.S. imperialism will be defeated."

The ARU wasn't a band of foreign terrorists. These revolutionaries were homegrown, and, as the communiqué made clear, they were fervently committed to fighting U.S.-backed "war, fascism, and genocide."

"We inside the U.S. are in the belly of the beast," they wrote.[1]

The terrorists revisited the nation's capital later that year. On August 18, the Armed Resistance Unit struck at another military installation: a computer center at the Washington Navy Yard.[2] The FBI described the damage as massive. Then the ARU started plotting additional attacks—something that would strike at the heart of the American state.

They decided on the gigantic domed structure that dominates the DC landscape. An off-white symbol of imperialism and a building erected by slave laborers whose descendants lived nearby in Third World squalor. It would send a message that could not be ignored.

INTRODUCTION

I n 1981, President Ronald Reagan announced that it was "morning in America." He declared that the American dream wasn't over—far from it. But to achieve that dream, the United States needed to lower taxes, shrink the size of the federal government, and flex its military muscles abroad. Some called his program the Reagan Revolution.

Meanwhile, a tiny band of American-born, well-educated extremists were working for a very different kind of revolution. They'd spent their entire adult lives embroiled in political struggles: protesting against the Vietnam War, fighting for black, Puerto Rican, and Native American liberation, and fighting against what they called U.S. "imperialism"—that is, U.S. military aggression, political domination, and economic exploitation, particularly in the Third World.

Many of them had been close to, or involved in, the violent far-left scene during the late 1960s and early 1970s. They were part of the so-called Generation of 1968, a worldwide cohort that embraced drugs, sex, rock music, and revolutionary politics with equal enthusiasm. "In the 1970s, a militant revolutionary ethos took hold in a substantial part of the American counterculture," wrote journalist Jeffrey Toobin.

"To a degree that is almost unimaginable today, the bomb became a common mode of American political expression."[1]

The Weather Underground Organization was among the most notorious elements in this extremist scene. An offshoot of Students for a Democratic Society (SDS)—possibly the largest left-wing student group in U.S. history—the Weather Underground, inspired by Third World revolutionaries, sought to foment domestic insurrection and confront U.S. imperialism from the inside, and with force. In an early manifesto, Weather declared that "We are within the heartland of a world-wide monster, a country so rich from its world-wide plunder that even the crumbs doled out to the enslaved masses within its borders provide for material existence very much above the conditions of the masses of people of the world."[2] What was needed, Weather said, was the "destruction of US imperialism and the achievement of a classless world: world communism."*

"We're tired of tiptoeing up to society and asking for reform," said Bill Ayers, a leader of the Weatherman faction. "We're ready to kick it in the balls."[3] By the mid-1970s, Weather had taken credit for dozens of bombings of government and corporate buildings.

Women were part of Weather—they were founders, they were members of its ruling Central Committee (also known as the "Weather Bureau"), and they were cadres in its underground cells. But while the group supported women's liberation in theory, Weather's largely male leadership was different in practice. The group's "Smash Monogamy" campaign, ostensibly designed to shatter repressive sexual paradigms, created new opportunities for male erotic aggression and domination.

---

* The title of the manifesto, "You Don't Need a Weatherman to Know Which Way the Wind Blows" (1969), was taken from Bob Dylan's 1965 folk-rock megahit, "Subterranean Homesick Blues." Inside SDS, the Weather faction quickly earned a reputation for bellicosity, fanaticism, and strutting self-regard. The SDS chapter at the University of Wisconsin lashed back, declaring that "you don't need a rectal thermometer to know who the assholes are."

Weather Bureau member Mark Rudd, a leader of the SDS uprising at Columbia University in 1968, confessed in his memoirs that the campaign "meant freedom to approach any woman in any collective. And I was rarely turned down, such was the aura and power of my leadership position."[4]

Members were often subjected to hours-long "criticism/self-criticism" sessions, and these blistering collective critiques were often directed at women who Weather males saw as particularly headstrong and independent. Susan Stern, a former Weather member, recalled a five-hour session in which she was charged with being "individualistic, egotistical, self-centered, power-hungry, manipulative, monogamous, dope-crazed, sexually perverted, dishonest, counterrevolutionary and arrogant."[5] Weather took a hard line on motherhood—women who appeared overly devoted to their babies were reprimanded for a purported lack of revolutionary commitment. And in some cases, children were taken from their mothers and given to other members of the group so they could refocus their energies on the cause.[6]

• • •

By the late 1970s, Weather was defunct. Most of the leadership, exhausted from nearly a decade on the run, surfaced from the underground, and those wanted on criminal charges surrendered to the authorities. Ultimately, Weather's clandestine enterprise had been a failure, wrote the journalist Bryan Burrough. The group had "failed to lead the radical left over the barricades into armed underground struggle; failed to fight or support the black militants they championed; failed to force agencies of the American 'ruling class' into a single change more significant than the spread of metal detectors and guard dogs."[7]

Many other Vietnam-era radicals also called it quits and returned to graduate school, started careers, and reentered ordinary American life. One left-wing militant observed that a lot of her comrades "had already stopped being active or said they wanted to check out doing other kinds of (non-revolutionary) political work. To me it looked like that choice led to becoming 'yuppies,' professionals and arm-chair activists."[8]

But pockets of militancy remained. In certain parts of New York, the Bay Area of California, Chicago, and Austin, Texas, a revolutionary sensibility "still smoldered and sparked," as one participant recalled.[9]

One of these militants characterized herself as "totally and profoundly influenced by the revolutionary movements of the sixties and seventies."[10] The Weather Underground was gone, but she and just a few others vowed to continue the struggle and to do so by any means necessary.

"We lived in a country that loved violence," she said. "We had to meet it on its own terms."[11]

In 1978, some of the militants created a new organization to wage a war against imperialism, racism, and fascism. They derived the group's name from the birthday shared by two of their ideological idols, Malcolm X and Ho Chi Minh: the May 19th Communist Organization.

May 19th was unique—unlike any other American terrorist group before or since. May 19th was created and led by women. Women picked the targets, women did the planning, and women made and planted the bombs. They'd created a new sisterhood of the bomb and gun.

To outsiders, these people must have seemed like ideological robots programmed for permanent rebellion. Like ghosts visiting from the past—unfriendly reminders of the ferocious struggles that had threatened to tear the country apart in the late 1960s and early 1970s.

May 19th certainly didn't see itself that way. Its members weren't automata, relics, or spooks but agents of history willing to sacrifice everything to transform the world. May 19th members prided themselves on their psychological toughness, analytical rigor, and lack of sentimentality. They were intellectuals but also warriors, with the purported science of Marxism-Leninism serving as their infallible guide. As Marxist-Leninists, they believed that men and women could bend the arc of history and usher in a new world free of injustice and oppression.

Their vision of what this heaven on earth would look like was hazy, but one thing was certain: creating it would require nothing less than violent revolution. This vagueness about ultimate objectives is typical among terrorists. As Georgetown University's Bruce Hoffman argued, groups as varied as al-Qaeda and the Red Army Faction "live in the future they are chasing after, [but] they have only a very vague conception of what exactly that future might entail."[12]*

May 19th had much in common with other ideological extremists. In her book *True Believer: Stalin's Last American Spy*, the author Kati Marton wrote that Soviet agent Noel Field's "commitment and his submission to his cause were as total, and ultimately as destructive, as those of today's ISIS recruits." Ideologies—whether communist, fascist, nationalist, or jihadist—can offer the promise of what Marton calls "a final correction of all personal, social, and political injustices."[13] For the captured minds of May 19th, their variant of Marxism-Leninism

---

* The Rote Armee Fraktion (Red Army Faction, or RAF) was a far-left terrorist group founded in West Germany in 1970. During the next twenty-nine years, the RAF robbed banks, bombed military installations, murdered policemen and U.S. soldiers, and in 1979, attempted to assassinate NATO commander and future U.S. secretary of state General Alexander Haig. The group, whose first generation was labeled the "Baader-Meinhof Gang," dissolved not long after the fall of the Berlin Wall in 1989, declaring, "The revolution says: I was, I am, I will be again."

was a pathway to total liberation. As another of their ideological he-roes, Fidel Castro, said in 1961, *"Dentro de la revolución, todo; contra la revolución, nada"* ("Inside the revolution, everything; against the revo-lution, nothing").

· · ·

Most of the members of the group were self-described lesbians, and they were feminists, but they weren't part of the bourgeois women's liberation scene represented by Betty Friedan, Gloria Steinem, and the National Organization for Women. Pay equity, day care, abortion rights—all well and good, but in May 19th's view, they were secondary to the real struggle at hand.

During the 1970s, some radical feminists insisted that "testoster-one poisoning" had saturated American life. Total separation from "parasitic male mutants," as one writer put it, was the only way to es-cape systemic male domination, violence, and aggression.[14] "This is the year to stamp out the 'Y' chromosome," one lesbian collective in-sisted in 1973.[15]

Thousands of women built penis-free enclaves in cities around the country—the Gutter Dykes in San Francisco; the Furies in Washing-ton, DC; and C.L.I.T. (Collective Lesbian International Terrors) in New York. The Van Dykes, a peripatetic band of motorized vegans, roamed southwestern highways in search of an imagined "Womyn's Land." Lamar Van Dyke, the group's founder, was "a kind of lesbian Joseph Smith," who, like the founder of Mormonism, traveled with an entou-rage of "wives and ex-wives and future wives in tow."[16] In New York, the Radicalesbians collective—known originally as Lavender Men-ace, a name chosen in reaction to Betty Friedan's remark that lesbi-ans were a "lavender menace" that threatened the women's liberation movement—declared, "A lesbian is the rage of all women condensed to the point of explosion."[17]

The women of May 19th couldn't have agreed more. But for them, "explosion" wasn't just a metaphor. They channeled their fury into violent insurrection. They took in the words of Leila Khaled, a member of the Popular Front for the Liberation of Palestine (and a purported Audrey Hepburn look-alike), who became a global revolutionary icon after her participation in an August 1969 airline hijacking.[18] "We act heroically in a cowardly world to prove that the enemy is not invincible," she declared. "We act 'violently' in order to blow the wax out of the ears of deaf Western liberals and to remove the straws that block their vision. We act as revolutionaries to inspire the masses and to trigger off the revolutionary upheaval in an era of counterrevolution."[19]

. . .

May 19th hated sexism, chauvinism, and misogyny, but its members weren't interested in the crunchy, women-only lifestyle embraced by the separatists. As one woman close to May 19th explained, "I think it was a reaction to . . . lesbian separatism, and being like, oh, if we just go back to our own land, and leave men out of our lives, then everything will be fine, and we can just wear our Birkenstocks, and have our women-only spaces, and live our own lives."[20]

For May 19th, revolutionary politics came first. Sexual oppression, capitalism, racism, imperialism—all of that horror went together. Lesbian liberation required national liberation.

Men would be allowed to join the struggle, provided they were tuned in to the correct ideological frequency. Men could be useful in all kinds of ways—one male member even donated his sperm to a female comrade who wanted to have children. But they had to know their place and be alert to and fight against any sexist or homophobic proclivities.

. . .

In 1979, just after May 19th's founding, the Talking Heads released "Life During Wartime." Reportedly inspired by accounts of terrorist groups such as the Red Army Faction and the Symbionese Liberation Army, the song is a driving, hallucinatory first-person chronicle of a hunted, unnamed figure moving through an unspecified underground realm: "Heard of a van that is loaded with weapons/Packed up and ready to go."

May 19th lived the band's lyrics, and in real time.

Terrorism is necessarily a secretive undertaking. Even minimally competent groups will do everything they can to conceal their underground activities from outsiders, understandably fearing that breaches in security will expose them to the repressive forces of the state. In their own minds, they're at war, and they work to maintain a warlike footing and focus. Ingrained habits of conspiracy tend to persist long after the "armed struggle" is over. Former terrorists tend to carry their deepest secrets to the grave.

Defining terrorism is something of a parlor game among specialists, with nearly every expert offering his or her own variation. The definition put forth by Georgia State University's John Horgan seems as good as any: "Terrorism is a strategy used to instill fear. It's a form of psychological warfare that uses violence or the threat of violence to create some social, political, or religious change. Terrorist violence, as opposed to other types of violence, is distinguishable because it serves a bigger picture."[21] For stylistic reasons, I use *terrorism* and *violent extremism* interchangeably.

Former Weatherman Bill Ayers's memoir, *Fugitive Days*, clocked in at nearly three hundred pages. Yet Ayers provided relatively few operational details about Weather's terrorist campaign, which had ended twenty-five years before his book was published. Any reader hoping to learn more about who was involved in Weather's scores of bombings, how the explosive devices were made, and how their attacks were planned and carried out, will almost certainly be disappointed. (Unfortunately for Ayers, his publication date coincided with the attacks of September 11, 2001, which overnight essentially eliminated the possibility that a memoir by a retired terrorist would find a large sympathetic readership.)

As Ayers wrote at the beginning of his book, there is "a necessary incompleteness here, a covering over of facts and a blurring of details which is in part an artifact of those fugitive days. . . . Most names and places have been changed, many identities altered, and the fingerprints wiped away."[22]

What explains Ayers's guarded approach? Perhaps his time underground really was a blur, and he was unable to reconstruct events with any fidelity. Alternatively, Ayers might have been worried that being too forthright might somehow open him up (or his former comrades) to prosecution for some still-unsolved Weather bombings. Or perhaps he's simply maintaining the discipline of a revolutionary, and the habits of conspiracy.

Despite the reticence of those who've engaged in political violence, it's still possible to draw back the curtain and reveal the inner workings of a terrorist group, and to tell, at least in part, the story that former members would rather see remained buried.

Trained as a historian of the Cold War, I first came across the May 19th Communist Organization while working as a terrorism researcher at the RAND Corporation, arguably the nation's preeminent defense think tank. Later at CNA, another government-funded research and analysis center, I had the opportunity to write about homegrown terrorist groups, including May 19th. The United States was in the midst of fighting what President George W. Bush had called the "global war on terror," or GWOT, and I was interested in the roots of counterterrorism. I discovered that during the 1970s and 1980s, the United States had waged an earlier "war on terror" against violent domestic extremists, and it was during that period that the government created many of the counterterrorism tools and approaches that continue to be used today.

During the course of my research for this book I was fortunate to spend considerable time with retired Federal Bureau of Investigation special agents who worked on cases involving May 19th. These individuals were generous, patient, and full of considerable insights.

Former members of May 19th, on the other hand, chose not to participate. Emails, letters, telephone calls, and entreaties through third parties went unanswered, with one exception. A former member, who served more than a decade in prison on terrorism-related charges, gave a terse but somewhat wry response to my interview request: "Having read your biography, what in the world makes you think I'd ever speak with you?"

Why indeed? Perhaps they feared that talking with me would reveal information that could expose them, or others, to prosecution, or that giving an interview would somehow fuel anti–left wing forces at work in American society. More simply, perhaps they concluded that they had nothing to gain from participating in research for this book.

Fortunately, I uncovered many other major sources of information on May 19th. The papers of group members are in the Sophia Smith Collection at Smith College and at the Columbia University Medical Center Archives and Special Collections, and include a wealth of material, such as unpublished autobiographies, diaries, and letters and other communications.

Court records were another invaluable source. For reasons that are unclear (to me at least), terrorism researchers have made scant use of legal documents, despite the amount and quality of otherwise unavailable information they can contain.

At U.S. district courts in New York and Washington, and at the federal records centers in Philadelphia and suburban Boston, I unearthed affidavits, sentencing memoranda, motions by the defense and prosecution, photographs and documents entered into evidence, transcripts, and even wiretap transcriptions and grand jury testimony. May 19th members put things down on paper, including surveillance notes, aliases, and operational assessments of their attacks, much if not all of which wound up in the hands of prosecutors and the courts.

The thousands of pages of once-secret FBI and other U.S. government files released to me under the Freedom of Information Act provided information on the pursuit of May 19th, the history and development of the group, as well as the relationship between May 19th and the revolutionary firmament of the 1960s, 1970s, and 1980s. Like any other records, public or private, these documents need to be treated with the proper degree of skepticism and caution. Names of living persons were redacted, as were the names of some sources and interview subjects. But when analyzed together with other sources, and with an understanding of U.S. law enforcement history, procedure, and culture, these files were invaluable.

Contemporaneous press reports, including in-depth accounts of criminal episodes involving May 19th and the manifestos and other material produced by the group, helped flesh out the story. Once behind bars, May 19th members often spoke to journalists they considered sympathetic, and although these interviews are larded with political rhetoric and sloganeering, they also contain some useful nuggets of personal information.

In the writing of this book, I have tried to reach the high standard set by Charles Nicholl, the author of a gripping historical and philosophical investigation into the murder of Christopher Marlowe, the enigmatic and ultimately unknowable Elizabethan playwright and spy: "I have not invented anything . . . this story is as true as I can make it."[23]

. . .

Typically, Americans see terrorism as something alien, foreign, and rare. But violent political extremism is woven deeply into our history. Consider the ethnic cleansing of Native Americans from the sixteenth through the nineteenth centuries; the counterrevolutionary terrorism carried out by white southerners during the era of Reconstruction; violent acts committed by (or attributed to) anarchists, including the bombing outside J. P. Morgan's bank in lower Manhattan on September 16, 1920, that killed thirty-nine people and wounded hundreds of others—"the day Wall Street exploded," Yale historian Beverly Gage called it.*

And sedition and armed insurrection by white supremacists during the 1970s, 1980s, and 1990s, which culminated in the bombing of the Alfred P. Murrah Federal Building in Oklahoma City on the morning of April 19, 1995, killed 168 people (including 19 children) and injured hundreds.

---

* The blast erupted from a horse-drawn wagon packed with dynamite—an early example of what would become known nine decades later in Iraq and elsewhere as a vehicle-borne improvised explosive device, or IED. Beverly Gage, *The Day Wall Street Exploded: A Story of America in Its First Age of Terror* (New York: Oxford University Press, 2010).

The U.S. government defines "domestic terrorist" acts as those that "occur primarily within the territorial jurisdiction of the United States."[24] "Homegrown" terrorism has its own definitions. The journalist and counterterrorism expert Peter Bergen, in an article written just after the June 12, 2016, Orlando nightclub massacre, noted that "every lethal terrorist attack in the United States in the past decade and a half has been carried out by American citizens or legal permanent residents, operating either as lone wolves or in pairs, who have no formal connections or training from foreign terrorist organizations." In other words, these attacks were by homegrown terrorists.[25]

The women of May 19th were part of a generation of violent left-wing militancy in the United States that stretched from the 1960s into the 1980s. Uncovering the history of the group can help us understand how and why a tiny band of Americans decided to wage a war against their own country.

That history isn't likely to produce tidy "lessons" about how such terrorism can be prevented, but it can help us understand the circumstances and contexts from which homegrown domestic terror emerged, and make us better prepared to grapple with the violent political extremism that remains part of the American landscape. After all, as the Black Power militant H. Rap Brown said in 1967, "violence is as American as cherry pie."

PART ONE

A NEW SISTERHOOD, 1978–1983

1

KEEPERS OF THE FLAME

. . . our dreams
will be the shell casings
that pierce the enemy
as our love, and resistance
continue.

—Susan Rosenberg, "Compañera"

(Fall 1986)[1]

NEW YORK, 1979

There is no record of the founding of May 19th. The closest thing to a formal beginning was a fiery manifesto the nascent group issued in 1979: "The Principles of Unity of the May 19th Communist Organization." Their creed was "revolutionary anti-imperialism," and like other millenarians, they wrapped their faith in reason. "Our science is Marxism-Leninism," they wrote.[2]

The United States, according to May 19th, was the ultimate "white oppressor nation," a "parasite on the Third World," a poisonous spider at the center of a noxious global web.

May 19th believed that national liberation wasn't just an international challenge: the United States had its own internal colonies filled with blacks, American Indians, and Puerto Ricans, who were just as ruthlessly exploited as the denizens of any sweltering tropical dictatorship. And it wasn't just racial minorities who were subjugated. The oppression of women in general, and lesbians in particular, was another symptom of a national sickness. Imperialism, capitalism, and racism were strong, but still, May 19th saw some hopeful signs. They heard revolutionary rumblings inside the guts of the American monster and detected systemic weaknesses that were ready to be exploited.

May 19th insisted that the "oppressed nations within the U.S. are preparing themselves to wage a full-scale people's war against the enemy that has entered its final decline."[3] The women offered apocalyptic visions and end-time prophesies: a "much more brutal fascist regime," the liberation of captive peoples, and the destruction of the United States.[4]

How could their tiny band of middle-class intellectuals contribute to the global struggle, and bend the arc of history to speed up the destruction of the "parasite" nation? One of their lawyers later described the women as "Revolutionaries. Dreamers. Lovers of Freedom. . . . Some are lesbians. All love women, people fighting everywhere for self-determination and dignity."[5]

But ushering in the new world required more than just good intentions and beautiful dreams. Mao Zedong had made that point back in 1927 when the Chinese Communist Party had been fighting for power. The revolution, Mao said, "is not a dinner party, or writing an essay, or painting a picture, or doing embroidery; it cannot be so refined, so leisurely and gentle, so temperate, kind, courteous, restrained and magnanimous. A revolution is an insurrection, an act of violence by which one class overthrows another."[6]

According to May 19th's analysis, the ruling class would never give up peacefully, and May 19th, one member said later, wanted to "ensure that all the shooting didn't come from one side."[7]

May 19th said that the First World mass movements of the 1960s had taken a wrong turn. Instead of doing all they could to support national liberation struggles in places such as Vietnam, South Africa, and Palestine, sixties radicals thought they were leading a global revolution. May 19th pledged to avoid that mistake. They vowed to shed their "white-skin privilege" and work as "North American anti-imperialists" under the leadership of black and brown people. "We, white women, say *NO* to amerika where white is a badge of acceptance of daily murder," they declared.[8]

May 19th didn't immediately reach for bombs and guns. They started off with nonviolent agitation and propaganda: demonstrations, picketing, speeches, film screenings, and politically informed graphic art. May 19th had a number of affiliated groups that promoted its agenda and served as recruitment pools.* The all-women Madame Binh Graphics Collective pumped out propaganda posters. Other affiliated groups raised funds for Robert Mugabe's wing of the Zimbabwe African National Union, a guerrilla movement fighting to end white minority rule in Rhodesia. They raised hell about imprisoned Puerto Ricans they called "freedom fighters." There was an "everlasting spiral of activity, urgency, and exhaustion," former May 19th member Mary Patten recalled.[9]

Two women were the heart and soul of the new formation. Although a decade apart in age, they had much in common: a solidly middle-class New York upbringing, early ideological commitment, ed-

---

* The FBI, among others, sometimes referred to these as "front groups," that is, nominally independent organizations with little or no apparent link to May 19th.

ucation at elite institutions—and an unwavering dedication to revolution, new values, and sexual self-actualization. Judy and Susan: sisters in arms.

· · ·

Judith Alice Clark was born to Joseph and Ruth Clark in New York on November 23, 1949. She described her childhood as happy, but it was an unusual upbringing, at least in her early years.

As a young man in Brooklyn, Joe had been a member of a Marxist-Leninist microsect that had followed the Bolshevik leader Leon Trotsky into anti-Stalinism.

Later, Joe concluded that Trotsky and his worshippers had been all wrong. Comrade Joseph Stalin, not Trotsky, was the true communist godhead. Joe switched sides and joined the Moscow-dominated Communist Party USA. He rose quickly through the Party's ranks, and before long he was a full-time high-level Party functionary, and an editor of the Party's newspaper, the *Daily Worker*.

Unsurprisingly, FBI Red hunters kept tabs on the Clarks. They had a sense they were being watched, but it didn't rattle them—they were on the right side of history, after all. Stalin's Soviet Union was their alpha and omega. They were utopians, like Tillie Olsen, a true-believing American poet who wrote in 1934 that the Soviet Union was "a heaven . . . brought down to earth in Russia." [10]

In 1950, Joe got to see his revolution's control center firsthand. He moved Ruth, their son, Andrew, and baby Judy to Moscow, where he took up a position as a *Daily Worker* correspondent. The relocation represented a remarkable devotion to the communist cause, given the harsh conditions that prevailed in the Soviet capital and the anti-communist sentiment that saturated postwar America.

After a three-year stint, the Clarks returned to New York, and Joe and Ruth continued their Party work. The family lived in Brooklyn: first in Bensonhurst and then in solidly lower-middle-class Flatbush. In the summer they would often go out to Mohegan Lake in Westchester County, where there was a colony of fellow communists. The folk singer Pete Seeger, a supporter of the Communist Party, made occasional appearances at lakeside hootenannies. Those annual excursions to the cozy summer community reinforced social bonds among Party members—being a communist meant total commitment.

But by the mid-1950s, Ruth and Joe had growing doubts about the communist cause. Even as pampered guests of the USSR, they had seen the pockmarked face of Stalinism up close. As with many other Party members around the world, the bloody Soviet suppression of a nationwide uprising in Hungary in 1956, and Soviet premier Nikita Khrushchev's "secret" speech in 1957 denouncing Stalin's crimes, forced the Clarks to reassess their slavish devotion to Moscow.

Ruth's Party-related activities dropped off, and in 1957, Joe finally checked out of the Party. There were repercussions: former comrades denounced him as a "deserter" and "liquidationist," [11] and it was tough for him to find work. Being a former Communist Party member, *Daily Worker* editor, and onetime Moscow resident was not exactly a formula for success in late-1950s America. But he managed to eke out a living at the Direct Mail Envelope Company and then at the American Cancer Society. Ruth helped support the family with odd jobs, including door-to-door interviewing for Trix cereal.

Although only a pre-teenager, Judy was developing a political consciousness, and she didn't like her parents' growing anticommunism. Weaned on Marxism-Leninism, she was a classic "red-diaper baby," who'd loved the Party's warm embrace. "Until I was about eight years old," she recalled, "I had lived in a home and in an extended 'Party family' that encouraged important ideals, like tolerance of diversity in the world; awareness of history, of racism, of other forms of injustice." [12] That all got yanked away. "I couldn't bear the loss of community and ideology and purposefulness in my life." [13]

According to Judy, Ruth turned rightward, trying to bring the family into the American mainstream. She was "getting more and more into wanting her family to be like from *Father Knows Best*." [14] But unlike the stereotypical 1950s mother, Ruth pursued a serious career. By the 1970s, she was a senior executive at Daniel Yankelovich's polling firm and the de facto inventor of the exit poll.[15]

Joe remained a man of the left, a socialist, but a staunch anti-communist and opponent of Stalinism. He was a cofounder of *Dissent* magazine, a lone voice of democratic socialism in midcentury America. In pungent prose, Joe attacked Stalinism, communism, and Fidel Castro, the tropical Spartacus, whose unfolding revolution in Cuba displayed a "distinctive, often mad character." [16]

•   •   •

Judy, however, kept the far-left faith. "I would be the 'keeper of the flame' in my family," she recalled.[17] By the time she was fifteen, she was politically active in her own right: she marched on a Congress of Racial Equality picket line outside a Woolworth's lunch counter in Queens. "I was always drawn to the most militant groups," she said. "And if the group I was in wasn't radical enough, I would push at the edge." [18]

Judy attended the academically rigorous Midwood High School in Brooklyn,[19] then the University of Chicago, where she joined Students for a Democratic Society. Agitation was part of the on-campus zeitgeist, and in January 1969, she and hundreds of other students occupied an administration building, demanding the rehiring of a sociology professor denied tenure and insisting on a permanent student voice in the faculty-hiring process.

The university's president, Edward H. Levi—whose diminutive frame, low-key manner, and modest lifestyle belied a formidable persona—weighed his options. He could have followed the lead of his Columbia University counterpart, Grayson Kirk, who had faced a similar challenge the year before. Kirk had called in the police, who'd kicked out the protestors and restored a semblance of order. But Levi was a shrewder character than Kirk: cops meant cracked skulls, bad press, and more anguish for his beloved university. Levi decided to wait it out, and sure enough, after two weeks, the militants voted to leave the building.

After the demonstration, the university disciplinary committee voted to expel forty-two protestors, including Judy. Though she and her father had bitter ideological differences (thirty years later, she wrote that he had subjected her to his "fits of fury and political harangues"), Joe was a loving man who wanted to help his only daughter.[20] He asked Irving Howe, *Dissent*'s coeditor, to reach out to the novelist Saul Bellow, who had deep Chicago ties. Bellow intervened with Levi, asking him to please give the Clark girl a second chance.

"No. She's a bad one," the university president said.[21] Judy was out.

No matter. By now she was a self-described revolutionary. "I felt that my parents had kind of failed, and so, if they failed, I had to do something different," Judy said in an interview in 2017. "I romanticized the revolutions going on around the world, and I sort of felt like I had to show I could do whatever was necessary."[22] Including violence.

As the Students for a Democratic Society self-destructed, Judy became part of what would become known as the Weather Underground. She lived in a collective of a dozen or so radicals—mostly women but led by men—and she was an enthusiastic part of violent Weather street

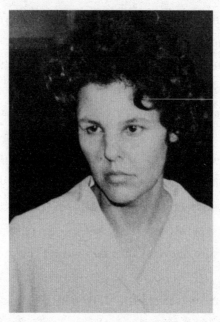

Judy Clark: A "red-diaper baby" who kept the faith

actions, including the notorious "Days of Rage" rampage on the streets of Chicago in 1969. On March 17, 1970, the feds issued a warrant for her arrest. The charge: interstate flight to avoid prosecution for "mob action." According to the FBI wanted poster that soon was hanging in post offices around the country, Judy was five feet, three inches tall, with brown hair and brown eyes and a medium build. And she had "sparkling eyes," according to one fellow activist's poetic tribute.[23]

Judy was on the run until December. Bureau men eventually nabbed her in New York at an Upper East Side movie house, where she was watching *Yellow Submarine*. She served nine months in the Cook County Jail, and after her release, she moved back in with her parents in Brooklyn.

Judy was eager to return to activism. She joined the Women's International Terrorist Conspiracy from Hell, or WITCH, a loosely connected feminist network founded in 1968 by the writer Robin Morgan and future Weather Underground member Naomi Jaffe. According to WITCH, men as such weren't the enemy. The true evil was late capitalism—corporations, consumerism, and commodification—as the group explained in a 1968 manifesto:

> *WITCH is a total concept, a new dimension of women. It means breaking the bond of woman as a biologically and sexually defined creature. It implies the destruction of passivity, consumerism and commodity fetishism. . . . Who is the enemy? WITCHes must name names, or rather we must name trademarks and brand names.*[24]

WITCH loved to put on a good spectacle—one Halloween, thirteen women dressed as witches went to lower Manhattan to "hex" the temple of modern capital, the New York Stock Exchange. WITCH also conducted what it called "invisible actions," such as the ex post facto "snuffing out" of Lurleen Wallace, the wife of Alabama governor George Wallace, who had succumbed to breast cancer in May 1968.[25]

During the mid-1970s, Judy edited *Midnight Special*, a publication for convicts sponsored by the far-left National Lawyers Guild. Her readers included Congressman Larry McDonald, a leader of the ultra-right John Birch Society known for his fanciful conspiracy mongering, his rabid commitment to fighting communism and subversion, and for his tenuous hold on reality. But the Georgia congressman stumbled upon the truth when he said in 1982 that *Midnight Special* "served as an inter-prison communications service by publishing messages from militant inmates and providing inflammatory accounts of prison strikes and disturbances."[26]

By the late 1970s, Judy had earned just about every radical creden-

Susan Rosenberg: Barnard dropout, acupuncturist,
"North American anti-imperialist"

tial. But the path of radicalism that lay ahead of her was likely beyond anything she imagined.

·   ·   ·

Susan Lisa Rosenberg was born in New York on October 5, 1955, the only child of Bella and Emanuel. Bella was a theatrical producer and Manny a kindly dentist who treated indigent patients at his clinic in Spanish Harlem.

Mr. and Mrs. Rosenberg were classic New York liberals. "We were always liberal, always into causes, taking part in Civil Rights demonstrations and anti-war marches," Manny recalled. "Susan asked to go with me even though she was only 11 or 12 at the time. I never pressured her."[27]

Susan's parents sent her to the private but progressive Walden School, not far from their Upper West Side apartment. Students were on a first-name basis with their teachers, no grades were handed out, and the school stressed personal expression over competition.[28] Susan was politically precocious and moving steadily to the left: in an eleventh-grade essay, she expressed a proto-Marxist notion when she wrote that "capitalist production does not begin or end with people's needs. It begins and ends with money."[29]

By age fourteen, she was a member of the High School Student Union, the youth branch of Students for a Democratic Society.[30] She was teargassed at an antiwar demonstration, and she started hanging out with the Black Panthers and their Puerto Rican analogue, the Young Lords.[31] Susan was part of a political demographic, summarized by one neoconservative scold as "liberal parents, radical children."[32]

Susan was an excellent student. Before her senior year, she was admitted to Barnard, entering in 1972. Her academic career flourished: in the back of a blue book, her English professor scribbled "very funny and perceptive exam." She got involved in the burgeoning women's liberation movement. A legendary professor of American history, James Shenton, ignited her interest in abolitionism and in the life of John Brown, the fiery white insurrectionist who believed that the evil of slavery could be ended only through armed rebellion. She also found inspiration in the revolutionary women of Vietnam. "I saw the women of Vietnam rise up as part of their nation to say, 'We're going to have our own destiny,'" she said in 1989. "I had never seen anything like that. And I wanted to be like that."[33]

Susan switched though from the well-heeled Barnard to the grittier City College of New York. Slender and with "magnetic green eyes" (as an interviewer later noted), Susan now coiffed her hair in an eye-popping foot-high Afro.[34]

In the mid-1970s, she doubled down on the revolution. She went to Cuba in 1976 as part of the Venceremos Brigade, an organization founded in 1969 by New Left *fidelistas* in solidarity with the Castro revolution.[35] Like other youthful leftists, Susan idealized Cuba and the bearded ex-guerrillas who were building socialism on the island. Venceremos participants cut sugarcane, smoked as many Havana cigars as they liked, and fraternized with Partido Comunista de Cuba dignitaries. If the North American pilgrims got lucky, Castro himself—the all-powerful Líder Máximo—might mingle and yuck it up with the visiting gringos.[36] Venceremos veterans typically returned from their island excursion even more dewy-eyed about Cuba's Marxist-Leninist experiment.

.   .   .

After she returned from Cuba, Susan found work as a drug counselor at the city-run Lincoln Hospital in the South Bronx. From its beginning in the early 1970s, conflict swirled around the hospital's drug treatment program, known as the Lincoln Detox Center. The program included an "acupuncture collective" run by Mutulu "Doc" Shakur (born Jeral Wayne Williams), who was close to the Black Panthers and the Young Lords.[37]

Shakur was also involved in the Republic of New Africa, or RNA, a pan-African revolutionary movement trying to carve out an independent black homeland from five states that made up the old "Black Belt" in the Deep South. The RNA saw itself as a state in being, complete with elected officials and its own "consulates" in cities such as New York, Washington, Chicago, and Los Angeles.[38] Their slogan: "Free the Land."

In 1970, RNA minister of defense Henry Hatches declared, "WE HAVE ENTERED THE ERA OF SELF-DEFENSE."[39] Mississippi attorney general A. F. Summer was apoplectic about the RNA. There was the whole "homeland" business, but much more troubling was the RNA's audacity to carry weapons in public—for people like Summer, the Second Amendment applied to whites only. There was an armed insurrection under way, Summer insisted. He appealed to the Nixon White House for help. Some functionary called over to the FBI.

The Bureau's boss, J. Edgar Hoover, hated black separatists and all other disrupters of the racial status quo, including nonviolent organizations such as the Southern Christian Leadership Conference. The Bureau called the RNA and the Panthers "black nationalist, hate-type organizations" and deemed them worthy of heavy surveillance, electronic eavesdropping, and aggressive counterintelligence measures designed to disrupt their operations.

The Bureau knew about Doc. Back in 1969 he'd spoken at length—and apparently wittingly—with an FBI special agent, telling the agent all about the RNA's convention in Detroit the previous year, when a local cop had been shot in a scuffle outside a church meeting hall.[40] Shakur said he'd told the Motor City cops that he had nothing to do with it, but they hauled him off to jail anyway. However, the police couldn't make anything stick, so he was released and soon he was back in Jamaica, Queens.

Shakur had a doctorate from an organization called the "Institut d'Acupuncture du Québec" in Montreal. His instructor, a Romanian refugee named Oscar Wexu, taught an acupuncture style the Chinese had used to fight the mass opium addiction that had come with British imperialism. In the Bronx, Doc touted the technique as a powerful nonchemical alternative to methadone, an opioid used to wean addicts off heroin, which was ravaging the South Bronx and other parts of the city. Methadone, Shakur and others claimed, was the poisonous fruit of an ongoing conspiracy to chemically enslave poor black and brown people. According to White Lightning, an organization of ex-addicts, "armies of slum-lords, script doctors, organized crime, greedy drug companies, methadone pushers, corrupt cops, and producers of rot-gut wine are plundering our communities."[41]

Susan learned acupuncture under Doc's tutelage and eventually earned a degree from the institute in Montreal. She was one of Doc's favorites, a youthful protégée who shared his medical interests as well as his political ideology.

Doc's agenda included more than getting ghetto residents off heroin; he also wanted to turn them into forces for the revolution. Toward that end, Shakur and his comrades handed out tracts such as "The Opium Trail: Heroin and Imperialism" and lectured drug-addled patients about the systemic political and social evils that underlay their addiction. National liberation in Africa was also a hot topic: Lincoln organized concerts and fund-raisers for the Zimbabwe African National Union, or ZANU.[42] Robert Mugabe, a leader of one of the movement's factions, would come to power in 1980.

Lincoln Detox started attracting attention, much of it unwanted. Lyndon LaRouche, the leader of an increasingly violent right-wing political cult, learned about the detox program from one of his followers who worked on the hospital's staff.

Like the left-wing acupuncturists at the South Bronx hospital, LaRouche believed there was a conspiracy afoot—but in his view, Lincoln Detox was a product, not a victim, of the master plan. He believed that the treatment program was part of an elaborate demonology that included the Central Intelligence Agency, Governor Nelson Rockefeller's political henchmen, the federal Law Enforcement Assistance Administration, and even the British royal family.

One of LaRouche's many obsessions was brainwashing, a technique he believed his enemies were using to create Manchurian Candidate–style automata programmed for political assassinations.

LaRouche personally handled the "deprogramming" of one hapless disciple suspected of being part of an assassination plot against him. A tape recording of the session captured sounds of sobbing, retching, and a sinister voice that issued a chilling command: "raise the voltage." [43]

According to LaRouche, Lincoln Detox had created legions of "ghetto zombies" poised to be exploited by his many perceived enemies on the left. Like Shakur and his comrades, LaRouche hated methadone, but for starkly different reasons. According to one LaRouche publication, white communities were under threat from gang members, "welfare loafer[s], and methadone-crazed dope fiend[s]." [44]

On May 15, 1974, members of a LaRouche group, the U.S. Labor Party, or USLP, held a press conference at the hospital to "expose" the sinister doings inside its walls. Predictably, a fight broke out. The USLP claimed that Lincoln Detox staff members "led a crowd of 50 zombies to attack the Labor Party organizers, shooting, stabbing and clubbing them." [45] Lincoln Detox personnel said they had merely been defending themselves against LaRouche's goon squad.

LaRouche and his underlings didn't succeed in shutting down the program. That came four years later, after Brooklyn democratic assemblyman (now U.S. senator) Charles E. Schumer, among others, accused Lincoln Detox of widespread waste and fraud, including no-show jobs, dubious expenditures, and "leakage" of methadone from the hospital's inventory. (Back in 1975, Lincoln Detox staffers had trashed the lower Manhattan offices of the city's Health and Hospitals Corporation after the agency threatened to cut the program's funding. Three years later, hospital administrators and city officials feared sabotage and more violence if they took any steps to rein in the program.)

But Shakur and his friends had gone too far. By now, mainstream opinion considered Lincoln Detox a taxpayer-funded playpen for left-wing lunatics. Mayor Ed Koch had had enough. He said that Shakur and his comrades had run Lincoln Detox like a Red reeducation center, with "Che Guevara as their patron saint, with his pictures all over the wall. It wasn't a hospital; it was a radical cell."[46] In November 1978, the mayor ordered city funding cut off and sent in the cops to shut the place down.

After Lincoln Detox shuttered, Susan moved with Shakur to his new enterprise, the Black Acupuncture Advisory Association of North America, or BAAANA, whose offices were on the second floor of Shakur's four-story brownstone at 245 West 139th Street in Harlem. Barbara Zeller, a medical doctor and activist, served as BAAANA's medical adviser. Her husband, Alan Berkman, also a physician, was another friend of Susan's from her stint at Lincoln Detox, and he dropped in from time to time. There were parties at the place, where Susan met black nationalists, assorted activists, and former Weatherpeople, including Judy. Lincoln Detox was a bust, but for Susan and the others, the struggle would continue, and their vehicle would be the May 19th Communist Organization.

2

CRACK THE FACADE

As May 19th coalesced, three other women became part of the group's core.

Silvia Baraldini was born into a well-to-do Italian family in Rome on December 12, 1947. Silvia's father was a brooding presence in the household. He'd spent seven years as a prisoner of war after being captured in Ethiopia, and the experience had scarred him mentally and physically. Still, Silvia and her sisters had a great childhood. "I lived a very privileged, protected life," she said.[1]

This pampered existence didn't last, though. There was some kind of reversal in the Baraldini family's fortunes, and when Silvia was twelve, they all left for the United States as economic migrants. There were a couple of tough years up in the Bronx and then a relocation to Washington. Silvia hated parochial school, and she persuaded her parents to send her to the local public high school, Woodrow Wilson, in northwest DC. She described herself as an outsider.

In 1965, Silvia enrolled at the University of Wisconsin–Madison, an emerging center of student radicalism. She was antiwar, antiracist, a part of what was called "the movement." She joined Students for a Democratic Society, and she heard Black Panther Party deputy chairman Fred Hampton speak on campus. After Chicago cops gunned him down on December 4, 1969, Silvia, like thousands of other students, was outraged—it seemed as though the state was at war with its own people. "The government would stop at nothing to kill the movement," she said. Later, she joined a Weather Underground front called Prairie Fire, and she was one of the few outsiders trusted by the violent Puerto Rican separatist group Fuerzas Armadas de Liberación Nacional, or FALN.

•   •   •

Unlike Silvia, with her once pampered lifestyle, Donna Joan Borup had a modest childhood in South Amboy, a small New Jersey town that she left right after high school. She moved to New York, earned a bachelor's degree and got jobs as a graphic artist, and taught part time at Cooper Union. According to the FBI, she was a speed reader with a photographic memory and an IQ of 164.

Susan Vicki Tipograph also linked up with the group in New York

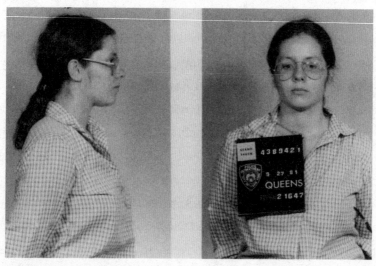

Donna Borup: A printmaker and dedicated revolutionary with an IQ of 164

City. Born in Brooklyn on October 12, 1950, she grew up in Teaneck, New Jersey. "Tip," as she was nicknamed, was a "slightly overweight, bespectacled tomboy," according to one newspaper profile.[2] In college, the Vietnam War and the killing of students at Kent State and Jackson State pushed her to the political left. "As the years went by, I got more and more radicalized," she said. "I realized there were people in the world who were fighting for their liberation."[3] After graduating from New York Law School in 1975, she passed the bar and set up shop, specializing in criminal defense work. As a "movement" lawyer, she took on radical clients: "She can be as charming in conversation as she can be ferocious in the courtroom," according to another profile.[4] Silvia, Susan Rosenberg, and another woman, Eve Rosahn, wound up working as paralegals in Tip's law office, which was run as a collective. Tip and Susan were particularly close. The two women, a federal judge said, "are more than just attorney and client. They have been associates, companions, and roommates."[5]

And then there was a fourth, secret member. Her exploits with the Black Liberation Army, her time behind bars, and her status as a federal fugitive have made her a legend among ultraleftists. One of her comrades praised her as "a bad sister, a woman totally about the get-down for the struggle."[6] She was a major addition to the fledgling group that was forming as the women connected, and her arrival augured new revolutionary possibilities.

• • •

Marilyn Jean Buck, born on December 13, 1947, grew up in Austin, Texas. The oldest of four children, she was the daughter of Virginia and Louis Buck. Her father, once a veterinarian, had become an Episcopal priest. The tall, 350-pound, sandal-wearing Reverend Buck cut an imposing, if eccentric, figure.

His politics are even more unusual—he was a certified liberal and integrationist in a reactionary and segregated city. In Buck's opinion, his church didn't have the guts to take a stand and fight against American apartheid. He told his bishop that his fellow clergymen were "wearing lace on their panties."[7] Louis drew national media attention in 1961 when he organized public protests against the exclusion of blacks from church-run schools. Local segregationists burned a cross on the Buck family's lawn.

By the mid-1960s, Episcopal leaders finally agreed to integrate church institutions, but by then Buck had worn out his ecclesiastical welcome. The church had tired of his outspoken support for civil rights, his prickly personality, and his vaguely beatnik vibe, so they took away his parish. He returned to veterinary medicine and part-time work as a U.S. Department of Agriculture meat inspector. His wife, Virginia, went to work as a secretary.

Still, life was good for the Buck family, which enjoyed a secure, upper-middle-class existence in midcentury America, complete with private-school education for the children. Marilyn was an ideal mid-century American girl—pretty, personable, and fully in synch with the zeitgeist. She wanted to fit in, and she did, both at home and at St. Stephen's Episcopal School. She was in the honor society, worked on the school paper and yearbook, and joined the drama club. A knitting and crocheting enthusiast, she was also an excellent shot, having received firearms instruction from her father, an avid hunter.[8] She harbored premarriage career ambitions to become a "woman stockbroker . . . [but] it wasn't really what I was interested in," she said.[9]

At St. Stephen's, Marilyn graduated at the top of her class and got offers from Brown, the University of Texas flagship campus in her hometown, and the University of California at Berkeley.[10] She picked Berkeley for its high academic standards, which was fine with her fa-

Marilyn Buck: From Texas teen to professional revolutionary

ther, who was happy to have her avoid UT—Louis was a liberal, but in his view, crazy student radicals were running the show in Austin.

In 1965, seventeen-year-old Marilyn enrolled at Cal. It was her first time away from home. Apparently, her father hadn't been following the news: Berkeley, the home of the Free Speech Movement, was the white-hot center of the country's left-wing student movement. The campus's turbulent politics aroused Marilyn's bred-in-the-bone sense of social justice. She made a lifelong commitment to waging war against what she called the "warmakers [and] white-skinned haters." [11]

Berkeley's freedoms were "too much for her," Marilyn's mother said, after she saw the effect that her new environment had on her, insisting that she had been "an innocent girl." [12] Louis agreed, and persuaded her to leave Berkeley after her first year.[13] She transferred to UT and moved back in with her parents.

Given her striking looks, considerable charm, and taste in knee-high boots, Marilyn no doubt drew the attention of the young men around Austin. She was "stunning and statuesque," as someone described her.[14] But she wasn't interested in distractions. In 1967, she was already committed—to the Students for a Democratic Society.

Nominally a Russian major, Marilyn didn't spend many hours curled up with *Anna Karenina*. The antiwar movement and the burgeoning countercultural scene took up most of her time. While campus Greeks were getting blitzed at keg parties, Austin's hippies were holding "Gentle Thursdays."[15]

Marilyn marched steadily leftward. Stokely Carmichael, the fiery leader of the Black Power movement, spoke at UT in early 1967. At speeches at college campuses around the country, Carmichael had electrified audiences with blistering oratory that linked racism at home with the war in Vietnam. "Why should black folks fight a war against yellow folks so that white folks can keep a land they stole from red folks?" he said in 1966. "Ain't no Vietcong ever called me nigger."[16]

She did manage to find time for Robert Pardun, a Students for a Democratic Society organizer, and when he decided to move to Chicago in March 1967, Marilyn went, too. She got a job in the SDS national office, where she coedited the group's newsletter, *New Left Notes*.

By July, Marilyn had won a seat on the SDS National Administrative Committee—and begun attracting FBI attention that would persist for nearly two decades.[17] In 1968, Bureau officials considered placing her on the "Agitator Index," a list of more than 1,000 radicals deemed worthy of special Bureau scrutiny.

But even as she continued to find work among the young radicals she admired, she was still a lonely feminist voice within the male-led, macho SDS organization. At a national conference, Marilyn walked on stage to deliver a report on women and revolution. A foul-mouthed, jeering chorus greeted her: One SDS member recalled that "men hooted and whistled, threw paper planes at the stage, and shouted out such gems as 'I'll liberate you with my cock.'"[18] Preternaturally calm and apparently unfazed, she ignored the sexist abuse and finished her presentation.

The Vietnam War was heating up; nearly 500,000 U.S. troops were in the country, the Vietcong and the North Vietnamese army were racking up hundreds of American casualties every week, and a large swath of the Vietnamese population was on the receiving end of U.S. artillery fire, napalm, and air-delivered five-hundred-pound bombs.

On October 21, 1967, Marilyn joined more than 100,000 antiwar protestors at the Pentagon. On the nightly news, all of America saw a parading rabble of peace creeps, potheads, and assorted deadbeats. But the protest also included habit-clad nuns, suited and sober Protestant preachers, and literary figures such as Allen Ginsberg, Robert Lowell, and Dwight Macdonald. The irrepressible Norman Mailer, also in attendance, described the Pentagon as it came into view: the building "rose like an anomaly out of the sea from the soft Virginia fields . . . its pale yellow walls reminiscent of some plastic plug coming out of the hole made in flesh by an unmentionable operation."[19]

For the antiwar throng assembled outside, the Pentagon was the ultimate symbol of an increasingly deranged U.S. military, a force that seemed hell-bent on incinerating the Vietnamese people or, for that matter, anyone else who resisted the rampaging American golem.

To the protesters, the five-sided structure seemed to throb with pure evil. Hippies conducted ancient Aramaic exorcism rites in the hope of driving out war-making "demons" from the building. Floppy-haired activists dropped daises into the bayoneted rifles wielded by the troops called in to deter potential mayhem. Secretary of Defense Robert S. McNamara, in the throes of a nervous breakdown, monitored the spectacle from the roof.

. . .

After Marilyn's relationship with her SDS boyfriend ended, she left Chicago for the San Francisco Bay Area, familiar territory that had become the West Coast epicenter of political and cultural rebellion. In May 1968, she landed a job as a clerk at the U.S. Postal Service's Ferry Annex. A year later, she was fired for chronic absenteeism. It's not surprising she got the sack—she was deeply involved with Newsreel, a filmmaking collective specializing in political documentaries.*

The films didn't do much at the box office, but that was hardly the point. The filmmakers were provocateurs and cultural assassins who wanted to weaponize the medium. Unlike the consensus-oriented liberals who dominated mainstream American life, Newsreel wasn't interested in offering policy solutions—rather, it wanted to showcase political, social, and economic evils and heighten the cultural contradictions.[20] As Marilyn said, "In our hands film is not an anesthetic, a sterile, smooth-talking apparatus of control. It is a weapon to counter, to talk back and to crack the facade of the lying media of capitalism."[21]

In 1968, Marilyn helped helm a documentary about the Black Panther Party and later moved into a house owned by someone close to the party. She and some Panthers read Mao and screened political films such as *The Battle of Algiers*, the gripping, lightly fictionalized account of the Front de Libération Nationale's underground campaign against French colonial rule. For budding insurrectionists, the documentary

---

* A typical Newsreel offering: *Garbage* (1968), a film about the agitprop antics of the Motherfuckers, a colorful New York anarchist horde. In the midst of a citywide sanitation workers strike, the Motherfuckers visited Lincoln Center. Just a few years earlier, the "master builder" and power broker Robert Moses had bulldozed the vibrant Puerto Rican neighborhood of San Juan Hill to create a new home for the Metropolitan Opera and the New York Philharmonic Orchestra. The Motherfuckers went on a preplanned rampage, dumping huge heaps of garbage at the entrances to the gleaming culture palace.

provided operational as well as political inspiration—in the words of one cultural critic, *The Battle of Algiers* "offered invaluable instruction in the language of communiqués, organization of cells, placement of terror bombs, and the value of cop killing." [22]

Like many in her cohort, she romanticized Third World revolutionaries, but she wanted to do more than just cheer on the forces of national liberation. "On an ideological level and practical level we felt we had to become guerrillas." [23]

It was time to become an urban insurgent.

●　●　●

In the early 1970s, the Bay Area's political landscape was rapidly destabilizing. The Symbionese Liberation Army, or SLA, led by Donald DeFreeze, an escaped convict who adopted the nom de guerre Field Marshal Cinque Mtume, murdered Oakland's first black school superintendant, robbed banks, and kidnapped the newspaper heiress Patty Hearst.* The SLA's slogan: "Death to the fascist insect that preys on the life of the people."

The equally bizarre and violent Tribal Thumb group was led by another charismatic ex-con named Earl Lamar Satcher, who peddled a home-brewed ideology that fused socialism with Reichean sexual psychology. It had a ranch in Honeydew, 180 miles northwest of San Francisco. In a crass and crude account of life in the group, one former member recalled lots of "revolutionary white girls," "beautiful non-armpit-shaving sexy-ass sisters," and plenty of "hot, hairy revolutionary pussy." [24]

Tribal Thumb drew recruits from the SLA, the Black Panther

---

* Like many terrorist groups, the SLA believed it was at war, but it was hardly an "army"— the organization never had more than thirteen members.

Party, and Charles Manson's murderous "Family." Sara Jane Moore, the would-be assassin who popped off a round at the hapless President Gerald Ford in San Francisco on September 22, 1975, reportedly used the Honeydew ranch for her target practice.

Adding to the Bay Area's early-1970s derangement was the presence of the Black Liberation Army, or BLA. Eldridge Cleaver, the leader of a major Black Panther Party faction, had ordered his followers to forget the party's moves toward mainstream legitimacy—running for political office, community empowerment, and feel-good, free-breakfast programs for neighborhood kids. Cleaver's faction formed the nucleus of a new, loosely knit underground organization. It was time to start killing cops, Cleaver said. "[This is] retaliation for ongoing atrocities," said Black Liberation Army leader Sekou Odinga, formerly known as Nathanial Burns.[25] The old Panther slogan—"Off the Pig"— was no longer mere revolutionary rhetoric.

The new armed group expanded its list of targets to include the social undesirables preying on communities of color, including "pimps, ho's [sic], howalkers [sic], trickwalkers, bodyguards, tricks, dope pushers, and owners/operators of trick houses. . . . Anyone found guilty . . . [will] be dealt with."[26]

In San Francisco, BLA mayhem included a string of bank robberies and the attempted murder of police sergeant George Kowalski on August 27, 1971. Two days later, a nine-person BLA team mounted an assault on the Ingleside station house. Just before the attack, somebody set off a diversionary bomb blast at a nearby bank.[27] Chaos ensued. A gunman killed Sergeant John Young with a shotgun blast to the chest. Another BLA guy drew his 9mm pistol, fired, and wounded Irene Grohman, the station house's civilian clerk. The BLA team had brought a bomb with them but couldn't get the fuse to light. "Let's get the fuck out of here," one of them said.[28] (Incredibly, the Young murder case remained open until 2009, when two former BLA members, Herman Bell and Anthony Bottom—already serving life sentences in New York—pled guilty to voluntary manslaughter.)[29]

Why would the BLA or any other revolutionaries attack a police station? According to former BLA member Sundiata Acoli (né Clark Edward Squire), cops weren't civilians or noncombatants—they were legitimate targets. The state was oppressing black people, and the pigs were "soldiers for the state," Acoli said.[30]

In "Terrorism as Strategy and Ecstasy," the scholar William F. May offered another explanation: that the plan was to assault the cops in order to *invite* government repression. "Go for the police station, sharpen the contradictions, because the police will club indiscriminately in retaliation, and thus will radicalize the uncommitted masses."[31]

The Ingleside attack didn't seem to incite any of the masses, but the BLA kept going. The violent campaign would stretch far beyond the Bay Area—it was a "coast-to-coast cop-killing conspiracy," according to one federal prosecutor.[32] Semiautonomous BLA cells targeted police officers in Illinois, New Jersey, Connecticut, Pennsylvania, and Georgia.

The FBI grew increasingly alarmed by what it called the "urban guerrilla terrorists." In an October 16, 1972, memorandum, the acting head of the FBI, L. Patrick Gray, warned about the BLA's apparent influence in "prisons, ghettos, and many other areas of malcontentment" and urged "full penetrative investigations" of the BLA and its supporters, who were working "to disrupt and destroy existing order in the United States."[33] But the BLA was elusive and next to impossible for the FBI to infiltrate.

The FBI also worried about the BLA's potential connection with dangerous foreign elements, particularly in the Middle East. The

Bureau had received reports that unspecified Arab terrorists were training U.S. blacks in guerrilla operations and that BLA might be involved in an "Arab terrorist plot" inside the United States, according to a May 17, 1973, memo.[34] The Bureau reached out to the intelligence community, including the Central Intelligence Agency, the National Security Agency, and the Defense Intelligence Agency. But the spies had next to nothing to report.*

New York City, according to one FBI report, was the "Mecca" of the BLA.[35] On May 21, 1971, BLA gunmen carried out a drive-by machine-gun attack that seriously wounded two police officers, Thomas Curry and Nicholas Binetti. The men were guarding the Riverside Drive apartment of Manhattan district attorney Frank Hogan, who had prosecuted many prominent Black Panthers.

Two days later, Officers Joseph Piagentini and Waverly Jones answered a call in the Colonial Park Houses, a public housing complex built on the site of the old Polo Grounds in upper Manhattan. Bell, Bottom, and a third BLA gunman, Albert "Nuh" Washington, ambushed them. Rounds smashed into Jones's head and back, killing him almost immediately. Piagentini pleaded for his life. The BLA members took their time, slowly firing twenty-two rounds into his body—it was a torture-murder.[36] "It's open season on the cops in this city," said the head of the Patrolmen's Benevolent Association.[37]

All told, the BLA murdered at least fifteen policemen.[38]

Marilyn started working again with former BLA comrades in the late 1970s, and she brought some of the May 19th women along with

---

* FBI investigations involve the relentless accretion of details—after all, it isn't always clear a priori what information might ultimately prove relevant. During the Bureau's probes into the BLA, special agents unearthed countless nuggets, including reports that the group's "Minister of War" (name redacted) had played a bit part as a dope addict in the now classic 1972 "blaxploitation" picture *Superfly*. FBI, "Black Liberation Army," New York, NY, May 2, 1973, 8 (FBI FOIA release).

her. On October 20, 1981, the renewed partnership carried out its most notorious operation, a botched armed robbery in upstate New York that left three men dead.

• • •

The FBI and local cops had long suspected that Marilyn was mixed up with the BLA. The San Francisco Police Department raided her apartment on October 29, 1970, and arrested her after they found a shotgun, an M1 carbine, a couple of 9mm pistols, ammunition, and some bags of weed and other drugs. A judge ruled that there hadn't been probable cause for the raid and turned her loose. The San Francisco Police Department had to return her weapons.

The cops believed that Marilyn had become pregnant by BLA member Ronald Stanley Bridgeforth and that she had had an abortion. According to the police, she was also a "paramour" of Richard Edward Brown, a purported member of both the BLA and Tribal Thumb.[39]

Four years later, Bell, Bottom, and Washington were convicted of premeditated murder and each received a sentence of twenty-five years to life. Washington died behind bars in 2000. In 2018, the New York State Parole Board voted to release Bell. He had a "sturdy network of supporters" and was capable of living a "law-abiding life," the board said. Officer Piagentini's widow, Diane, said that the board's decision "devalues the life of my brave husband who was taken from his two daughters and for whom there is no parole." Bottom remains behind bars.[40]

In 1968, Bridgeforth shot at three police officers outside the White Front discount store on El Camino Real in South San Francisco. By 1969, he was a fugitive, having jumped bail after pleading no contest to an assault with a deadly weapon. Cops suspected that Bridgeforth was a getaway driver during the Ingleside attack. He would spend four decades on the run—in Senegal, in the Gambia, in Atlanta, and finally, in Ann Arbor, Michigan, where he taught at a community college under the name Cole Jordan. In 2011, Bridgeforth turned himself in to California authorities, pled guilty to the 1968 shooting, and was sentenced to a year in the San Mateo County Jail.

San Francisco detectives liked Marilyn for the Ingleside attack; a white woman matching her description had reported a stolen bicycle at the station house a few days before the assault—a reconnaissance mission, no doubt.[41]

Marilyn was, in fact, working as the BLA's quartermaster—the group's "only white member," according to press accounts.

An FBI bulletin quoted from what the Bureau said was a BLA manual for prospective urban guerrillas: "We do not need to take weapons from iced [killed] pigs, especially those who have been righteously baconized. There are better places to rip-off weapons—not where they can be linked to butchered hogs."[42]

Marilyn didn't steal firearms. She had no need to: she simply bought them at gun stores. Well educated, poised, savvy—not to mention a WASP from Texas—Buck was far less likely than her trigger-happy comrades to draw police attention, or so it would seem.

For a couple of years, nobody could pin anything on her, but evidence started to pile up, and on March 22, 1973, Bureau of Alcohol, Tobacco, and Firearms agents and San Francisco cops raided her place at 136 Peralta.[43] The charge: using fake IDs to buy more than a thousand rounds of ammunition and 9mm Browning Hi-Power pistols in Arizona, Oregon, and Austin—federal offenses.[44]

Later, U.S. marshals hauled her to Phoenix to stand trial. Wearing a stylish pink suede coat, Marilyn giggled with her lawyer and spent much of her time in court smiling at two female supporters. "She is very intelligent, very clever, and very dangerous," the judge said during sentencing. He gave her ten years, the most severe sentence possible under the law—he said he wanted "to save others from being killed."[45]

The state saw her as "terrorist and traitor," a "white woman dangerous to white Amerika," Marilyn wrote in an autobiographical poem.[46] She'd been handed a preposterous, politically motivated sentence, she insisted. Just look at Dean Martin, Jr., busted in 1974 for possessing an illegal arsenal that included machine guns and an eight-foot-long anti-tank weapon. The son of the celebrity had gotten off with probation.[47]

In 1974, Marilyn began her sentence at the Federal Reformatory for Women in Alderson, West Virginia. She was assigned to the Special Treatment Unit, the prison's strictest regime. Prison shrinks did an assessment—she was "seductive and provocative in an intellectual way," they concluded, adding, "This woman had a strong masculine identification. She tends to equate male strengths with power and is heavily identified with male aggressiveness."[48]

Back in the mid-1970s, prison authorities, prosecutors, and judges still maintained the notion that convicts could and should be rehabilitated—prison, in their view, wasn't just about punishment, and short-term releases were considered therapeutic. In November 1976, Marilyn got a six-day furlough to visit her parents in Galveston, Texas. The following June, she got a second respite—this time to visit her lawyer in New York, Susan "Tip" Tipograph.

However, Marilyn never returned to Alderson and added "federal fugitive" to her list of crimes. She found sanctuary in New York's radical community and dug into the underground.

3

THE WHITE EDGE

In the imperialist metropole, where the organization of the anti-imperialist struggle must have both legal and illegal components, the political struggle and the armed struggle, bank robbery cannot be dispensed with. It is, in practice, expropriation.

—"SERVE THE PEOPLE: THE URBAN GUERILLA
AND CLASS STRUGGLE," APRIL 1972[1]

Some May 19th members chose to enter clandestine realm and support "people who were not public" and "people who : doing illegal things," Judy Clark said.[2]

One of those people was Mutulu Shakur.

. . .

In the late 1970s, Doc Shakur was running his acupuncture operatic the Black Acupuncture Advisory Association of North America, BAAANA, out of his Harlem brownstone. He taught classes, treat patients, and engaged in other, more surreptitious activities.

He'd assembled a criminal crew that included Tyrone Q. Rison (aka "Little Brother," aka "Osedrick Lalupe"), a U.S. Army veteran, and Sekou "Big Daddy" Odinga. Most were veterans of the Black Panther Party and the BLA. The crew committed armed robberies, ostensibly to raise money for the Republic of New Afrika (the spelling had by then been changed). But helping homegrown freedom fighters wasn't Doc's only motive. He and some of the crew were heavily into cocaine—"sniff," they called it.[3] There's no evidence that they sold any serious amounts of coke, but they regularly robbed small-time dealers.*

They called their ensemble "the Family," apparently not caring that Charles Manson and his murderous band of acid-crazed followers had already made the name notorious. The first job they plotted was an armored car robbery in Pittsburgh, but they got cold feet at the last minute.[4] They retreated to New York but were soon over whatever fears had stopped them in Pennsylvania.

During an eighteen-month period beginning in May 1977, "the Family" did three jobs: the House O' Weenies hot dog factory in the Bronx; a Citibank branch in suburban Mount Vernon, New York; and a Chase Manhattan Bank on lower Ninth Avenue in Manhattan. These were relatively crude operations: Doc's men fired shots and dropped money on the stairs during the House O' Weenies job. During the Mount Vernon heist, wrote the journalist John Castellucci, "Rison had to rush inside the bank and yell 'Let's go' to Odinga, who had stayed beyond the thirty-second time limit."[5] The three robberies netted the men a total of $22,180—not bad but not great, considering the risks involved.

---

* During the late 1970s and early 1980s, illegal narcotics trafficking was a billion-dollar-a-year business. Once largely controlled by the Italian Mafia, the drug trade was increasingly dominated by colorful, ruthless figures such as Leroy "Nicky" Barnes, aka "Mr. Untouchable" (who made the cover of *The New York Times Magazine* in June 1977), and Frank "Superfly" Lucas, whose criminal exploits served as the inspiration for the *Superfly* film.

WANTED BY THE FBI

BANK ROBBERY; CONSPIRACY TO COMMIT BANK ROBBERY

MUTULU SHAKUR

DESCRIPTION

Age, 31; Born, August 8, 1950, Baltimore, Maryland; Height, 5'8"; Weight, 150 pounds; Build, medium; Hair, black; Eyes, brown; Complexion, dark; Race, Negro; Nationality, American; Occupations, practices acupuncture, census taker, laborer; Scars and Marks, scar left side of face; Social Security Number used: 083-40-7447. Remarks, may wear ear pin or earring in left ear.

CRIMINAL RECORD

A Federal warrant was issued on April 21, 1982, in New York, New York, charging Mutulu Shakur with the crimes of bank robbery and conspiracy to commit bank robbery.

CAUTION

SHAKUR IS BEING SOUGHT IN CONNECTION WITH THE ARMED ROBBERY OF AN ARMORED TRUCK WHICH RESULTED IN THE KILLING OF TWO POLICE OFFICERS AND ONE GUARD AND THE WOUNDING OF ONE OFFICER AND TWO GUARDS. SHAKUR IS KNOWN TO ASSOCIATE WITH REVOLUTIONARY ORGANIZATIONS WHICH HAVE A GREAT PROPENSITY FOR CRIMINAL ACTIVITY AND VIOLENCE AGAINST LAW ENFORCEMENT. CONSIDER SHAKUR ARMED AND EXTREMELY DANGEROUS.

FBI/DOJ

Mutulu "Doc" Shakur: The Republic of New Afrika,
armed "expropriations," and the "white edge"

Doc was looking for help—some way to boost his yield and shore up his bottom line. He had an idea: enlist some savvy white women who could carry out relatively sophisticated robbery-related missions without the unwanted attention that the men of color in his crew were sure to attract from police.

Shakur put out feelers to May 19th, telling the women that he was raising money to pay for weapons, ammunition, safe houses, and anything else that Afro-American freedom fighters might need to wage the armed struggle. And he wanted to bankroll land buys for the Republic of New Afrika down South. He said he'd been involved in several felonious fund-raising ventures—"expropriations," he called them.[6]

David Gilbert, a former Weather Underground member who was part of the Family's most notorious and deadly operation, said decades later that such high-risk fund-raising activities were a necessary part of the revolution. Militants "were not going to be awarded grants from the Rockefeller or Ford Foundation."[7] A former BLA member made a similar point: armed "expropriations" were "revolutionary compulsory tax."[8]

Doc had a proposition for the May 19th women: come join the Family. He and the guys would supply the firepower and the muscle—the all-male "primary team," as he called it. The women would print fake IDs, line up safe houses, provide perimeter security during operations, and drive getaway cars. It was a criminal-revolutionary take on Cold War America's division of domestic labor. With the women on board, the Family could carry out more advanced—and more lucrative—armed operations.

To the women of May 19th, Shakur seemed like a righteous soldier, a real revolutionary who'd do just about anything to "heighten the contradictions" and usher in the revolution. "I am not a militant; I am not a rabble-rouser; I am not macho," Doc once said.[9] Maybe so, but the women were still mesmerized by Shakur's tough-guy persona, rhetoric, and street cred.

And he was offering them a chance to do more than organize demonstrations and print posters. His offer resonated with the women.

According to one internal May 19th paper, white leftists had spent far too much time simply "mouthing revolution—always years in the future—and abandoning Third World comrades on the front lines." It was a priority for "white communists to participate in armed struggle" under the leadership of "Third World" groups such as the Black Liberation Army and the Puerto Rican *independistas* fighting for the liberation of that island.[10]

May 19th was in. The women would refer to themselves as the "white edge." However, Doc and the guys called them "the crackers."

Shakur gave the orders, and Marilyn was the go-between who passed them along to the other women. Each got a nom de guerre: "Dee" (Marilyn), "Elizabeth" (Susan), "Alex" (Judy), and "Louise" (Silvia).

The Family hatched plots at the BAAANA building. Its prime targets were "cans of corn"—Family lingo for armored trucks. New Jersey was a target-rich environment, and they robbed Coin Depot armored cars outside Bamberger's department stores in Livingston and Paramus, for a total take of $300,000. May 19th helped bring in a whole new level of sophistication: surveillance, false identification, safe houses, and "switch cars" to throw off any pursuing police. Bringing in the white edge seemed to be paying off.

But the Family's activities weren't limited to armored-car stickups. Revolutionary fund-raising was necessary, but not sufficient. If you weren't having real political impact, you were just another criminal. Doc started thinking big. Two high-profile revolutionaries were languishing behind bars, and Shakur and the May 19th women wanted them out.

· · ·

Morningside Heights, according to one 1981 *New York Times* piece, "is, in many ways, as eclectic and tolerant as the great domed presence [of Columbia's Low Library] that is at its center. Its transient population moves every couple of years in a welter of secondhand furniture, toaster ovens, textbooks and hanging plants." [11] Housing was relatively cheap, and rent-controlled apartments were still available if you greased the right palms.

The area was perfect for a fledgling revolutionary formation.

May 19th had a bunch of places near Columbia. There was a spacious three-bedroom apartment at 211 West 106th Street, and another at 526 West 111th Street. Some of the women lived a little farther south, at 243 West 98th Street, and others at 200 West 95th Street.[12] The endless meetings, the comings and goings at all hours, and the apartment full of women in their twenties and thirties didn't seem to attract much attention. The would-be insurrectionists were able to hide in plain sight.

Given her federal fugitive status, Marilyn needed something more secluded. She liked the anonymity of working-class East Orange, New Jersey. It wasn't too far from the city, it was dirt cheap, and it had good lines of communication—in other words, it was a great place for a safe house. Marilyn, using the name "Carol Durant," rented an apartment at 223 Prospect Street.

Living was communal—hippie-style. Money was always tight, and living together was a way to cut down on expenses. More important, being in a collective meant that you were almost never alone and that everybody was watching everybody else. Just as in the Weather Underground, the May 19th communards conducted harrowing, and lengthy criticism/self-criticism sessions, in which members would face their comrades, confess to ideological deviations, bourgeois affectations, or even simple laziness, and then "fight for oneself" and demonstrate that they were on the path to political and personal reconstruction.* This hothouse environment reinforced the group's values—it was 24/7 indoctrination. Real revolutionaries didn't have time off.

---

* A former member of a Maoist group in Philadelphia described in 1981 how their cell used criticism/self-criticism: "In a follow-up discussion to a cell meeting one cadre made the un- contested statement: 'We just have to admit that we are essentially bad people.' Members were expected to evaluate weaknesses and errors made throughout their lives and then to develop all-inclusive self-criticisms (typed out in triplicate) in much the same manner as one collects their sins and purges themselves for the confessional, and then becomes cleansed in one fell swoop." "The PWOC: Degeneration into Ultra-Leftism," Encyclopedia of Anti-Revisionism On-Line, Fall 1981, https://www.marxists.org/history/erol/ncm-7/ex-pwoc-members.htm.

4

HANDLESS TERRORIST ESCAPES

During the 1970s, New York was an arena for extremist groups that were looking to air their international grievances. As the media capital of the world, the city was a soundstage for anti-Castro exiles, Croatian nationalists, Puerto Rican *independistas*, and other groups trying to draw global attention to their causes.* Among the most formidable was the Fuerzas Armadas de Liberación Nacional, or FALN, which fought to create an independent, socialist Puerto Rico aligned with Fidel Castro's Cuba. The extreme left was in awe of the Puerto Ricans—they were America's very own anticolonial movement, and they were willing to use any means necessary, including deadly violence.

The FALN was responsible for more than a hundred bombings, including an August 3, 1977, attack on Mobil Oil headquarters in midtown Manhattan that killed one office worker and severely wounded others.

---

* For example, Croatian separatists were suspected in the December 29, 1975, bombing at New York's La Guardia airport that killed eleven people and wounded seventy-five more. Omega 7, a violently anti-Castro group, carried out multiple bombings of the Cuban Mission to the United Nations during the late 1970s, and attempted to assassinate the mission's chief diplomat with a car bomb on March 25, 1980.

The group did more than bomb—it was also responsible for an attack on the federal electoral system. On March 15, 1980, the FALN stormed the Carter-Mondale presidential campaign office in Chicago and the George H. W. Bush campaign office in New York, where they held campaign workers hostage while they ransacked the facilities and stole lists of supporters. A Carter-Mondale campaign worker, Bruce Moran, told reporters about a man with a pump-action shotgun and a woman with a pistol. Ordering Moran to get down on his knees, one of the FALN members said, "This is a takeover." In New York, ten campaign workers were bound and gagged. According to retired FBI special agent Donald R. Wofford, "on the days that followed these incidents, the group sent threatening letters to around 200 Carter-Mondale supporters including [Democratic] National Convention delegates living throughout the State of Illinois."[1]

But their most notorious attack took place downtown in the financial district: on January 24, 1975, the FALN planted a bomb inside an entrance to Fraunces Tavern at 101 Broad Street. The place was drenched in American history—General George Washington had bidden farewell to his officers there in 1783. The private Anglers Club and the offices of the Sons of the Revolution were upstairs.

At 1:29 p.m., during the lunch service, the device went off, killing four people and wounding sixty more.

QUEENS, JULY 1978

By 1978, the NYPD knew plenty about William Morales; it had been on his tail for years. He'd held a lot of jobs over the years: airline reservation agent, schoolteacher, lab technician, lifeguard, photographer. But there was only one that really mattered to the cops: he was the FALN's go-to explosives guy, its IED guru, its bombmaker-in-chief. The NYPD believed he had built the Fraunces Tavern device but they didn't have enough evidence to arrest him.

They would get the evidence they needed in a spectacular fashion. On a warm afternoon in New York in the summer of 1978, Morales was in his seedy two-room apartment at 26-49 96th Street in the Elmhurst section of Queens, assembling a new IED. As he put on the finishing touches, something went wrong. Maybe it was some static electricity, a little vibration, a slight temperature change. Morales's creation detonated. The blast sheared off nine of his fingers and a chunk of his face. You could hear the explosion for blocks around.

The NYPD hauled a massive load of bomb-making materials out of the FALN factory—enough to build 28 explosive devices and 2,632 incendiary devices, according to the bomb squad.[2] Still Morales refused to go down without a fight: Investigators found bloodstains on the knobs of his gas stove. It looked as though he'd dragged himself postblast across the floor and used his mouth to turn on the stove. His goal? To fill the place with gas; responding cops might inadvertently set off an explosion, sending out the bomb-maker and anybody else in the apartment in a blaze of glory.

A detective tried to question him.

"Fuck you, fuck yourself," Morales said.

"It's you that are fucked, pal," said the cop. "You'll be wiping your ass with your elbows."[3]

They locked him up in the federal Metropolitan Correctional Center on Park Row in lower Manhattan. Morales was a mess, and he needed some serious medical treatment. Doctors wanted to reattach his blown-off digits, but the FBI insisted on holding them as evidence. He was transferred to the third-floor prison ward at Bellevue Hospital at 30th Street and First Avenue.

Although Morales was behind bars, the FALN's violent campaign continued. On New Year's Eve 1982, bombs went off at 26 Federal Plaza and at NYPD headquarters at One Police Plaza. According to one policeman, the headquarters blast "hit Detective Rocco Pascarella, blowing away most of his left side." Another detective, Richard Pastorella, was also hit by the explosion, which threw him "twenty-five feet, blew off all the fingers of his right hand and left him blind in both eyes. He has had thirteen major operations and twenty titanium screws inserted just to hold his face together."[4]

Morales had been languishing in the ward for nearly a year, waiting to be fitted with a pair of artificial hands. He knew for certain that if he were convicted for Fraunces Tavern, he'd be going away for life.

The May 19th women knew all about Morales and decided to help. Morales was a bona fide Third Worlder, a righteous freedom fighter, and one terrifyingly effective anti-imperialist. Moreover, in their judgment it was a political necessity—according to one May 19th discussion paper, "Fighting to free the freedom fighters [like Morales] helped fulfill a critically important role in people's war: building conscious,

Willie Morales: The FALN's bombmaker-in-chief

mass support, building a mass base that can be mobilized to fight fascism and white supremacy in all [its] forms."[5] Breaking Morales out would be a major coup.

From the outside, the Bellevue ward looked wide open. People wandered in and out, there was little prisoner supervision, and guards napped on the job. The FBI complained about Morales's move out of the federal lockup downtown—Bellevue simply wasn't secure enough to hold somebody as dangerous as him.[6] But an escape plan was already in place. It would be a big operation, involving some thirty people from the FALN, the BLA, and May 19th.[7] By mid-May of 1979, everything was lined up.

On May 18, Morales's lawyer, Tip Tipograph, visited her client between 6:20 and 7:10 p.m.[8] Alfredo Mendez, a convicted FALN member and government informant, claimed later that Tip had a fourteen-inch bolt cutter strapped to her thigh and covered by her frock.[9] However delivered, Morales ended up in possession of a bolt cutter. On the night of the twenty-first, he got to work. His stumps frantically working the strapped-on bolt cutters, he snipped through the thin wire mesh covering the windows and somehow managed to shimmy down a rope improvised from Ace bandages. Fellow revolutionaries were waiting for him below. Comrades took Morales to the safe house that Marilyn rented in East Orange, New Jersey.

Tip has consistently denied playing any role in the Bellevue breakout and she has never been charged in connection with the escape. "I think if (the allegations) could have been substantiated, I would have been arrested four years ago," she said in 1983. "Every time I saw Mr. Morales, I was searched," she said. "If they had the slightest bit of evidence other than these lies and innuendos, I assume I would have been arrested."[10] However, according to federal prosecutors, "For a few weeks prior to the date of the escape, Tipograph became increasingly vehement in asserting that the attorney-client privilege protected her from a search by correction officers. On one occasion, when correction officers denied her request to be exempted for a search, she surrendered a knife only after repeated questioning. On the day of her last visit with Morales, her bag was not searched, nor did she go through a metal detector, nor was she physically searched." [11]

"HANDLESS TERRORIST ESCAPES," a *New York Post* headline screamed the day following the escape. One press account said Morales had been plucked up by somebody in a borrowed New York Telephone cherry picker. The truth was more prosaic: the improvised rope had snapped under the strain of Morales's weight, and he had fallen a couple of stories. A window air-conditioning unit had broken his fall. [12]

No one has ever revealed the details of how he did it, but eventually Morales made it across the border into Mexico—an impressive feat, given that he was a wanted man with a pair of stumps and a horribly mangled face. Things were copacetic for a couple of years. Then the FBI found out where he was and tipped off the Mexican federal police. [13] On May 26, 1983, the cops surrounded his place in the small city of Puebla, sixty-five miles southwest of Mexico City, and a shoot-out ensued. A cop and two of Morales's associates were killed, but Morales was captured. In custody, he was uncharacteristically chatty, telling a local Bureau agent that it was Tip who had slipped him the bolt cutters. [14] (Morales claimed that Mexican security personnel had tortured him with "electric prods" and beat him while FBI agents and New York City police officers stood next door.) [15] Morales was sentenced to twelve years in Mexico but was released early, in 1988. The United States asked for his extradition, but Mexico refused and Morales was allowed to go to Havana.

Today Morales remains a guest of the Cuban government. The FBI still wants him back, and it's offering a $100,000 reward for information leading to his arrest. Politicians such as U.S. senators Marco Rubio and Robert Menendez periodically demand that the Cubans turn him over.*

As of 2015, Morales was living in an apartment building on 3rd Street in the capital's Vedado section.[16] Even after mutilation, prison, and exile, Morales has kept his revolutionary discipline: "It's a shame that things happened to me, to cops, and to innocent people," he said. "But that comes with the job."[17]

NEW YORK, 1979

May 19th had had a major asset to aid it in breaking out Morales: Alan Berkman, MD, who was one of the doctors who treated Morales at Bellevue and also happened to be a supporter of the cause. He was a man, but that was offset by his impeccable radical credentials, and moreover, he was a licensed, practicing medical doctor. He had skills that proved helpful in the planning of the breakout and would be critical if one of the group was injured.

Born at Israel Zion Hospital in Brooklyn on September 4, 1945, Alan was the second of Samuel and Mona Berkman's four children. In 1948, the Berkmans relocated to Middletown, New York, a town of 22,000 people about seventy miles northwest of New York City. Sam owned a modest wholesale plumbing and heating supply business. Semirural Orange County in the 1950s had all the markings of classic small-town life—unlocked doors, a bustling downtown, and telephone numbers with only five digits.

---

* In December, 2006, the New York *Daily News* reported the existence of the "Guillermo Morales/Assata Shakur Community and Student Center" at City College. The City University of New York chancellor ordered the sign taken down, but the center remained open until October 2013, when the college abruptly closed it, sparking student protests and arrests.

Alan was a normal, straight-arrow kid with an astronaut-style crew cut. He spent his free time hanging out with pals and watching *Howdy Doody*, *Sea Hunt*, *Have Gun—Will Travel*, and other Eisenhower-era TV favorites. He hunted in the woods outside town. His transgressions were minor, even Tom Sawyer–like. In his unfinished memoirs, he recalled swiping apples from a neighbor's tree and "waiting for the cops to come. They never did."[18]

His social conscience emerged early, though. Alan "couldn't live with the idea of prejudice," his brother Steven wrote in 1990. Alan "befriended Skippy Seploin, a Puerto Rican who lived nearby. He was chastised and threatened by fellow students but never gave in to the peer pressure."[19] He attended Middletown High School, an impressive twin-turreted structure that the town's residents were rightly proud of. He was a standout: National Merit Scholar, class salutatorian, track star, Eagle Scout. His future seemed bright.

Like most parents, Sam and Mona wanted a better life for their kids. A college education was central to their American dream. "My father had done manual labor for years before getting his little business," Alan told a reporter in 1985. "They always wanted me to do better, to be a doctor, to have money, but they never wanted me to be as disrespectful as other people had been to them because they had never gone to college."[20]

After graduating from high school in 1963, Alan went to Cornell and graduated in the class of 1967. He played defensive tackle on the lightweight football team, and served as president of his fraternity. Fully grown, Alan was five feet eleven and 170 pounds. He had black hair and a pronounced cleft chin—a feature noted in the early 1980s when he began appearing on FBI wanted posters.

• • •

During the mid-1960s, once-sleepy Cornell started to boil. SDS was growing. The Black Power movement had a presence. In March of Alan's senior year, Cornell's fraternity council sponsored a "Soul of Blackness" week. Stokely Carmichael, the leader of the Student Non-Violent Coordinating Committee, gave a blistering speech to a standing-room-only crowd, blasting assorted evils including the Vietnam War, white supremacy, and the draft. As with Marilyn at the University of Texas during that same year, Carmichael's scorching speak had a powerful effect on Alan, and he started to develop a new political consciousness.

Originally a mild, Kennedy-style liberal, Alan moved steadily leftward as the 1960s wore on, and, like many of his cohorts, he burned with rage over poverty, racism, and the insanity of the war in Southeast Asia.

After getting his BA, Alan attended Columbia's College of Physicians and Surgeons in New York. The oldest medical school in the country, Columbia was very traditional: jackets and ties, and no facial hair. There were very few blacks or women and no Latino students at all. But there was a small group of white activists. Alan got involved in antiwar teach-ins and joined sit-ins calling for affirmative action, pass-fail grading, and an end of the dress code.

In April 1968, there was a student uprising at Columbia's main campus in Morningside Heights. SDS members, unaligned revolutionaries, and various outside agitators occupied buildings and issued fiery antiwar and antiestablishment proclamations. A handful of radical celebrities, including Dwight Macdonald and Stokely Carmichael, came to observe the spectacle. One photo imprinted on the mind of the culture was of a protestor in dark glasses easing back in university president Grayson Kirk's swivel chair and lighting one of the president's cigars.

The Student Afro-American Society took over Hamilton Hall, the heart of Columbia College. To Kirk it seemed as though events were spinning out of control, and he decided to call in the NYPD to clear out the protesters. A thousand policemen showed up. Helmeted cops cracked student skulls, and plainclothes agents swung blackjacks. Alan stitched up scalps and comforted the walking wounded. He was shocked by the police violence. "Calling them pigs was not an abstraction to me anymore," he said.[21]

Alan started reading Karl Marx and was wowed by the nineteenth-century theorist's approach to understanding society. He joined a Marxist-Leninist study group and concluded that the time for reform and incremental change was over.[22] By the beginning of the 1970s, he had become a committed revolutionary. That didn't hinder his studies, though, and in 1971 he graduated near the top of his med school class. His clinical and diagnostic skills were highly regarded. The newly minted MD took an internship at Presbyterian Hospital on the Upper East Side, one of the best hospitals in the country.*

His family expected the usual doctor's trajectory—residency at a top hospital, a well-paid specialty, wife and kids parked out in the suburban hinterlands of Scarsdale or Ho-Ho-Kus. But for Alan, that kind of life was out of the question. "I couldn't simply go back to a medical career and occasional demonstrations," he recalled. "It felt like betrayal."[23]

He didn't give up medicine; instead he fused it with his Marxist ideology. Rather than go on to a medical residency, he decided to focus on community health as a doctor to the downtrodden. He worked at

---

* Two days into the job, Alan became part of one of the most famous food poisoning cases in American history. While caring for a woman in the intensive care unit who was suffering from some unknown affliction, he came to a shrewd diagnosis: botulism poisoning, a relatively rare condition. The botulism was traced to the can of Bon Vivant vichyssoise she and her recently deceased husband had eaten a few days before. Mrs. Cochran lived but spent the rest of her life in a wheelchair.

*Alan Berkman, MD: Eagle scout, Cornell and
Columbia man, and revolutionary desperado*

a Black Panther–founded health care clinic in the South Bronx and cared for prisoners at the Bronx House of Detention. Off duty, he organized potluck suppers to raise funds for Third World groups such as the Front for the Liberation of Mozambique, or FRELIMO. Then he began taking more dramatic and direct action.

On September 9, 1971, inmates at New York's Attica Correctional Facility revolted. The place was an upstate penal hellhole packed with black and brown prisoners guarded by pissed-off whites. Convicts wanted an end to the squalor, overcrowding, and brutality. A few prisoners spouted fiery revolutionary rhetoric, but most of the jailbirds just wanted to reclaim their human dignity.

When the convicts grabbed forty-two staff members as hostages, the authorities were ill prepared.

New York State's prison commissioner, Russell Oswald, couldn't decide on a plan. Eventually Oswald's liberal Republican boss, Governor Nelson Rockefeller, demanded an end to the Attica standoff. The time for talk was over. "Rocky," likely thinking about a future run for U.S. president, green-lighted the retaking of Attica.

At 9:46 on the morning of September 13, salvos of tear gas signaled the beginning of the operation. Guards and state troopers opened fire on the prisoners and hostages massed in the central prison yard, known as Times Square—a poignant reference to the crossroads in a city many of the Attica denizens called home. Forty-three convicts and prison staffers died, and hundreds of prisoners were wounded. Alan and some of his fellow med school students made it to Attica and treated casualties.*

In 1973, Alan used his considerable medical talents to comfort the sick and wounded in another violent standoff: on February 27, armed members of the American Indian Movement took over the town of Wounded Knee on the Pine Ridge reservation in South Dakota. The activists grabbed hostages and demanded that the U.S. government abide by the terms of the treaties it had signed with the Oglala Lakota in the late nineteenth and early twentieth centuries.

The National Guard, the FBI, and the U.S. Marshals Service sealed the place off. A seventy-one-day siege ensued. The sides traded gunfire on a daily basis. Two Native Americans were killed, and a federal agent was shot and paralyzed.[24]

Alan and his girlfriend, a short, frizzy-haired fellow doctor named Barbara Zeller, sneaked through the federal cordon to bring supplies and medical care. They arrived at Wounded Knee after a hair-raising two-day, thirty-mile overland trek. Day and night, they had to evade armed patrols and armored vehicles and sneak across a no-man's-

---

* Three years later, Rockefeller made it to the White House, but only as Gerald Ford's un-elected vice president. In 1979, atop his twenty-five-year-old assistant, Rocky succumbed to a massive coronary attack. A joke soon made the rounds. Q: How did Rocky kick the bucket? A: Low blood pressure, 70 over 25.

land.[25] One woman in labor needed care in a fully equipped hospital, but she refused to leave the reservation. "'I want the baby born free, and this is the only place,'" Alan recalled her telling him.[26] The incident sent him reeling. "Here she was, willing to risk her life. It told me something about this country," he said. "People [should be] able to determine their own destiny."[27]

Back in New York, Alan's political commitments grew. His family "knew he was into some heavy things," his brother Steven wrote.[28] Most of his time was taken up with the Prairie Fire Organizing Committee, or PFOC, the aboveground transmission belt for the Weather Underground's pronouncements and theoretical musings. Alan met Laura Whitehorn and Susan Rosenberg, both PFOC leaders. Technically he wasn't in Weather, but he was a sympathizer—a "fellow traveler," as the old Communist Party USA called its unofficial adherents.

Most Prairie Fire members believed the group was independent, but in reality, PFOC was controlled by Weather. Not all Weatherpeople lived subterranean lives. Some, like Laura, lived and worked aboveground while keeping their Weather affiliation hidden. They shaped PFOC's agenda. It was a time-tested Leninist approach.

In late January and early February 1976, PFOC convened the "Hard Times" conference in Chicago. Thousands of assorted leftists attended, including radical notables such as the lawyer William Kunstler and Boston University history professor Howard Zinn. The conference's theme: "Hard Times Are Fighting Times." Expectations were high.

But Hard Times was a fiasco. The Weather Underground Organization, pulling PFOC's strings, pushed a narrow, rigid political line: the international working class had *the* central role in worldwide revolution. The inert wage slaves toiling in factories, mines, and power plants had to be aroused and alerted to their world-historical role. Puerto

Ricans, Palestinians, Namibians, homosexuals, women—all of them could help, of course. But they were ideological second-stringers.

A black caucus and a women's caucus were frozen out. Conference goers gagged on the workers-first political line. Susan later called the conclave "male-defined and not pro-lesbian."[29] An anti-imperialist and profeminist gay men's collective hammered the Hard Times organizers as sellouts and reactionaries. Revelations that the Weather Underground had used PFOC as its stooges added to the general outrage.

The ideological flailing continued into the following year. Clayton Van Lydegraf, a grizzled sixty-two-year-old communist militant who had helped Weather spring LSD guru Timothy Leary from prison back in 1970, ripped into Weather's Central Committee in a 1977 collection, *The Split of the Weather Underground Organization*. The document was "creepily hermetic, dogmatic, sloganistic, and censorious—almost unbelievably dated and Byzantine," as historian Jeremy Varon described it.[30] *The Split* was part of the miasma of despair, self-loathing, and confusion that permeated the late-1970s ultraleft.

Laura did a public mea culpa a few months after the Hard Times shambles. "As a founder of the PFOC and as organizational secretary . . . I take full responsibility for leading the organization in a revisionist direction," she said.[31] Post–Hard Times, Alan also self-flagellated: he confessed to being a male chauvinist, Weather stooge, anti-lesbian, and anti-anti-imperialist.

· · ·

Alan's partner, Barbara, gave birth to a daughter, Sarah, in October 1976. The baby's middle name was Machel, no doubt given in honor of Samora Moisés Machel, a charismatic FRELIMO guerrilla leader who became Mozambique's first postindependence leader. Sarah's arrival caused Alan to reflect on his life's direction. He considered abandoning radical activism and concentrating on his medical practice and family.

But the lure of revolution was too strong. During the late 1970s, Alan worked at a variety of clinics and hospitals around the city. He treated indigents down on the Lower East Side and up in the Bronx, and part-time at the Bellevue prison ward.

PFOC had split bicoastal, as had the Black Panther Party before it. The West Coast faction kept the name. On the East Coast, Susan helped rebrand PFOC as the May 19th Communist Organization, and after the success of the Morales breakout, Alan was inspired to take a more active role in its actions.

· · ·

Alan used his medical skills to make an important contribution not long after becoming part of May 19th. Judy longed for motherhood. She said she wanted to become pregnant as a "conscious lesbian."[32] Conventional procreative sex was out of the question.

Pamphlets such as "Artificial Insemination: An Alternative Conception for the Lesbian and Gay Community" offered solid tips: "Some women prefer using a turkey baster. This is fine. But remember not to place it against the cervix at the opening [os]. It can be dangerous to put air into the uterus and a turkey baster holds alot [sic] of air." The guidebook offered words of caution about semen: "the unfamiliar or well-forgotten smell and consistency might take some getting used to."[33]

She had a better idea: Alan. He was in decent physical shape, he was highly intelligent, and he came with the correct ideological alignment. He willingly donated his sperm and assisted with the insemination. Harriet Josina Clark was born on November 13, 1980.

Judy was a doting new mother, but some of the other May 19th women weren't so excited about her new focus. The May 19th women were single-minded in their pursuit. There was no room for motherhood. At least at that moment.

Judy was conflicted. She loved her child, but she also loved her comrades. "I loved being a mother and I also felt very split because I didn't think it was legitimate, I guess, according to my political philosophy and group commitments," she said. "It felt . . . very individualistic, and so I had an incredible desire to just do nothing else but mother her."[34]

Divided between the two loyalties, Judy ultimately decided to go with May 19th women. After all, she was a self-described "single-minded fanatic" who was "'at war' with America."[35] From then on, she spent a lot less time with little Harriet. Her daughter would be raised collectively, with the responsibilities for child care divided among multiple May 19th members—as had sometimes been the case in the Weather Underground.

5

"AMERIKKKA IS TRYING TO LYNCH ME"

Not long after the Morales breakout, the May 19th women joined an even more audacious plot. Not far from New York, another revered revolutionary figure sat behind bars.

Joanne Chesimard was one of the brightest stars in the revolutionary firmament. Back in the 1960s, she'd ditched what she called her "slave name"—henceforth, she'd call herself Assata Shakur.* She had been a Black Panther, and after the party split, she joined the Black Liberation Army. Law enforcement considered her a major threat— she was "the soul of the gang, the mother hen who kept them together, kept them moving, kept them shooting," said NYPD deputy commissioner Robert Daley.[1]

In the spring of 1973, Chesimard was wanted for questioning in connection with a string of armed robberies and BLA-connected

---

* During the 1960s, a number of black militants related by blood or marriage took the Shakur surname. Jeral Williams became "Mutulu Shakur," and his adopted brother, Anthony Coston, became "Lumumba Shakur." Lumumba married Alice Faye Williams, who took the name "Afeni Shakur." In 1971, she gave birth to future hip-hop great Tupac Amaru Shakur, who was named after an indigenous Peruvian ruler executed by the Spanish in 1572. "I felt that giving my child a racist, cracker's name would be like cussing my child," Lumumba said. Geronimo Pratt, a senior Black Panther Party figure, was his godfather; Assata Shakur was his godmother. After her divorce from Lumumba, Afeni married Mutulu, her former brother-in-law.

*Assata Shakur: The BLA's "mother hen who kept them
together, kept them moving, kept them shooting."*

cop killings. The crimes included the murders of NYPD patrolmen Gregory Foster and Rocco Laurie, killed on January 27, 1972, outside the Shrimp Boat luncheonette at 173 Avenue B on the Lower East Side.

On May 2, 1973, two New Jersey state troopers, Werner Foerster and James Harper, pulled over a white Pontiac LeMans on the southbound side of the New Jersey Turnpike near East Brunswick. Three people were inside the car: Zayd Malik Shakur (born James F. Costan), a leader of the Harlem branch of the Black Panther Party; Sundiata Acoli; and Chesimard.[2]

Zayd and Sundiata had been defendants in the Panther 21 case, accused of attempting to bomb police stations and other targets in New York.* The prosecution had failed to convince the jury, and on May 13,

---

* It was a riotous eight-month trial. Adding to the spectacle was the striking courtroom attire of one of the codefendants, Michael Tabor, who appeared in a "fly blue leatherette jacket with matching Lenin cap" and a "Metternich overcoat," according to the ace columnist Murray Kempton. Afeni Shakur was another Panther 21 defendant, as was her then husband.

1971, all of the Panther 21 had been acquitted. Six days after the verdict, the BLA retaliated with a drive-by machine-gun attack that badly wounded NYPD patrolmen Nicholas Binetti and Thomas Curry, who were on duty protecting district attorney Frank Hogan.[3]

The violence continued during the traffic stop on the New Jersey Turnpike. Within moments, Trooper Foerster lay dead, shot in the head at point-blank range with his own service revolver—an "execution style" murder, as the FBI described it.[4] Trooper Harper was badly wounded. Zayd was shot and killed. While Sundiata escaped on foot, Assata was struck by at least three bullets.

She survived but faced major felony charges, including first-degree murder, assault with intent to kill, and illegal possession of a weapon.

After lots of legal maneuverings by both the defense and the prosecution, Assata finally went to trial. She didn't think much of the judge, Theodore Appleby: "He was a real died-in-the-wool craka [*sic*]," she said. "The kind that could wipe out the 'natives' in Africa, make Central America safe for United Fruit Company, or run a sterilization center in Puerto Rico."[5] On March 25, 1977, the jury returned its verdict: guilty on all counts. She received a life sentence, with an additional twenty-six to thirty-three years for good measure.

"Like all other Black revolutionaries, I have been hunted like a dog," Assata said after her conviction, "and like all other Black revolutionaries, Amerikkka is trying to lynch me."[6] Her case was a cause célèbre for leftists around the world. They called her a political prisoner, a victim of official racism, a revolutionary martyr.

· · ·

Two years later, the Family wanted Assata out. This operation was going to be strictly political, like busting out Morales, only bigger. Springing Assata (aka "Cleo" and "Sister Love") would be a major triumph—a shock to the system and a morale enhancer for freedom fighters the world over.

As with the Family's armed robberies, Doc and the guys handled the guns and the rough stuff with the May 19th women taking on supporting parts. The Madame Binh Graphics Collective cranked out political material that laid out the ideological line. One leaflet described the "police ambush" of Assata, Zayd Shakur, and Acoli on the New Jersey Turnpike as part of the U.S. government's broader campaign to neutralize the black liberation movement.[7] In addition to making posters, May 19th rented vehicles, served as lookouts and getaway drivers, and rented safe houses. Marilyn, using the alias "Delia Richards," rented a short-term hideout for Assata in East Orange at 358 Park Avenue, apartment A-15.[8]

They'd budgeted carefully for what they called the "Cleo trip."[9] Their armed fund-raising campaign in and around New York was supposed to cover Assata's exfiltration-related expenses. (Marilyn kept careful track of Family finances in a red ledger.)[10]

Assata's lawyers had managed to get her assigned to the low-security Clinton Correctional Facility for Women in central New Jersey. Doc handled the casing of the inside of the prison, visiting Assata several times, signing in under his birth name, Jeral Williams. "Big Daddy" Odinga visited her as well, and on several occasions they discussed an escape plan. Assata was housed in South Hall, which visitors reached by a shuttle van from the reception center at the main gate. Even with the lax security they took their time and plotted out the extraction over a nine-month period.

NOVEMBER 2, 1979

Odinga arrived at the reception center and signed in. Nobody searched him, and there were no metal detectors. A shuttle van driven by a prison guard, Stephen Ravettina, took Odinga to South Hall, where a prison matron, Helen Anderson, buzzed him in. After greeting Assata, he discreetly passed her a .357 Magnum revolver he had concealed against the small of his back.

Meanwhile, Ravettina got a radio call and was told to come back to reception and pick up two more visitors. The two men were Doc's guys, and when they got inside the van, one of them, Mtayari Shabaka Sundiata (né Samuel Smith), put a gun to the guard's head and told him to get moving. When they reached South Hall, they met Big Daddy and Chesimard, who was wielding the .357 Magnum. Somebody cuffed Ravettina and Anderson, and everybody left the building and got into the van.

A short while later they reached the designated switch-point in a parking lot outside the prison grounds. Marilyn, Silvia, and Susan were waiting for them. They hustled Assata and Odinga into the trunk of a white Lincoln Continental and headed east on Interstate 78. The entire operation took just ten minutes. The white edge was in effect. In the immediate aftermath of the breakout, the cops were looking for a black man, not two white women.

They arrived at the East Orange safe house. Doc showed up later with a wad of cash he'd retrieved from another safe house in Mount Vernon, New York—$50,000, half of the proceeds from the Paramus heist, the Family's most recent armed robbery.[11] Chesimard would have plenty of expense money while she was on the run. There was a multistate manhunt on, so everybody kept moving. Marilyn drove her car west, with Assata in the trunk, to a safe house in Pittsburgh.[12]

The FBI later found loads of prints at 350 Omega Street, apartment 2. It looked as though just about every revolutionary had been there at one time or another—not just Marilyn and Assata but Susan, Rison, Odinga, Mutulu, May 19th member Susan Rautenberg, and even Willie Morales. Federal prosecutors called the place a "cross-section of terrorists."[13]

Bureau agents also discovered Marilyn's after-action assessment of the breakout, in her own handwriting. She judged the operation a "victory qualitatively," one that would "be felt internationally."[14] There had been only one hiccup: Odinga had received a parking ticket in the name of "Edward Holmes" during one of his surveillance missions at Clinton, and Marilyn worried that it might somehow lead the cops to the Family. It didn't.

•   •   •

Back in Brooklyn, May 19th continued to pump out pro-Assata material. The women at Madame Binh designed and printed a poster with an image of the fugitive and the words "Assata Welcome Here." Silvia and others passed out copies on the Lower East Side, in Harlem, and in Bedford-Stuyvesant, neighborhoods where May 19th thought Assata might find a sympathetic population.

Assata was constantly on the move—she had to be, the cops were looking for her everywhere. Back in New York on the morning of April 16, 1981, she was in the back of a van, riding through the St. Albans section of Queens. Two ex-BLA guys, James Dixon York and Anthony LaBorde, were up front. At 10:30 a.m., NYPD officers John Scarangella and Richard Rainey, on patrol in a radio car, saw the van near the corner of 202nd Street and 116th Avenue; it matched the description of the vehicle used in a string of recent robberies, so they hit the lights and signaled to the driver to pull over. As they rolled up to the back of the van, 9mm gunfire poured out of the rear window and through the patrol car windshield. Rainey was hit fourteen times, but he survived. Scarangella wasn't so lucky: he suffered two shots to the head, and after two weeks on life support, he died.*

Assata knew she had to get out of the country, and she considered Libya, Angola, Cuba, and China as possible destinations. The Bahamas was chosen as a suitable short-term refuge. None of the details of Cleo's escape from the United States has ever come to light—certainly none of the participants has ever revealed anything about the operation. But we do know from the trial testimony of a Family member that Big Daddy, Dee, and Doc smuggled Cleo out of the United States in the summer of 1980 and ensconced her in a comfortable seaside villa.[15]

In 1984, Assata eventually arrived in Havana. "Cozy in Cuba," blared a *Newsday* headline. She got political asylum and became an honored guest of the Castro brothers. It was an easy way for the Cubans to give the Americans some political heartburn. The regime lined up a place for her in building 502, number 33, also in the Vedado district, a few miles west of Old Havana. She even got a phone number (326-170)—a luxury in revolutionary Cuba.[16]

Thirty-five years later, Assata's still in Cuba, under the government's protection. Her supporters portray her as a martyred revolutionary living in exile. "The struggle Assata and her comrades took bullets for is still not over," according to the writer Mychal Denzel Smith. "Hands off Assata, now and forever."[17] The radical activist and academic Angela Davis declared that Assata should be allowed to come home and

---

* In June 1986, LaBorde and York were convicted of second-degree murder. Both spent the rest of their lives in prison.

live out her life "with justice and peace."[18] The hip-hop artist Common wrote an ode to the fugitive, and conservatives seethed after the rapper got an invite to a 2011 White House poetry party.

There are others who want to see Assata back in the United States: Foerster family members, the State Troopers Fraternal Association of New Jersey, and the New Jersey State Association of Chiefs of Police have all demanded her return to U.S. soil to face charges. Prominent politicians, including President Donald Trump, have also clamored for her repatriation. And the FBI still wants her: In 2013, on the fortieth anniversary of Trooper Foerster's murder, Assata became the first woman to make the Bureau's "Most Wanted Terrorists" list. "Bringing Joanne Chesimard back here to face justice is still a top priority," said a New Jersey detective on the Joint Terrorism Task Force in Newark.[19]

President Barack Obama reportedly raised the Assata issue with the Cuban government during his visit to the island in 2014. However, as long as she has political asylum status and stays in the regime's favor, it's unlikely that the Cubans will throw her out. Assata has kept a low profile in recent years and no longer grants interviews. That's an understandable move, given that U.S. federal and state authorities continue to offer a $2 million reward for information leading to her arrest.

NEW YORK AND CONNECTICUT, 1980

After the Assata breakout, the armed revolutionary fund-raising continued: led by Doc and his usual crew, and supported by Susan, Marilyn, Judy, and Silvia. Three armored car jobs were botched or aborted, but one in Inwood, New York, paid off big. On April 22, 1980, they hit a Purolator truck doing a run from the European American Bank just over the Queens line in Nassau County. They made off with $529,000, a new Family record.

By 1981, the Family had collected a large stash of money, at least according to the red ledger that Marilyn kept. But Doc and the guys needed more. Running BAAANA wasn't cheap; there were monthly mortgage payments, salaries, utilities, and other expenses. And there was the cost of cocaine to consider: with the price of cocaine on the rise and the male Family members' growing consumption of the white powder, fresh cash infusions were vital.

In the winter of 1981, they executed their next job, the robbery of an armored car outside a Read's department store in a Danbury, Connecticut, shopping center.[20] Susan, Judy, Marilyn, Silvia with Doc, Rison, Big Daddy, Mtayari "Sonny" Sundiata, and Kuwasi "Maroon" Balagoon (formerly Donald Weems) were all part of the job. Balagoon was a real tough guy who'd been a member of the Black Panther Party and the BLA, as well as a Panther 21 defendant. Back in September 1973, he'd broken out of Rahway State Prison in New Jersey, and in May the following year he'd been shot while trying to free a BLA convict, Richard Harris, who was attending a family funeral in Newark in the custody of a prison guard.[21]

They had to call off the Danbury heist at the last minute—the Purolator guy made the cash pickup so quickly that he caught the robbers off guard, Rison testified in 1982.[22] So they went back a second time. Again, no luck: Doc had somehow spooked the armored car personnel, so they left. The crew went back a *third* time. Doc and a couple of the guys subdued one of the guards, but the other managed to get behind the wheel of the armored truck and drove off with all the department store's cash. As the truck roared away, the guys opened fire with automatic weapons and shotguns. "They sprayed the truck up," Rison said. "They used automatic weapons and shotguns on the truck."[23]

Back home in New York, the Family plotted a similar attack in

Co-op City. Deep in the Bronx, Co-op City is the largest cooperative housing complex in the world—a city within a city, complete with high schools, firehouses, and shopping centers.

Marilyn, Susan, and Judy cased the place repeatedly, clocking the coming and going of armored trucks. The Family scheduled expropriations on two different occasions, and each time they called them off when the truck failed to arrive at the appointed time. They tried once more. Doc assembled some of his usual players for the job: Odinga, Rison, Sundiata, and Balagoon. On June 2, 1981, they hit an armored truck idling outside Co-op City's Chase Manhattan Bank branch. The women did the getaway driving, and they made off with $292,000.[24]

But the trigger-happy Rison opened up with his M16, killing one Brinks courier, William Moroney, and wounding another, Michael Schlachter—the Family's first victims.

Doc's considerable drug intake, his carousing at after-hours night-spots, and his increasingly erratic behavior might have suggested that he was losing his grip. But if the women of May 19th had any doubts about Shakur's leadership, they didn't act on them. They still revered Doc as a righteous warrior, a leader, an engine for the national liberation of his people.[25]

And the women didn't seem to back away from Doc's steering of the group into more violent actions. He wanted to target the police, and Sundiata agreed: the police were the enemy of the black community, he said. They wanted to pick up from the Black Liberation Army and target cops in order to show they weren't invulnerable and to demonstrate to the community and progressive forces more generally that there was a new revolutionary force to be reckoned with.

Doc instructed "the crackers" to check out station houses, monitor foot traffic, and see when police shift changes took place. The women were on board. They visited at least six precincts in Manhattan and

Brooklyn.[26] The women drew some schematics, so that the Family could pick the right locations to plant "champagne"—its code word for bombs.

But the Family was thinking about more than dropping off some cases of champagne. They were also tracking individual policemen: when they went to work, what kind of cars they drove, where they lived, where they drank. The women watched them at cop-friendly bars and restaurants, such as Farrell's Bar & Grill near Park Slope.[27] They scoped out Evelyn's Kitchen, not far from the 9th Precinct station house at 321 East Fifth Street on the Lower East Side. According to one restaurant reviewer, the bar had a jukebox that played "loud, slurry gems from the '60s," it was open late, and there were plenty of "boys in bleu" with "bulging holsters" around the place.[28]

Before long, the Family had lists of police officers selected for assassination. May 19th women were now part of a cop-killing conspiracy.

6

DEATH TO THE KLAN

As a movement we have developed [a] program against organized white supremacy. We have struggled to [i]mbue ourselves with the principle of non-collaboration with the state.

—UNDATED INTERNAL MAY 19TH PAPER, "DEDICATION"

May 19th's inner circle might have been only a handful of dedicated militants, but the group's wider network of affiliated organizations brought the numbers up to a hundred to two hundred people. Most were in New York, but there were May 19th groupings elsewhere, including Chicago, Boston, and Austin. Leafleting, street protests, film screenings, and fund-raisers kept members engaged and busy, often to the point of exhaustion. May 19th was a "dogmabound sect" that required complete commitment and submission to the cause.[1] Aboveground member Mary Patten described an "ever-escalating spiral of activity urgency, and exhaustion—the driving machine to will into being an army of white revolutionaries."[2]

Brooklyn was home to a major May 19th affiliate. The dimly lit

Moncada Library was on the second floor of the building at 434 Fifth Avenue in Park Slope. The place was named after Fidel Castro's assault on the Moncada army barracks on July 26, 1953, which had served as the Cuban Revolution's opening salvo. May 19th supported Moncada in the hopes it would draw in supporters and potential recruits. Moncada wasn't exactly a library—there wasn't a lot to read besides left-wing tracts that were strewn around the place. Posters produced by Madame Binh provided a little decoration. Moncada periodically screened agitprop documentaries such as *Women of Telecommunications Station #6*, which chronicled a unit of North Vietnamese women tracking and shooting down U.S. bombers. The suggested donation was $3, child care provided, coffee and danish available.

The library's publications hit on time-tested May 19th tropes: national liberation forces in Zimbabwe, Grenada, and Nicaragua "have seriously weakened the power and world hegemony of u.s. [sic] imperialism."[3]

Moncada proclaimed its solidarity with the "growing armed clandestine forces of the Puerto Rican independence movement" and with Willie Morales, who had "escaped the grip of his captors."[4]

Moncada routinely denounced "killer cops," as well as the "rock 'n' roll industry," which was working to "destroy the minds and drain the energy of youth by promoting disco and drugs."[5] But the biggest issues for Moncada were local. Early in 1981, Mayor Ed Koch held a public question-and-answer session at John Jay High School in Park Slope. Koch was a polarizing figure at the time, and many liberals and leftists loathed the abrasive, combative, pro-Israel Democrat. Koch's appearance presented Moncada with an opportunity: they showed up in force and heckled him mercilessly. Koch quickly left.

Then there was gentrification. During the 1970s, middle-class Manhattanites were snapping up run-down, sandstone-clad row houses in neighborhoods that had once been lumped together as South Brooklyn, and "brownstone Brooklyn" was being born. Traces of an older, scruffier Brooklyn remained: the annual Grecian Festival; free folk dancing with Karl Finger; and the "Good Ol' American" musical stylings of the Wonder Beans at the Good Coffee House. But signs of incipient gentrification were everywhere. The Kings Bay YMCA offered "Inside My Mom: Afternoon of Childbirth Films." Surging real estate prices were pushing out many longtime residents with lesser means, including many African Americans. Beloved mom-and-pop stores, luncheonettes, and candy stores were disappearing fast. James Fixx's *The Complete Book of Running*, a sacred text within yuppie ranks, topped the Brooklyn best-seller list. Brunch spots sprouted up and buried well-heeled Slopers in eggs Benedict, cantaloupe slices, and whole wheat pancakes.

"Gentrification = mass murder," Moncada proclaimed. The library convened a public meeting on January 18, 1980: "The Brownstone Movement and the Ku Klux Klan: A Forum Against Urban Genocide." Moncada condemned neighborhood watch groups such as the Slope Citizens Anti-Crime Network as "vigilante motor patrol" in league with the cops and the KKK. Killer cops, the Klan, gentrification, apartheid, white supremacy—those evils were all linked in a great chain of oppression fostered by a capitalist, imperialist system.

However, many Park Slope residents were genuinely panicked by crime. What is still called "vice" was rampant. Brothels dotted the neighborhood, as they had since the Second World War, when priapic seamen from the Brooklyn Navy Yard had prowled the Slope.* Every week, a neighborhood paper, the *Phoenix*, recounted in lurid detail as-

---

* Even today, brothels continue to operate in Park Slope: the *New York Times* reported in November 2018 that 483 Fourth Avenue was used as a brothel, with the connivance of the eight-unit building's landlord.

sorted ruptures in the public order. An ax-wielding maniac hacked two homeless men to death in nearby Carroll Gardens. The Ching-a-Ling motorcycle gang was busted after cops from the 76th Precinct found dope, handguns, and a blackjack in their clubhouse. Neighborhood delinquents had robbed and assaulted a man and tossed him into the United States' filthiest waterway, the toxic, reeking Gowanus Canal.

Slope residents must have been bewildered by Moncada's claims that brownstoners were the ones waging genocide. Moncada's rhetoric, said the *Phoenix*, "alienates most people—including many who describe themselves as leftists."[6] Moncada was becoming a public nuisance.

On May 9, 1981, six Moncada members—Richard Ruth, Jonathan Keller, Terry Bisson, Lisa Roth, Donna Borup, and Susan Rautenberg—were doing their usual leafleting at Fifth Avenue and 15th Street.* They got into an argument with Ralph Busti, a resident of Sheepshead Bay, Brooklyn. The cops arrived, and Busti said the activists assaulted him. The Moncada people claimed he came at them with a table leg. The NYPD sided with Busti. Donna Borup recalled what happened next, as reported in a Brooklyn newspaper: "They [the police] walked over and said, 'you're under arrest.' Then one woman said, 'wait a minute, what is going on?' Then the police started clubbing us."[7]

Ruth et al. were hauled off to the 72nd Precinct and charged with resisting arrest, disorderly conduct, and assaulting an officer. According to Moncada's account of the episode, the cops "threatened to burn down the Moncada Library, to punch out our teeth, to rape the

---

* Bisson would go on to become a Hugo Award–winning science fiction writer and the author of a novel about John Brown, *Fire on the Mountain*. "My novel was inspired by the Republic of New Africa . . . revolutionary Black nationalists dedicated to liberating the Deep South," he told an interviewer in 2009. Terry Bisson, *The Left Left Behind* (Oakland, California: PM Press, 2009), p. 105.

women."[8] In his mug shot, Ruth's head is swathed in a turban-sized white bandage.

. . .

There was another May 19th affiliate, much larger than Moncada, with outposts in Chicago, San Francisco, Washington, Austin, and Northampton, Massachusetts.

The John Brown Anti-Klan Committee, or JBAKC, regularly denounced abortion clinic bombers, Zionism, imperialism, fascism, killer cops, and high-security prisons such as Attica, Marion, and San Quentin—"Amerika's Koncentration Kamps," as the committee called them.[9] But as its name suggested, the group's focus was on the Ku Klux Klan. The title of the JBAKC's periodical said it all: *Death to the Klan!*

They did more than just publish. Although they didn't use the name, the committee was an early forming of the "antifa" (short for "antifascist") movement that would come to prominence in the United States after the "Unite the Right" rally in Charlottesville, Virginia, in August 2018. The JBAKC counterprotested at Klan marches, threw rocks and bottles, and brawled with Klansmen.

Antifa began in Germany after the Second World War to confront and resist neo-Nazis, by violence if necessary. By the 1970s, antifa reached the United States. "After Treblinka and Auschwitz," wrote the historian and activist Mark Bray, "anti-fascists [in Germany] committed themselves to fighting to the death the ability of organized Nazis to say anything." In Bray's *Antifa: The Anti-Fascist Handbook* (2017), he quoted a Baltimore activist who explained the antifa approach: "You fight them by writing letters and making phone calls so you don't have to fight them with fists. You fight them with fists so you don't have to fight them with knives. You fight them with knives so you don't have to fight them with guns. You fight them with guns so you don't have to fight them with tanks." [10]

An event in Greensboro, North Carolina, in 1979 energized the JBAKC. The Workers Viewpoint Organization, or WVO, a minuscule Maoist sect, was organizing textile mill workers in China Grove, in the state's rural interior.

During the summer of 1978, the Maoists protested when the KKK tried to screen *Birth of a Nation*, a 1915 film that had its world premiere in Woodrow Wilson's White House and helped revive the dormant KKK. The Maoists torched a Confederate battle flag and chanted "Nazis, Klan, scum of the land." Klansmen screamed "Hitler was right, Hitler was right," and whipped out weapons. [11] Somebody called the incident the China Grove Standoff. [12] Eventually everybody stood down and went home.

A few months later, the WVO announced a protest march and conference in nearby Greensboro, to be held on November 3. The theme: "Death to the Klan." Before the event, the Maoists ditched their anodyne name and rebranded themselves as the Communist Workers Party, or CWP. Like the JBAKC, the CWP was an early (if unstated) part of the antifa movement: the Maoists called for "armed self-defense" against fascists, Nazis, and white supremacists. [13]

Long-suffering African American residents had serious doubts about the CWP's plans. Memories of civil rights–era KKK violence were still fresh, and a march by avowed communists would almost certainly invite Klan mayhem and collateral damage to black citizens. "We questioned why the Communist Workers chose to march in our community, a community that was already going through its own private hell," one resident said. [14]

In an open letter to the KKK, local CWP leader Nelson N. Johnson called the organization "one of the most treacherous scum elements

produced by the dying system of capitalism" and "two-bit cowards."
Johnson vowed to "physically smash the racist KKK wherever it rears
its ugly head." [15] On the day of the demonstration, local cops took an
early lunch. A rabble of Klansmen and Nazis arrived in a nine-vehicle
caravan, pulled shotguns and rifles out of their car trunks, and opened
fire.

The CWP managed to return a few rounds. In the end, four communists were dead and five others seriously wounded. "I didn't know
there was going to be a fight," one Klansman said, "but if you smack
a man in the face with an egg, you got to expect to get your butt
whipped." [16] The following April, an all-white jury acquitted five Klansmen charged in the shootings.

• • •

Racial terrorism wasn't confined to the South. Not far from Syracuse,
New York, the Knights of the KKK held a "patriotic rally" in July 1975.
The KKK's invitation was extended to "All White, Christian, Patriotic
Americans. For God, Country and Family. Others Please Stay Away."
To the horror of May 19th, the Klan was even on the move in New
York City. In the Rockaways, a narrow peninsula in the outer reaches
of Queens, African Americans were moving in, and some of the white
residents didn't like the change in the area's racial makeup.

A few Rockaways residents formed their very own Klan Klavern.
The Queens Klansmen nurtured grievances and rubbed racial sores.
They handed out hate literature, including pamphlets with an image
of a sheeted man brandishing a fiery cross atop a rampant steed. Off
duty, the Klansmen would slip out of their robes and booze and brawl
at taverns in the Irishtown section of Rockaway Park. The Ku Klux-
ers had even infiltrated the ranks of police and prison guards in New
York state prisons. Prison Commissioner Benjamin Ward told them to

hang up their sheets for good or they'd be terminated, but the problem persisted.

Both Susan and Alan were JBAKC leaders, but they didn't advertise the fact that they were part of May 19th, and few if any of the rank and file knew about the connection.

Unbeknown to most of the JBAKC's members, fighting the Klan likely wasn't the group's most important purpose. Even more critical may have been its role as a recruiting ground for May 19th: activists who demonstrated a rock-solid commitment to revolutionary anti-imperialism were ideal candidates. JBAKC leaders worked as talent spotters.[17] The May 19th inner circle did the final vetting. If those who made the cut weren't already living in key May 19th cities, they were expected to relocate. Some ended up joining the underground apparatus itself.

• • •

Timothy Adolf Blunk was from the Jersey suburbs, born in Princeton on May 21, 1957. His mother, Mary Ann, was a pianist and music teacher, and his father, Theodore, a Presbyterian minister. Tim's middle name was an unusual one to give to a child in post–World War II America, but apparently it was something of a family tradition. Tim had a couple of brothers, Jonathan and Seth, and the Blunks had a nice spread in upper-middle-class Bridgewater Township. "Our household was filled with love, music and creativity," Tim recalled.[18]

The Blunks weren't typical New Jersey surburbanites. Social justice concerns percolated within the household—through the Presbyterian church, the Blunks got involved in the anti–Vietnam War movement. The entire family worked for a time on a dirt-poor Papago Indian reservation in southwest Arizona, and they helped out in an antipoverty program in Newark, about forty miles away.

In the seventies, Newark was an urban husk that hadn't recovered from rioting a decade earlier. On July 12, 1967, an African American cab driver, John Smith, was hauled in by Newark cops for allegedly tailgating and driving the wrong way up a one-way street. Smith supposedly mouthed off—a dangerous thing to do when facing members of the lily white Newark force. Police administered a savage beating, and after some time in a cell, Smith was stretchered out to Beth Israel Hospital.

Five days of rioting ensued. The demonstrations had all the elements of the violent unrest that plagued other American cities during that long, hot summer: Molotov cocktails, National Guard troops, city block after city block in flames, false rumors of "negro snipers" on the rooftops. New Jersey Governor Richard J. Hughes, apoplectic and red-faced, told reporters that a "criminal insurrection" was under way.[19] By the time it was over, twenty-six people were dead, more than seven hundred were injured, and $10 million in property was destroyed.

The mayhem in neighboring Newark had made a profound impression on ten-year-old Tim. As a teenager, he grew increasingly concerned about the gap between the country's rich and poor and about his own position of economic and racial privilege, and according to family members, Tim felt guilty about being a white male.

Still, Tim flourished at Bridgewater-Raritan High School East. His freshman biology teacher called him the brightest student he ever had. Blond-haired and blue-eyed, Tim was described by many as smart, caring, and idealistic.[20] He served as vice president of the senior class and was a standout on the basketball court. He graduated in the top 5 percent of his class of 489 students and earned a National Merit Scholarship. Tim was "blessed with it all," his guidance counselor said.[21] Even his penmanship was stellar.

Tim landed athletic and academic scholarships to Denison University in Granville, Ohio. The campus style was preppy, and the place was full of rich, conservative white kids who didn't have the wattage to get into Stanford or Brown. Tim soon realized he'd made a mistake; after his first year, he transferred to Hampshire College in Amherst, Massachusetts.

Hampshire was a much better fit. An "experimental" college packed with hippies, health food, and geodesic domes for faculty members offered Tim the freedom he was seeking. He took up modern dance and studied jazz and classical guitar. But he had multiple talents and interests, and he aced his biology and chemistry courses and landed a summer job as a research assistant at science-heavy Rockefeller University in New York.*

Campus politics skewed far left—if there were any conservatives at the place, they kept themselves well hidden. Tim got involved in the movement to end the college's investments in apartheid South Africa and took a college-sponsored trip to communist Cuba. His senior thesis was on the social construction of gender. In his free time, he helped set up the Amherst chapter of the John Brown Anti-Klan Committee.

Tim met Susan during his time at Amherst. Although Susan was a committed lesbian, she had a crush on him. He was funny and whimsical, and there was "a quiet beauty about him," she said. "He had a lithe dancer's body." [22] Some sexual frisson, perhaps, but nothing more. Later, in the underground, Susan and Tim would work together. He looked up to her, and she considered him her protégé.

Tim moved to New York in 1981. The country was in the midst

---

* Tim coauthored a scientific paper, "Correction of Ongoing Motor Output of the Cat." Back at Hampshire, he read an article about other medical experiments on felines and sat up all night brooding about their mistreatment. "He felt such empathy for the poor cats," his Hampshire roommate recalled. Tom Kehoe and Beverly McCarron, "The Making of a Radical: From Bridgewater to Prison He Turns to Armed Struggle," *Courier-News* (Bridgewater, NJ), March 4, 1985, A-4.

of a deep recession—the worst economic downturn since the Great Depression—and he was lucky to land a job as a gym teacher at the private St. Ann's School in Brooklyn Heights. He had already made the decision that he wasn't going to pursue a professional career.

His left-wing political enthusiasms were all-consuming: "Political activism came to define my life above all else," he said. "I grew increasingly distant from my family as my politics grew more radical and my judgment more clouded."[23] He thought about going to El Salvador to join the guerrillas fighting to overthrow the U.S.-backed regime. Instead, he reconnected with his old friend Susan, who convinced him to join her in fighting for the cause right at home in New York City.

Tim joined May 19th. Like Alan and his sperm donation, the new member of the inner circle would be asked to make a specific contribution. Silvia had been living in the United States for two decades, but she had remained an Italian national. She felt that a marriage to an American could shield her from any potential problems with the Immigration and Naturalization Service. Tim readily agreed to be her husband as part of his initiation into the revolutionary group.

· · ·

In May 19th's inventory of evil, the apartheid regime in South Africa was at or near the top. In 1981, the country's national rugby team, the Springboks, embarked on a U.S. tour. The tour's sponsor, the Eastern Rugby Union, had received a $25,000 gift from a South African businessman eager to polish his country's international image as a rogue state hell-bent on maintaining white supremacy. May 19th member Eve Rosahn called the Springboks "ambassadors of genocide."[24] Media coverage of the touring Springboks was considerable, and May 19th concluded that the rugby team was a perfect target for radical antiapartheid protests.

On September 22, a bomb went off in the Eastern Rugby Union clubhouse in Schenectady.* The incident's still unsolved, but there is a good chance that Doc and the May 19th women were responsible—after all, they'd given a lot of thought to planting "champagne" at one of the matches; however, their involvement was never proven.[25] Wherever the Springboks played, antiapartheid activists met them. New York mayor Ed Koch vetoed a proposed match in the city, saying it would be too hard to provide police protection.

As the tour wound down, activists learned the date and time of the British Airways flight that was supposed to take the Springboks home. Some sixty demonstrators, calling themselves the "Coalition to Stop the Apartheid Rugby Tour," showed up at John F. Kennedy International Airport late on the afternoon of September 26, 1981. At 6:40 p.m., a handful of protestors, all members of May 19th, slipped past security and into the departure lounge.

It turned out that somebody had gotten the flight information wrong; the Springboks weren't there. But no one was going home without doing some vigorous protesting. Tim punched a cop (in self-defense, he said later). Donna splashed a Port Authority policeman, Evan Goodstein, in the face with a burning liquid—described variously by the press, cops, and prosecutors as lye, a vinegar mixture, and butyric acid.† Whatever the stuff was, Goodstein lost 80 percent of his

---

* At least one May 19th member seemed to hate rugby itself. "It's a horrible scene," Donna said. "I hope I don't offend anybody, I'd like to know why you do it, it's a very violent game [and] there is a whole drinking scene." Transcript of Interview by Clayton Riley WBAI of Donna Borup, Mary Patten, and Denise Lewis on March 29, 1982, Susan Rosenberg Papers, Sophia Smith Collection, Smith College.

† Butyric acid, according to the New Jersey Department of Public Health, "is a colorless, oily liquid with a strong, characteristic smell. Contact with the substance can severely irritate and burn the skin and eyes with possible eye damage." More recently, the militant Sea Shepherd Conservation Society has used butyric acid stink bombs in its confrontations with Japanese whaling vessels on the high seas.

vision in one eye. A total of twenty-three policemen and two security guards were hurt.

Eve, Donna, Tim, and two other May 19th members, Mary Patten and Margo Pelletier, were hauled off to jail. The *New York Post* headline the next day was "Rugby Riots: No Bail for 5." There was no mention of May 19th, but there was an accompanying photo of their perp walk, the women shuffling along in chains. Tim, shaggy-haired and sporting a meaningful mustache, had his fist thrust straight up in the classic left-wing gesture of defiance.

But Tim was putting on a brave face: his arrest was a nightmare, he said. While he was handcuffed and facedown in a police van, cops kicked him repeatedly. His balls swelled up to the size of grapefruits, and he hobbled around with a cane for weeks afterward.[26] He lost his job at St. Ann's—the school had a progressive reputation, but an alleged rioter on the staff was too much.

Tim agreed to an interview with a reporter from a Brooklyn weekly. Looking a bit pale, he projected "a shadowy and quiet image," according to the paper, as he fulminated about the Springboks ("organizing for white supremacy in this country") and "killer cops."[27]

The "Anti-Springbok Five," as May 19th dubbed the arrested protesters, were charged with a slew of offenses, including rioting, mob action, criminal trespass, and resisting arrest. In May 1982, they appeared before Judge Arthur Lonschein at the State Supreme Court in Queens. (Except Donna, who skipped bail. The FBI put out the word that she might be in Nicaragua, helping to build the socialist state.[28] Thirty-seven years later, Donna is still a fugitive, and the Bureau is offering $100,000 for information leading to her arrest.)

Mary went for a jury trial. The verdict: guilty. Tim, Eve, and Margo decided to plead out. On July 8, 1982, the four appeared for sentencing. The courtroom was packed with supporters from May 19th and its associated groups. Eve and Tim got nine months each, and Margo received six. Mary drew a full year behind bars. After the judge passed sentence, May 19th members and their supporters shouted fiery political slogans, and he gave each of them an extra thirty days for contempt.

. . .

Eve, Tim, Margo, and Mary served their time at the city's sprawling Rikers Island penal colony, a 444-acre island in the East River, just a hundred feet from the end of Runway 22 at LaGuardia Airport and only six miles from Times Square.

Ring-necked pheasants, woodcocks, and grouse flourished beyond the razor wire. So did packs of wild dogs. Inside the wire, in the damp concrete cell blocks, seven thousand men, women, and teenagers, about a third of them with histories of violent crime, awaited trial or the end of their sentences. Rikers was a "crowded, noisy, and potentially dangerous place," *New York* magazine's star reporter Nicholas Pileggi wrote in 1981. In point of fact, Rikers was, and remains, one of the most violent lockups in the United States. In 2018, New York mayor Bill de Blasio announced plans to shut down Rikers and replace it with a "modern community-based jail system that is smaller, safer and fairer."[29]

The four May 19th members managed to keep busy and stay out of trouble. Mary Patten said the women had "created 'prison art' with permitted materials . . . collages made from torn-up magazines, toothpaste substituting for glue."[30] During his ten months behind bars, Tim played a lot of basketball—the only white guy the black prisoners allowed into their games.

The last few months had been traumatic for Tim. He wasn't some regular street punk, somebody who might consider a police beating

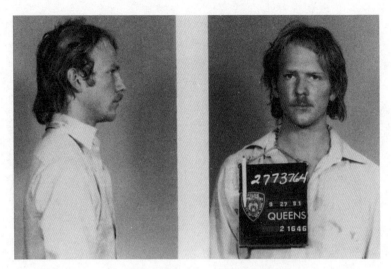

Tim Blunk: After a stretch in Rikers Island, ready for the armed struggle

and a stretch in Rikers as just the cost of doing business. But he didn't leave Rikers broken—far from it. He was boiling with fresh revolutionary passions. "I left jail ready to sacrifice myself for 'the struggle,'" he said.[31]

There was to be no more of the mainline Protestant liberalism that had suffused his New Jersey childhood. Now Tim called himself a "communist resistance fighter."[32] He decided that the struggle required what he called "the judicious application of a few rounds of ammunition pointed in the right direction for a limited number of years [which] will be able to resolve an enormous problem of violence which has been our experience for 400 years."[33] He was ready to serve in the armed campaign and fight U.S. imperialism directly.

Susan Rosenberg and the others were waiting for him.

7

ELIZABETH FUCKED UP

Cocaine use by Doc and some of his crew was out of control. In the past, some of the money from their armed robberies had gone to support "freedom fighters" such as Joanne Chesimard and underwrite the BAAANA operation, but now they had one priority: raising money to buy coke. The FBI concluded later that by that point, the group had "deteriorated into nothing more than a band of greedy, cocaine-addicted criminals, oriented toward immediate material acquisitions, and personal financial gain."[1] They were looking for the next big score.

They found a potential target about twenty miles northeast of Manhattan, in Rockland County, New York. Then, as now, the mall in Nanuet drew affluent shoppers from upstate New York, New Jersey, and the City. May 19th women did multiple reconnaissance runs and noted the coming and going of Brinks armored trucks at the mall. The Brinks men handled large bags loaded with cash. The guards were armed, but they didn't look particularly imposing. This had the promise to become the Family's biggest haul yet.

As the planning for the operation got under way, the women must have had doubts about where the Family was going and what their role had become. After previous robberies the proceeds went into a central fund. But things would be different this time: rather than pooling their haul, the money would be split among the participants—just as ordinary criminals handled their robbery hauls. But if the women had doubts, they didn't act on them. As in previous heists, they lined up vehicles, printed fake IDs, and made sure the safe houses were ready.

The preparation for the job was extensive and meticulous and included seven training sessions: running, martial arts, and on at least three occasions, dry runs of the robbery. Kamau Bayete (né Peter Middleton) worked as an acupuncturist at Doc's BAAANA clinic up in Harlem. He was also one of the crew addicted to coke, and he spent a lot of time hanging out with Shakur. He was at a couple of planning meetings that Doc convened at apartments in the West 90s and later gave evidence. He said that Doc's code name for the operation was "the big dance."

Also, according to Bayete, they discussed ahead of time what to do with anyone who got in the way. Sonny, he said, gave instructions on how to deal with noncomplying guards or troublesome civilians: "You tell them to freeze. If they don't freeze, you shoot them. You take them out."[2]

There would be an all-male component made up of Doc, Sonny, Balagoon, Samuel Brown, and two other African American Family members, Cecilio "Chui" Ferguson and Edward Joseph, aka "Jamal Baltimore."[3] And, as with previous operations, there was an all-women team that included Marilyn, Susan, and Judy.[4] Silvia would help out. The women enlisted Eve Rosahn, who loaned Judy her tan Honda and rented a red Chevrolet van for Family use.[5]

The white edge had a couple of fresh faces, both of whom had been members of the Weather Underground: David Gilbert and Kathy Boudin, a survivor of the Village town house explosion in 1970.* They agreed to help their old pals with the logistics. Gilbert rented a U-Haul in the Bronx.

The staging area was the safe house at 590 East Third Street, apartment 4-C, in New Rochelle, New York, which Marilyn had rented using one of her favorite aliases, "Carol Durant"—the same one she had used to register her white Oldsmobile.[6]

On October 20, 1981, everybody assembled at the apartment, and in the early afternoon, they headed out, convoy style, toward the Tappan Zee Bridge and Rockland County. There were four vehicles: the Olds, a tan Honda, and two rented vans. They had 9mm pistols, M16 rifles, ski masks, and bulletproof vests.

Two of Doc's best men, Odinga and Rison, dropped out of the heist. They'd been in on the planning but could see huge holes in the operation. Odinga worried about the time of day when the job was supposed to go down: late afternoon, rush hour, when the streets would most likely be clogged with traffic. It didn't seem to him conducive for a getaway. He also wasn't blind to the fact that at that point Doc and his crew were trigger-happy and jacked up on coke half the time. Odinga said he wasn't going on some death trip. Rison had his own worries about the job. He wasn't confident in Doc's plan—there was no African American neighborhood to disappear into if things went bad.

• • •

Two Brinks guards, Peter Paige and Joseph Trombino, were making a collection at the Nanuet National Bank, their last call of the day. At

---

* Boudin, a Bryn Mawr graduate, was the daughter of Leonard Boudin, a renowned left-wing New York lawyer. Among his clients in the early 1960s was the revolutionary Cuban government, which was fighting in U.S. courts for the right to expropriate a billion dollars' worth of assets on the island controlled by multinational U.S. corporations. Boudin biographer Susan Braudy wrote that Leonard did more than argue in court on Fidel Castro's behalf; he was also sharing a twenty-year-old mistress with him, a Cuban dancer named Kassana Worszeck.

3:55 p.m., the red Chevy van roared up, and masked men jumped out and started firing before their feet even hit the ground. Paige died instantly from multiple gunshot wounds to his neck and torso. A burst from an automatic rifle tore into Trombino's shoulder and upper arm, nearly severing the limb. "I've got no arm!" he screamed.' He fortunately survived and kept his arm, but it was never the same.

Almost exactly twenty years later, Trombino was still on the job with Brinks. On a bright morning in early September, he was in the basement garage of a skyscraper in lower Manhattan, guarding a truck carrying $14 million. At 8:46, a jet crashed into the building. At 9:03, another plane crashed into the tower next door. At 9:15, Trombino got on the radio to the Brinks dispatcher and said that a cop was telling him to get the hell out, move that truck, the building's unstable. It was the last anyone heard from Trombino.

Shakur and the guys roared off with six bags totaling $1.6 million in cash.[8] They were in the red van, heading east down Route 59 toward the switch point outside a vacant Korvettes discount store, where Susan, Judy, and Marilyn were waiting along with Boudin and Gilbert. They needed to ditch the Chevy, move Shakur and his men and the cash into the waiting cars and U-Haul truck, and take the New York State Thruway back across the Hudson. They assumed that the cops would be looking for a red van driven by black men—not some cars with white chicks and a rental truck with a heavily bearded white dude behind the wheel.

But things didn't work out as they'd planned.

Sandra Torgersen, a college student, had been spending a long weekend at her parents' house and eagerly awaiting a Dan Fogelberg concert scheduled for that night. The family home faced the Korvettes parking lot, and from the living room window she saw people moving from two vehicles into the U-Haul truck, and some had weapons, she recalled.[9] She immediately phoned the police. Cops from all over the county had been swarming in ever since radio calls had gone out about the savage gunplay at the mall. BOLO: be on the lookout for a red van, a tan Honda, and a U-Haul. There were a few escape routes, and the trip back to New York meant using the Thruway and going across the Tappan Zee Bridge.

At the intersection of Route 59 and Mountainview Avenue, right by the Thruway on-ramp, Nyack policemen pulled over the U-Haul and told Gilbert and Boudin to get their hands up in the air and get out of the van. Sonny cracked the rear door and peeked out. "Shit, it's the police," he said.[10]

The cops came around to the back and rattled the door. There was some noise on the other side, and then the door burst open. Ski-masked men opened up with their M16s. There were loud cracks, and the reek of cordite. Detective Arthur Keenan was hit and Officer Waverly "Chipper" Brown, the only African American on the Nyack force, was shot and fell to the pavement. A masked man stood over Brown and shot him dead with a 9mm pistol.

Another Nyack cop, Sergeant Edward O'Grady, returned fire with his .357 magnum service revolver—just six shots, then he had to reload. Then a guy in a mask shot him with an M16. O'Grady later died on the operating table at Nyack Hospital. Witnesses identified Samuel Brown as one of the trigger-pullers who had gunned down the cops.[11]

It was rush hour, and just as Odinga had predicted, the streets were clogged with traffic. Sirens wailed, pedestrians panicked—it was total chaos. An off-duty New York City corrections officer, Michael Koch, happened to be in the vicinity. He heard the shots, saw Boudin running, and drew his .38-caliber service revolver. He chased her on foot and managed to run her down. "Move and I'll blow out your fucking brains," Koch said.[12] She didn't put up a fight and kept repeating that it wasn't she who had shot the cops.

Boudin pled guilty to murder in the second degree and to first-degree robbery, was sentenced to a twenty-year-to-life term, and was released in 2003. Today she's an assistant professor at Columbia and a codirector of the university's Center for Justice. Gilbert stood trial, was convicted, and received three consecutive sentences of twenty-five years to life for second-degree murder. He's serving his time at the maximum-security Wende Correctional Facility in western New York State and will be eligible for parole in 2056.

The rest of the teams kept moving. Balagoon found a white BMW idling on the overpass, with a woman named Norma Hill and her mother in the front seats.[13] He waved his gun, kicked them out, and carjacked his way out of town and back to New York. Separately, Shakur and Ferguson headed off into the woods on foot and disappeared. Chui buried his M16 and 9mm pistol, and he (and almost certainly Shakur) hid for more than a day before they were rescued by Family members.[14]

Meanwhile, Gilbert and Brown were still in the Honda with Judy, who was driving wildly. On Christian Herald Road, the police spotted their careening car. Judy lost control and crashed. Gilbert crawled from the wreckage, and Brown was immobilized inside with a broken neck.

As the police moved closer to the car, they saw Judy reaching for something on the back seat: it was a 9mm pistol. Before she could grab it, the cops overpowered her. They popped the trunk and discovered more weapons, ammunition, a bulletproof vest, ski masks, and bags of stolen cash. While patting everyone down, they also found a 9mm clip with fourteen live rounds in Brown's sock.

In a photo taken shortly after her arrest, Judy looked crazed, with wild hair and a freakish smile. While being processed, she was also spitting and screaming the whole time. An FBI special agent said later that Judy reminded him of the diabolically possessed Regan MacNeil character in *The Exorcist*.[15] Tip Tipograph represented her.

When the shooting started during the getaway, Marilyn had drawn her 9mm pistol and attempted to join the fight but accidentally shot herself in the leg instead. It was a nasty wound, and a lot of blood was pumping out. "Hold on," someone told her, "medical help is coming."[16]

Marilyn got back into her Olds and powered through the pain. Sundiata took the wheel, having turned down her suggestion to ride in the trunk. "I'll take my chances up front," he said.[17] "I didn't think we were going to get out," Sundiata said, but the Olds sped off and somehow they made it across the Tappan Zee Bridge.[18]

Susan's job was to get members of the primary team back across the Hudson.[19] But she had lost her nerve and melted down instead. She was reduced to babbling: "We're never going to get out of here," she said over and over again.[20] Sonny took over the driving, and they, too, managed to avoid the police.

Brown would receive a seventy-five-year sentence for his Brinks-related crimes. While in custody, he told the FBI about Balagoon's role in the operation. Police arrested Balagoon in the Bronx on December 20, 1981. During his trial for armed robbery, grand larceny, and murder, he told the court, "Money couriers are safe as long as they don't put their bodies in the way of somebody else's money. . . . This is because the goal of an expropriation is to collect revolutionary, compulsory tax and not casualties. Had Peter Paige not acted the fool he would've lived and his co-worker would not have been injured." Balagoon was convicted on all counts and was sentenced to seventy-five years to life. He died in 1986 in a New York State prison of pneumocystis pneumonia, an AIDS-related illness. After his death, Judy described him as "simply lustful of life and life's sensuous pleasures—food, people, wine and laughter. Lustful too, for battle against the enemy."[21]*

The survivors made for the Mount Vernon safe house, roughly twenty miles from the scene of the crime. Somebody had called Alan, who was in the Bronx working in outpatient care at Lincoln Hospital, to come and work on Marilyn's blasted-out leg.

Alan already had plenty of experience treating gunshot wounds: Attica, Wounded Knee, overnight shifts in the Bronx. He stopped the blood flow and gave Marilyn a transfusion, splinted her leg, and wrapped her in a blanket. Alan likely saved her life, although she would walk with a pronounced limp from then on. They took her to recover at another safe house, at 2819 Barker Avenue in the Bronx.

FBI agents later overheard Shakur talk about Susan in a Bureau-bugged apartment. He'd relied on her as a getaway driver, but in the frenzy surrounding the shoot-out, she'd wigged out. "Elizabeth fucked up," he told his companions.[22]

Susan wasn't the only one. Not only did the big dance expose the Family as more criminals than revolutionaries, it now made them cop killers, too.

The cops also recovered all of the $1.6 million and would soon find out about the safe house in Mount Vernon. Somebody had already cleaned the place out but had left behind some evidence, including ammunition, a bloody mattress, and gore-soaked clothing. The police also found a fingerprint belonging to William R. Johnson, aka "Bilal Sunni-Ali," aka "Spirit," who was part of Doc's crew. Eleven months

---

* Two other Brinks defendants, Jamal Joseph and Chui Ferguson, were acquitted of murder and robbery charges but convicted as accessories for harboring Mutulu Shakur, and each received a sentence of twelve and a half years. Joseph served his time in the federal prison in Leavenworth, Kansas; Ferguson was behind bars in the U.S. penitentiary in Lewisburg, Pennsylvania. Today, Joseph is a professor at Columbia University's School of the Arts and the author of *Tupac Shakur Legacy* and *Panther Baby: A Life of Rebellion and Reinvention.*

later, local cops in Belize picked up Spirit on a drug charge, learned that the FBI wanted him back in the United States, and packed him off on a plane to Miami.

. . .

The first principle of terrorist tradecraft—what the nineteenth-century Russian revolutionaries called *konspiratsiya*—is: don't write anything down, and if you have to, destroy it as quickly as you can. In the hands of the security forces, things such as diagrams, ledgers, and letters can become lethal weapons.

But terrorists, guerrillas, and insurgents the world over have routinely violated this rule. For example, the Islamic State in Syria and Iraq kept detailed accounts of strategy, personnel, revenues, and expenses. During the invasion of Afghanistan in 2001, coalition forces recovered mountains of papers ranging from al-Qaeda membership application forms to notes on weapons of mass destruction. And when U.S. Navy Seals raided al-Qaeda leader Osama bin Laden's compound in Abbottabad, Pakistan, in May 2011, the special operators found multiple computer hard drives full of documents, videos, and the jihadists' inevitable porn collection.

Scaling up requires administration, and administration means paperwork. There's much to keep track of: aliases, phone numbers, addresses, way too much for anyone to remember accurately. Well-planned operations require surveillance, and that meant taking notes and drawing diagrams. After-action analyses help the learning process: What were the tactical, operational, and strategic effects, if any? What did we do right, what went wrong, and how can we do better?

Post-Brinks, there was a lengthy paper trail for the FBI to follow.

8

WHAT THIS COUNTRY NEEDS IS A LITTLE MORE CHAOS

Two important May 19th members were in Texas during the botched Brinks heist. At the time they weren't on the FBI's radar, but that would soon change.

Elizabeth Anna Duke was born on November 25, 1940, in tiny Beeville, Texas, to Martha and Howard Weir. Betty Ann and her sisters, Mary and Kathleen, grew up in San Antonio, where Martha taught school and Howard ran a medical supply business. The Weirs were solidly middle-class, churchgoing Methodists.

At Jefferson High School, Betty Ann was an outstanding student—on the honor roll for three years and a member of the National Honor Society—and the leader of the pep squad. A relative described her as "cheerful, happy, friendly, and lovely."[1] As an adult, Betty Ann could mostly fit in anywhere, at five feet, six inches tall and with "nondescript features," according to the FBI.[2] But there was one striking thing about her appearance: her distinctive hazel blue eyes.

After high school, Betty Ann enrolled at Southwestern University in Georgetown, Texas, where she joined a sorority—a "prom girl with a beehive hairdo," according to friends.[3] She wasn't particularly politi-cal, although Mary said that even as a child, her sister "abhorred racist language, ideas and their perpetuation in any form, including jokes."[4] After graduating from Southwestern in 1962, Betty Ann married David Haylon and became a Dallas housewife. By 1965, they had two kids, Russell and Cheryl. Betty Ann and David split up that year.

Betty Ann's otherwise ordinary life story took a new direction in the mid-1960s, shortly after she remarried. "My world view was shaken up by the civil rights movement—the freedom riders, the riots, the sit-ins," she said. "It made me look at the world differently. I was raised when blacks rode in the back of the bus, and when they started fight-ing for their civil rights it moved me."[5] She supported a farmworkers' strike in the Rio Grande Valley in 1967. Then she and her family joined a lay religious community in Chicago focused on social justice.

The year 1970 was a tumultuous one. On April 28, President Rich-ard M. Nixon ordered a U.S. and South Vietnamese invasion of ostensi-bly neutral Cambodia. Two days later, in a nationally televised address, Nixon described the operation as an "incursion" aimed at eliminating North Vietnamese sanctuaries. His opponents said he was widening the war he had pledged to wind down.

Across the country, the antiwar movement erupted. Thousands of college students went on strike. Radicals torched university buildings, trashed Reserve Officer Training Corps facilities, and rained rocks down on police cars.

Things got particularly ugly in Ohio and Mississippi. At Kent State University on May 4, ill-trained, jittery National Guardsmen opened fire during a campus protest, killing four students and wounding nine others. Crosby, Stills, Nash & Young memorialized the outrage in "Ohio," which soon became a countercultural anthem. Eleven days later, at predominantly African American Jackson State College, local cops unloaded into a dormitory, killing two students and wounding twelve.

That year, Betty Ann and her second husband divorced, apparently over political differences—he didn't support the civil rights movement that had so inspired her. She decided to pursue a PhD on the prairie at North Texas State University in Denton, just south of the Oklahoma border. She had a fellowship and a teaching assistant job in the English department.

The counterculture and radical politics had penetrated even this remote and conservative corner of the country and Betty Ann wanted to be part of the new scene. During student orientation week in late July and early August 1970, she did a little leafleting. It was reported to university administrators that she was hoping to make an unspecified "subculture group" part of the official orientation program. One of the handbills asked, "What's happening to your head? What part are you going to play in a world in revolution!" and invited students to come down to the park on campus "to dig on some music and to rap about where we are and what we can create."[6]

On the evenings of July 30 and August 3, Betty Ann shouted out her political thoughts in the campus park to whoever had come to listen. The university said the gatherings were unauthorized and that Betty Ann had used profane language. According to a security guard who was monitoring the get-togethers, Betty Ann called the board of regents a "stupid bunch of motherfuckers" and said that "the girls would be locked up in the dorms like a bunch of whores."[7]

She denied the obscenity charge, and she claimed her First Amendment rights to say whatever she wanted. The regents didn't agree, and in September, she lost her teaching assistant gig and her graduate fellowship. Betty Ann fought the decision in an angry open letter. The once beehived Texas gal had adopted a radical new stance:

the regents, she said, were guilty of crimes that were "far more serious than mother-fucking."[8] She closed her letter with a dramatic counter-cultural flourish: "We have already begun to define ourselves and the world we live in. We know that we are fucked over, yet we are not victims. We affirm life! . . . Live the revolution! All power to the people!"

Betty Ann went to court to get the decision overturned but got nowhere. To support herself and her children, she held down a variety of jobs: teacher, bartender, nursing home attendant. In 1979, she was hired as a researcher in the House of Representatives at the state capital in Austin. A supervisor described her as a rigorous analyst and an outstanding writer.[9]

In Austin, Betty Ann became further radicalized, but she didn't go underground yet. She actually spoke about her anti-Klan work in 1980

Betty Ann Duke: May 19th in the Lone Star State

on *Donahue*, the nationally syndicated daytime TV talk show. She also started making regular trips to New York, where she stayed with Barbara Zeller and readily agreed to become part of May 19th's cause.

Then, in the early morning hours of March 2, 1980, there was a theft at the Bland Construction Company in Austin. Robbers made off with ten fifty-pound boxes of Hercules Unigel Tamptite, "a semi-gelatin dynamite designed to satisfy the vast majority of explosive applications in soft to medium rock types," according to the manufacturer.[10] No one was ever charged for the theft, but it is almost certain May 19th was responsible. It appears that the women shared some of the dynamite with the FALN and other violent extremists, keeping the rest for themselves in storage sites in New Jersey and Connecticut.

• • •

A self-described "corn-fed girl," Linda Sue Evans was born on May 11, 1947, in Fort Dodge, Iowa, to Rachel Evans, a schoolteacher, and John, a general contractor.[11] The family, loving and close, were rock-ribbed Republicans who lived a comfortable if unostentatious small-town life.

Linda was a Girl Scout, a volunteer at an old folks' home, and a sought-after babysitter. She was a standout at Fort Dodge Senior High School—the only girl on the varsity debate team, a straight-A student, a National Merit Scholar, and the valedictorian of the class of 1965. She also nurtured dreams of becoming a surgeon and applied to Radcliffe, Harvard's women's college. After Radcliffe turned her down she settled instead on the School of International Studies at Michigan State University in East Lansing. It wasn't Harvard, but the land-grant college offered a solid education at a reasonable price.

Linda had a political transformation at MSU. Like Marilyn at Berkeley, Laura at Radcliffe, and Alan at Cornell, Linda was aroused by the most burning issues facing the republic in the mid-1960s: civil rights and the war in Vietnam. One field trip to Detroit made an indelible mark. "I was appalled, really overwhelmed, by the conditions in which black people had to live in the ghetto," she said. "It really changed my life in some very basic ways. I couldn't accept, or reconcile, the gap between the life I was being directed into as a privileged white person in our society, with the poverty and suffering I witnessed."[12]

Vietnam was what Linda called her "second seminal experience."[13] Her own university's once obscure role in the conflict helped radicalize her. In the mid-1950s, officials in the administration of President Dwight D. Eisenhower had turned to MSU to help with a problem in Southeast Asia. The government of South Vietnam's president, the autocratic nationalist Ngô Đình Diệm, had security problems, internal and external, communist and noncommunist. Eisenhower said that keeping the former French colony in the Free World's orbit was a Cold War imperative. The United States was trying to build up the Vietnamese armed forces, but that wasn't enough—the Diệm regime had to have stronger police and intelligence services to fight the enemy within. That's where MSU came in.

The U.S. government couldn't do the job in-house. Michigan State had a well-regarded criminal justice program. The university's president, John Hannah, was a friend of Eisenhower. Moreover, an on-the-make academic, Wesley Fishel, knew Diệm personally. So Washington and MSU worked out an agreement, and the university sent a team of professors, with their families in tow, to Saigon. Their task was to professionalize the country's police forces, including the sûreté, which specialized in rooting out regime opponents, communists, and suspected subversives. But the MSU mission served another purpose: it was a cover for CIA officers, who could use their university affiliation to provide covert assistance to the U.S.-backed regime—and at the same time gather intelligence inside the Saigon government's own surveillance organs.

The police project kept going into the administration of President John F. Kennedy. The professors continued to propose what they thought were sensible reforms—organizational, administrative, and operational changes that might have worked in Schenectady, Baton Rouge, or Terre Haute but were not based in the reality of what was happening in Vietnam.

Diệm needed the United States to keep South Vietnam afloat. He was one of many U.S. clients around the world, but he wasn't an American flunky, and he wasn't going to listen to lectures about how he should run his internal security forces. According to one American official, Diệm was a puppet, but one "who pulled his own strings—and ours as well." [14]

In 1962, MSU concluded that the university shouldn't continue to be in the business of training internal security services and shut down the Vietnam operation. After the project wrapped up, some of the professors published a monograph about the university's Vietnam activities. They mentioned the CIA's involvement. As with most academic books, nobody paid much attention. The whole episode was forgotten.

Then, in 1966, everything changed. The war in Vietnam was rapidly losing its appeal, particularly among male campus youths facing the prospect of being drafted for military service in Southeast Asia. A muckraking magazine, *Ramparts*, brought Michigan State's police training activities to the public's attention with a scorching exposé, "University on the Make, or How MSU Helped Arm Madame Nhu," a reference to Diệm's sister-in-law, who was the de facto first lady to the bachelor Diệm. Madame Nhu had a reputation for being ruthless and diabolical—she got global press attention in 1963 when she dismissed an antigovernment protest by self-immolating monks as a mere "Buddhist barbecue." In the wake of the *Ramparts* piece, MSU students erupted in protest. The revelations were a major blow to the university's reputation—MSU looked like it was a bought and paid-for stooge of the U.S. intelligence community.

Meanwhile, Linda was wrapped up in SDS. She was a self-described revolutionary, and it was time to become a full-time activist. She left MSU for good in 1967. Later, she came out as a lesbian. "Being a lesbian has always been an important part of the reasons why I'm a revolutionary," she said. "I don't separate 'being a lesbian' from any other part of my life, or from my politics." [15]

She was part of an SDS delegation to North Vietnam in June 1969. "I entered a country at war on a mission of peace," she said.[16] North Vietnam and the United States were at war; Hanoi's forces were killing American GIs; and navy and air force pilots were POWs held under the harshest conditions.

Going to Vietnam was a huge step. The American antiwar movement had entered its most militant and uncompromising phase. During the three-week trip, Linda spoke at a mass rally in Hanoi, which the North Vietnamese regime broadcast across Southeast Asia. She saw landscapes cratered by B-52 raids, ruined villages, human casualties of war. She was "uncontrollably angry, unbelievably sad," she said, and "unable to express the depth of what I was feeling—I wept." [17] At one point during the trip, she was shown an antiaircraft gun. She caressed it, and "wished an American plane would fly over," she told an antiwar crowd after her Vietnam tour.[18]

Back in the United States, she gave blistering antiwar speeches and wrote articles about her Vietnam visit. In "Motor City Sister in North Vietnam," a piece for an underground paper in Detroit, she announced that the time for marching against the war was over. "We have begun to understand that the peaceful demonstrations and marches that we've had are not enough," she said. "The rulers of America have not been affected by our protest, or by our demonstrations, or by our anger. The time has come that they must not be allowed to have peace in this country while the war in Vietnam and while our wars of American aggression continue." [19]

The time for peaceful protest was over. Marching had failed to stop the war machine. It was time to "bring the war home," according to SDS.[20] Linda adopted an antinomian stance: henceforth, the rebels, revolutionaries, and insurrectionists would make all the rules.* "What this country needs is a little more chaos," she said in an interview with the underground *Berkeley Tribe* in 1969. "It's our job to create a chaotic situation in this country so that those of our brothers and sisters engaged in armed struggle can move and move fast." [21]

As SDS imploded in 1969, Linda was quick to join the Weathermen. On September 4 that year, she was arrested after she and other Weatherwomen rampaged through the halls of South Hills High School in Pittsburgh, shouting antiwar slogans, smearing paint on the walls, and reportedly scratching teachers and policemen.† She was also among the dozens of Weatherpeople rounded up during the Days of Rage rampage in Chicago in October 1969. The cops got Linda for battery of a police officer, resisting arrest, and mob action. She skipped

---

* In "The Antinomian Personality: The Hippie Character Type," published in 1968, the psychologist Nathan Adler called this troubling creature a by-product of a "new ideology and culture of the 'drop-out'; the epidemic diffusion of drug abuse; the changing patterns and blurring of differentiated sex roles [and] the enthusiastic propagation of the Hippie ethos in both its evangelical and apocalyptic forms." Nathan Adler, "The Antinomian Personality: The Hippie Character Type," *Psychiatry* 31, no. 4 (1968): 325.

† According to one press account, about a hundred Weather "girls," some bare from the waist up, were part of the protest. "Girls Go Topless in Protest," *Desert Sun* (Palm Springs, CA), September 5, 1969.

*Linda Sue Evans: A "corn-fed" Iowa gal, Weather Underground
member, and "North American anti-imperialist"*

bail, though, and fled town. The police eventually caught up with her
in 1971, and she pled guilty, receiving three years probation and three
months behind bars.[22]

Even after serving her time, she assumed that the cops and the FBI
were still watching her. She decided she needed a different look, so she
replaced her long hair with a self-inflicted shag haircut. She had "a bril-
liant smile and intelligent eyes that speak volumes," a journalist wrote
decades later.[23] At the time, the FBI offered a more clinical description:
"5'5", approximately 160 lbs., wide hips, small-breasted."[24] An interview
subject later told the Bureau that Linda "looked hard like a man" and
"looked weird."[25]

During the early1970s, Linda returned to her rural roots, working as a farmhand and organizer in Arkansas and Texas. In 1975, she
moved to Austin, where she joined the progressive scene.

At a graphics collective, the Red River Women's Press, she learned how to work an offset printing press, a skill that would later prove useful in the May 19th underground. She also played in an all-women band, joined a guerrilla street theater troupe, and was part of Dollars for Bullets, a fund-raising campaign for the South West African People's Organisation, which was fighting to liberate Namibia from South African domination.

She was no longer preaching "chaos" or armed revolt, but she did some protesting. Three times a year, the Austin Boat Club held drag boat races on the city's Town Lake, hard up against a poor, heavily Mexican-American neighborhood. By the spring of 1978, residents were thoroughly fed up with the noise, congestion, and filth generated by the thousands of people who flocked to the event. The races were "degrading and dehumanizing," said one community organizer. Drunken race goers routinely urinated on private property, and residents demanded that the city shut down the annual disturbances.

On race day, activists, including the militant Brown Berets, a Mexican American group modeled on the Black Panthers, staged a lakeside protest. Mayhem broke out. Helmeted riot police manhandled demonstrators. A long-haired undercover cop in a rugby shirt whipped out a nightstick and wailed mercilessly on a protester. A news crew videoed the melee and managed to record a couple of seconds of Linda mixing it up with a burly policeman.

Linda met Betty Ann through Texas activism networks, and they started working together on anti-Klan messaging in the capital and around the state. Klan members didn't take kindly to that and threatened Linda's life.[26] "My name was put on a death list along with other Black, Mexican, and white anti-Klan activists," she said. "The list was displayed inside a coffin surrounded by stacks of automatic weapons at a Klan rally."[27]

Together, Linda and Betty Ann formed May 19th's outpost in the

Lone Star State. They initially served the important aboveground roles of making speeches, raising money, and buying guns.[28]

Linda became May 19th's armorer, just as Marilyn had been with the BLA. Using the alias Louise Robinett, Linda got herself a Louisiana driver's license and routinely went gun shopping around the Bayou State. In Gretna, she bought an Uzi rifle and a box of 9mm ammunition. In Arabi, another Uzi. And in Norco, a Ruger Mini-14 rifle, a Browning Hi-Power pistol, and two boxes of .223-caliber ammunition.[29]

Linda and Betty Ann were all in as North American anti-imperialists.

PART TWO

THE ARMED STRUGGLE, 1983–1984

9

MORNING IN AMERICA

During the late 1970s, the national political winds were blowing steadily rightward and in 1980, former California governor Ronald Reagan was elected president. He ran on a staunch anticommunism platform that pointedly made Jimmy Carter, the sitting president, seem weak in the face of threats from the Soviet Union and an uprising in Iran that resulted in some fifty U.S. embassy personnel being held hostage by "students" in Tehran—a national humiliation that Carter seemed incapable of ending. At home, Regan had accused Carter of coddling convicts and welfare cheats while hardworking, everyday people worried about their jobs, "stagflation," gas prices, and drug dealers preying on the country's youths.*

Reagan beat Carter by ten points in the popular vote and ten to one in the Electoral College. He had built a powerful coalition that included evangelical Christians (the "Moral Majority"), libertarian-minded businesspeople who wanted to shrink the bloated, overweening federal government, militant Cold Warriors, and angry blue-collar

---

* Adding to the president's misery were his brother, Billy's embarrassing escapades: publicly urinating on an airport runway, selling his name to a brewer of cheap "Billy Beer," and accepting cash from Libya's sinister strongman, Colonel Moammar Gadhafi.

workers who were watching their good-paying factory jobs disappear in the face of foreign competition. In 2016, Donald Trump put together a similar coalition of Americans who were despondent over the state of the country and longed to "Make America Great Again."

Political opponents called Reagan an antigovernment extremist, a fantasist, a warmonger, an unhinged anticommunist. Others dismissed him as a washed-up actor who was a master at dispensing political bromides. But even his opponents came to concede that he had an uncanny talent for channeling, and even shaping, the zeitgeist.

• • •

Terrorism was constantly in the news in the United States and the rest of the world in the 1970s. It had been around in one form or another for centuries, of course, but the threat had "taken on a new and, I think, a more sinister complexion," according to one congressman.[1]

Spectacular incidents occurred with alarming frequency. In Athens in December 1975, members of the 17 November group assassinated the CIA station chief. In Entebbe, Uganda, the following July, Israeli commandos stormed a plane hijacked by a band of Palestinians and Germans and freed the hostages.

The purported mastermind of the plot was Ilich Ramírez Sánchez, better known as Carlos the Jackal. Carlos was a member of an upper-class Venezuelan family and an adventurer par excellence whose fun-loving ways distinguished him from run-of-the-mill terrorists. He enjoyed fine food, Havana cigars, handmade shoes, and the company of beautiful women. "I am an epicure," he said. A photograph of the Jackal became iconic: a "chubby dark-haired Latin with tinted shades, his fleshy sensual lips stretched in a faintly ironic smirk," as the writer Matthew Carr described the man in the picture. During the 1970s and

'80s, Carlos was a worldwide brand and the embodiment of the menace of global terrorism.[2]

In Cologne in September 1977, the Red Army Faction kidnapped and murdered Hanns Martin Schleyer, a leading industrialist and former high-ranking Nazi. In Evanston, Illinois, in May 1978, a bomb accidentally detonated and wounded a security guard.[3] The perpetrator wouldn't be discovered until years later, after he'd sent a series of mail bombs (sometimes with lethal results) and forced the *New York Times* to run his manifesto. Theodore "Ted" Kaczynski, later known as the Unabomber, was a shaggy-headed former mathematics professor and was caught only after his brother turned him in. And in December 1979, in San Juan, Los Macheteros ("the machete wielders"), a violent, Castro-linked Puerto Rican separatist group, machine-gunned a U.S. Navy bus, killing two sailors and wounding ten others.

Regular Americans might have been slow to pick up on the changing tides from hippie revolution to armed revolution, but they were now alarmed. A 1977 poll revealed that 60 percent of the country considered terrorism a "very serious" problem. And the public wasn't in a particularly forgiving mood when it came to punishing terrorists who killed or injured Americans at home or abroad; according to the same poll, 55 percent favored giving them the death penalty.[4]

In 1981, Reagan declared that it was "morning in America." The new president said that the American dream wasn't over—far from it. America *was* great, but for it to *stay* great, some drastic measures were in order, namely lowering marginal income tax rates, shrinking government, and forming a more muscular foreign policy—measures he promoted long before he reached the Oval Office.

The need to fight international communism was central to Reagan's worldview. Back in 1964, in a pungent turn of phrase, he'd called the Soviet Union "the most evil enemy mankind has known in his long climb from the swamp to the stars." As president, he expounded on the "phenomenology of evil," labeling the Kremlin the "focus of evil in the modern world" and an "evil empire." [5]

Reagan got Congress to agree to double-digit rises in Pentagon spending. Cash poured into defense industry coffers. Critics blasted bloated, pork-barrel military programs, sleazy corporate lobbying, and rampant waste, fraud, and abuse.

The president was captivated with a decades-old, but so far unsuccessful, program designed to shoot down enemy warheads before they could hit the U.S. homeland. The Pentagon called it the Strategic Defense Initiative. Opponents labeled it "Star Wars." Some politicians, defense officials, and think tanks said it really didn't matter whether the initiative actually played out as advertised, or indeed whether *any* of the Pentagon's new wonder weapons worked. It was all about superpower competition. The USSR would spend itself into oblivion trying to keep up with its archrival's military marvels.

But spending more money and fielding exciting new weapons systems wouldn't be enough to bring down the Soviets. The United States also had to show some force. Reagan pumped up covert aid to the mujahideen, the Muslim holy warriors fighting to push the Soviet invaders out of Afghanistan. In 1982, Reagan sent U.S. marines to Lebanon to serve as peacekeepers, an ill-fated mission met with an Iranian-backed suicide bomb attack that killed 241 U.S. service members.

Closer to American shores, the administration dispatched the CIA to organize, train, and equip the contra rebels fighting the left-wing Sandinista government in Nicaragua. Fearing the emergence of another procommunist regime in the hemisphere, the United States bankrolled the right-wing regime in El Salvador, which was locked in a savage civil war with nominally pro-Cuban leftist rebels.

The administration perceived other hemispheric threats. On the northeastern coast of South America, tiny Suriname was flirting with Castro's Cuba, prompting national security officials to consider deploying an exile force to topple the regime in the former Dutch colony. When Senator Barry Goldwater got wind of the proposed plot, he offered his unvarnished opinion of the plan: it was "the dumbest fucking idea I ever heard."[6]

The administration was also worried about little Grenada—a Cuban client state that had descended into chaos following an October 1983 coup d'état. Just days after the coup, Reagan green-lighted Urgent Fury, a "no-notice" military operation aimed at rescuing American medical students on the island and restoring order. U.S. forces met unexpectedly stiff armed resistance, but the students made it back to the United States safely. The president and his supporters considered Urgent Fury a big win—a lightning-fast operation that had achieved its immediate objectives.

There was a not-so-subtle message for Moscow: Washington was shaking off the so-called Vietnam Syndrome and was ready to use force to defend its interests.

·   ·   ·

During his inaugural address, Reagan mentioned terrorism—the first U.S. president to do so. He and his top lieutenants believed firmly in the existence of a global conspiracy directed from Moscow that the best-selling author Clare Sterling called the "terror network." Working with its international friends, the Kremlin supposedly backed violent, subversive groups such as the Palestinian Liberation Organization, Italy's Red Brigades, the African National Congress, and the Red Army Faction. The Red Brigades (Brigate Rosse, or BR) was the largest and most notorious Italian far-left terrorist group during the 1970s and 1980s. Its armed campaign included bank robberies, kidnappings, and assassinations, which, according to the BR, were part of a "concentrated strike against the heart of the State, because the State is an imperialist collection of multinational corporations."[7] Terrorism, in this view, was a frightening and deadly new weapon in the East-West struggle—it was war against the West being waged by other means.

The Senate Judiciary Committee's Subcommittee on Security and Terrorism, created in 1981, became the leading congressional platform for terrorism hard-liners. Its chairman was Senator Jeremiah Denton, a mossbacked Alabama Republican, retired navy admiral, and former long-term guest of the communists at the notorious "Hanoi Hilton" prison in North Vietnam. Denton was all in with the terror network thesis: he said it was obvious that the trail of terror led straight back to the Kremlin. In an antecedent to President George W. Bush's "Axis of Evil" hypothesis, Denton postulated that there was a "Radical Entente," an array of mischief-making countries such as Syria, North Korea, and Iran, doing Moscow's dirty work.[8]

Samuel T. Francis, PhD, a portly, spectacled far-right polemicist, served as the committee's in-house terrorism guru. A former Heritage Foundation analyst, Francis had penned a widely circulated pamphlet, "The Terrorist Underground in the United States," which posited a world of violent left-wing formations—almost certainly with international connections—that included Weather Underground veterans, the BLA, and the FALN. In his view, Watergate-era legal shackles had kept the Bureau from investigating dangerous dissent.

As far as Francis was concerned, the terrorist threat was confined to one end of the political spectrum—namely, the far left. Neither he nor his Senate bosses showed interest in the revived Ku Klux Klan, the emergence of antiabortion extremists such as the Army of God, and the spread of the fanatically antigovernment groups like Posse Comitatus, whose members were responsible for the murder of peace officers.

In other words, the terrorists that alarmed Francis and the Senate subcommittee weren't cross burners, far-right seditionists, or brown-shirted neo-Nazis: they were ultraleft insurrectionists who looked an awful lot like Marilyn, Susan, Silvia, Alan, Betty Ann, and Linda.

Francis was on the fringes of a loose group of experts who were try-ing to make sense of the frightening phenomenon of terrorism. A new field called "terrorism studies" was gaining a toehold in the academic world. Think tanks, well funded with foundation and government money, were piling on, eager to enlighten a perplexed and fearful nation.

Specialists wondered: Who became a terrorist, and why? Were these people misguided idealists? Rational utility maximizers? Youth-ful thrill seekers? Or just ordinary criminals masquerading as revolu-tionaries?

Then there was the terrorism-as-nut hypothesis. Look at the Symbionese Liberation Army, filled with troubled souls who seemed to delight in creating lurid public spectacles and carrying out outland-ish acts of violence.[9] And what about the Weather Underground? They must have been deranged—consider their drug-fueled orgies, their bizarre "Smash Monogamy" campaign, and their unholy celebration of the Manson Family's murder of the actress Sharon Tate and her unborn child as a revolutionary act. (Weather's group-sex sessions were referred to as "wargasms"—an interesting choice of words. Ear-lier in the decade, RAND Corporation strategist Herman Kahn, one of the models for Stanley Kubrick's Dr. Strangelove—and the "heavy-weight of the Megadeath Intellectuals," as *The New Yorker* called him—characterized all-out nuclear war as "wargasm.")

"That's what we're about, being crazy motherfuckers and scaring the shit out of Honky America," Weather leader Bernardine Dohrn announced in 1969.[10] Manson, who died in prison in November 2017, espoused an apocalyptic racist ideology ("Helter Skelter") that inspires some of today's neo-Nazi terrorists, including Atomwaffen Division, which, according to the Southern Poverty Law Center (SPLC), is made of cells that "work toward civilizational collapse. Members . . . believe that violence, depravity and degeneracy are the only sure way to establish order in their dystopian and apocalyptic vision of the world."[11]

Public officials and the press liked the terrorist-as-nut idea. It seemed self-evident that anyone who bombed a building, took hostages, or mowed down policemen on behalf of some half-baked political "cause" must be some kind of lunatic. California attorney general Evelle Younger declared that terrorists "are simply unstable people" who read the works of insurrectionists such as Mao, Che Guevara, and Frantz Fanon and "became confused."[12]

Back in 1971, FBI director J. Edgar Hoover stressed to Congress the need to "discourage the terrorist radical in his insane desire to intimidate and destroy."[13] And according to one newspaper editorial, terrorists were "life's losers" and "deranged malcontents," nonentities who yearned to become somebodies, as in the case of one would-be hijacker, described as "44, unemployed and divorced, a nobody thirsting for a moment of fiery notoriety."[14]

A decade later, some experts continued to advance the terrorist-as-nut hypothesis. According to one FBI investigator, the SLA had "played a fanciful game with self-made intrigue and persistent paranoia. They made their vain attempts to give meaning to their empty lives and status to their weak egos."[15]

The question of women and terrorism was a particularly vexing one for the specialists. Even though women had been key figures in terrorist groups during the 1970s—Dohrn of the Weather Underground and Ulrike Meinhof of the Baader-Meinhof Gang were two notable examples—experts at the time tended to frame terrorism as a largely male enterprise. The women who participated in such violence were characterized as particularly dangerous deviants. How could women participate in such savagery? The journalist Eileen MacDonald described the popular anxieties that female terrorists generated:

> *If the male members of a movement committed to violence are seen as mad, bad, and evil, how much more then are the females? In taking up arms they commit a double atrocity: using violence, and in the process destroying our safe, traditional view of women.*[16]

Take, for example, the writings of the terrorism expert H.H.A. Cooper. Writing in an academic volume titled *The Criminology of Deviant Women*, Cooper wondered about these "alienating, questing women" and the motivations underlying their barbaric behavior.[17] He arrived at a startling conclusion—that a "primary cause of female terrorism is erotomania"—and warned that "the female of the species is deadlier than the male." *

On the other side of the Atlantic, the press drooled over the women-terror-sexuality nexus. London's *Sunday Mirror* published "Sexy Secrets of a Terror Girl," which chronicled the fugitive adventures of Astrid Proll, another member of the Baader-Meinhof Gang: "Friends told of her lesbian loves, and her delight at being a mechanic." Coverage in other London papers was equally lurid, with the *Daily Express* claiming that Proll "was a woman's libber and had no boyfriends. In fact she was a self-confessed lesbian."[18]

---

* The National Institutes of Health defines erotomania as "a rare disorder in which an individual has a delusional belief that a person of higher social status falls in love and makes amorous advances towards him/her." In earlier times, the term was a label for excessive sexual desire. Erotomania can also simply mean "oversexed." What Cooper had in mind is not clear.

Meanwhile, over at the RAND Corporation, the analyst Konrad Kellen detected a link among sexuality, class, and terror. "There is a higher percentage of lesbians among the female terrorists studied (7 percent) than is estimated to prevail in the population at large (1 to 2 percent)," he claimed, adding "Individual cases show that the lesbian tendency often emerges coincidentally with the exit from the bourgeois fold." [19]

The notion that female militants were more dangerous than their male comrades would persist for decades. Germany's elite counterterrorism force, Grenzschutzgruppe 9, purportedly issued a standing order: "Shoot the women first." [20]

• • •

Denton and his Senate allies insisted that the terrorist threat wasn't confined to the actual trigger pullers and bomb throwers. For terrorists to operate, they needed aboveground helpers, and, according to Denton, "members of the overt and front groups can aid and abet acts of terrorism or 'armed struggle' by locating targets, carrying out 'intelligence gathering,' [and] providing logistical support."

The senator didn't stop there; he claimed that there were all kinds of enablers, equally threatening. "When I speak about a threat, I do not just mean that an organization is, or is about to be, engaged in violent criminal activity," he said. There was also the peril posed by the support groups that "produce propaganda, disinformation, or 'legal assistance' [that] may be even more dangerous than those who actually throw the bombs."

The implication was clear: fighting terrorism meant casting a wide net. Nonviolent groups could be part of a broader web of subversion. In a 1983 Senate report, staffers cited the work of Philip Selznick, a former RAND sociologist, to shed light on the slippery concept of subversion—what Selznick called "the manipulation of social institutions for alien ends, this manipulation being conducted covertly in the name of the institution's own values."[21] Subversives, Denton said, weren't necessarily criminals. Nevertheless, they had to be fought; they were the enemy within, working covertly to destroy the system.

Denton decided to name and shame. He called out three prominent leftist institutions: *Mother Jones* magazine, the National Lawyers Guild, and the Institute for Policy Studies.[22] Another subcommittee member, Senator John P. East, a North Carolina Republican, called for deeper probes into America's subversive realms. "We ought to know who these people are and what they are up to," he said.[23]

In Reagan's America, plotting to overthrow the government wasn't going to be treated as 1960s-style fun and games. If the administration was correct, all terrorists had at least *some* foreign ties. And if those ties weren't readily apparent, they'd have to be uncovered. It was war against the state, and it was time for the state to hit back hard. The terrorism hard-liners insisted that the FBI needed to be unleashed.

• • •

J. Edgar Hoover's views on crime, dissent, and subversion dominated federal law enforcement and domestic intelligence gathering for nearly fifty years. Although every president from John F. Kennedy to Richard Nixon considered sending the FBI director into retirement, Hoover remained in office until his death at age seventy-seven on May 2, 1972. His *New York Times* obituary described him in his declining years: "The once ruddy face was puffy and pale. The brushed-back, gray-brown hair was straight and thin—not the wiry dark curls of a few years ago. He walked stiffly, although his figure was trim and erect. Behind his glasses, his dark brown eyes looked fixed, and he seemed to be daydreaming."[24]

During the Great Depression, as colorful crooks such as Ma Barker, Pretty Boy Floyd, Machine Gun Kelly, and Bonnie and Clyde roamed the American landscape, Hoover worked to secure the Bureau's reputation and image as the nation's premier crime-busting force. Through movies, radio, press accounts, and eventually television, his masterly campaign shaped the public's imagination. Hollywood called Hoover's agents "G-men," that is, government men. Ever vigilant and incorruptible, and using the latest crime-fighting technologies, the Bureau's special agents were on the front line, battling the nation's criminal multitudes—bank robbers, car thieves, grifters, joyboys, dopers, white slavers—and the agency's size and resources grew along with its prestige. What had been founded in 1908 as the Justice Department's Bureau of Investigation was by 1935 the *Federal* Bureau of Investigation.

During the Second World War, the Bureau rooted out Axis spies; it was classic counterintelligence work. And although the Office of Strategic Services, or OSS, the predecessor of the CIA, was supposed to be in charge of intelligence-gathering operations overseas, the wily Hoover, a consummate bureaucratic operator, managed to outmaneuver the OSS chief, General William "Wild Bill" Donovan, and grab responsibility for espionage in the Western Hemisphere for the Bureau.

After the conflict ended in 1945, the FBI continued its war on crime, with Hoover constantly refreshing the image of the Bureau's agents as the nation's crime fighters supreme.

And Hoover expanded the Bureau's clandestine portfolio. Special agents kept tabs on the so-called lavender lads who were supposedly cavorting in the nation's homosexual netherworld and enthusiastically corrupting civil servants, politicians, and military men and women.* In 1950, U.S. Senator Millard Tydings claimed that the State

---

* Gossip about Hoover's own sexuality persisted for decades, including claims that he liked to dress up in women's clothing, participated in homosexual orgies, and was "married" to a top aide, Clyde Tolson. Many of those rumors, including those spread by some of Hoover's liberal opponents, have a strongly homophobic undercurrent. Moreover, absent any definitive evidence, the thruth is unknowable.

Department was overrun with "sexual perverts," and that same year, Senator Kenneth Wherry claimed that as many as three thousand homosexuals were employed by State.[25] In 1953, President Dwight D. Eisenhower issued an executive order banning federal employment for anyone engaging in "any criminal, infamous, dishonest, immoral, or notoriously disgraceful conduct, habitual use of intoxicants to excess, drug addiction, sexual perversion."[26] The "Lavender Scare" was on, and thousands of Americans would lose their livelihood and endure public and private humiliation.

Hoover worried about the country's growing civil rights movement—it posed a direct threat to the white-dominated racial order Hoover supported with enthusiasm. He also hated the Ku Klux Klan—not so much for its poisonous beliefs and its reign of terror against African Americans but for its temerity in challenging government power and authority.

But in the director's view, the main internal threat was the Communist Party USA.

During the 1930s and early 1940s, the United States had been crawling with Soviet spies. Moscow Center directed intelligence networks made up of hundreds of American citizens. Moscow's U.S. spies were in the State Department, the Office of Strategic Services, and the Treasury, in the defense industry, and in the most important target of all: the top secret Manhattan Project, which produced the world's first atomic bomb.

Overt Party members, and communist supporters and sympathizers ("fellow travelers" and "comsymps," as they were called), helped marshal public support for "Uncle Joe" Stalin, a crucial U.S. and British ally. During the war years, none of this attracted much of Hoover's attention.

As the Cold War began, the American Communist Party was

already in terminal decline. Reds, foreign or homegrown, had about as much popular support as a plague of measles. Soviet intelligence continued its operations in the United States, but the pool of dupes, stooges, comsymps, and true believers available for espionage and subversion was drying up.

Hoover didn't see it that way. With the full support of Congress, the executive branch, and most of the media, universities, and trade unions, the director doubled down on rooting out the enemy within.

Hoover began gathering intelligence on U.S. citizens, not so much for the purpose of investigating federal crimes—the FBI's nominal mandate—but to disrupt organizations and movements he deemed antithetical to American goals, values, and security.

It wasn't the first time for Hoover. During the so-called First Red Scare of the 1920s, the young Hoover had been a tenacious hunter of Bolsheviks, anarchists, and labor radicals.

During the "second Red Scare," in the late 1940s, Bureau agents tapped phone lines, spread disinformation, and conducted "surreptitious entries" and "black bag jobs" to install bugs and carry out warrantless searches, all in the name of "domestic security," an all-encompassing but vague mission.

Over time, some Bureau men (the ranks of special agents were all male until 1972, when the first woman was admitted) came to see such activities as dubious, sleazy, and at odds with the squeaky clean G-man culture and image Hoover had fostered since the 1930s.

By the mid-1960s, even some of the director's senior lieutenants were worried about the questionable legality of some clandestine FBI operations. "We do not obtain authorization for 'black bag' jobs from outside the Bureau," top Hoover aide William C. Sullivan wrote in a July 1966 memo to the director. "Such a technique involves trespass and is clearly illegal; therefore, it would be impossible to obtain any legal sanction for it."[27] But the break-ins and bugging continued.

President Richard M. Nixon came to power in part because of his promise to crack down on campus revolts, ghetto rebellions, and left-wing extremism. Hoover was on board with Nixon's get-tough stance. Hairy hippies, acid heads, champagne socialists, pro–North Vietnam protestors—they were the antithesis of everything Hoover believed in.

For the director, SDS and then the Weathermen were particularly abominable. Enjoying every advantage of American life, these privileged and pampered radicals sought not just the destruction of the Republic but the victory of communism worldwide. In 1970, the FBI announced the largest manhunt in Bureau history.

But the Bureau's hunt for Weatherpeople would be largely futile—none of the big Weather fish was caught. The Bureau tied itself in knots in a search for fugitives that employed questionable if not outright criminal methods, including warrantless searches and eavesdropping.

"Even though we had hundreds of FBI agents looking for them, they couldn't find the fugitives," said retired FBI agent William E. Dyson, Jr. Weatherpeople were "more sophisticated than we gave them credit for," he conceded. "They were more than a bunch of college kids."[28]

In the end, most of the Weatherpeople who had been underground surfaced on their own accord. Those who faced outstanding earlier charges—such as those stemming from the Days of Rage—were often able to get them dismissed. Nobody went to jail for any of the Weather Underground's bombings.

There was major fallout from the Weatherman hunt. Top FBI officials, including former deputy director Mark Felt, would be prosecuted for illegal surveillance.* Felt tried later to explain his actions as a necessary response to the politically motivated violence that saturated the American landscape during the late 1960s and early 1970s:

> *There were dissidents who talked of kidnapping Dr. Henry Kissinger and visiting heads of state. There were plans to paralyze the nation's Capital by widespread sabotage. Policemen were being ambushed and murdered. . . . Hundreds of bombs were exploding all over the country.*[29]

Felt was right about the scale of violent extremism: in 1971, there were more than four hundred terrorist attacks in the United States. But congressional probes and revelations in the press about illegal domestic snooping had tarnished the FBI's image. The political climate had changed, and much of the public had lost its appetite for rooting out subversives, radicals, and bomb throwers. The FBI's budget dropped, and the number of special agents shrank.

In 1976, Attorney General Edward Levi—who as the president of the University of Chicago had resisted Saul Bellow's entreaties on behalf of Judy Clark—issued a directive known as the Levi Guidelines. For the first time in its history, the FBI was compelled to operate under a set of Department of Justice rules about domestic security investigations.

The number of security-related probes plummeted. As of March 31, 1976, the FBI was conducting 4,868 domestic security investigations. Two years later, the number was down to 102.[30]

---

* Felt publicly confirmed in 2005 what many insiders (including Richard Nixon) had long suspected: that he was "Deep Throat," the Watergate source for the *Washington Post*'s Bob Woodward.

The FBI could investigate terrorists. Indeed, the Bureau was the federal agency with the lead responsibility for incidents involving attacks on U.S. citizens. But there was to be no more political snooping: from now on, the focus had to be on prosecution of federal crimes, such as bombing, bank robbery, and kidnapping.

•   •   •

In April 1981, Reagan pardoned Felt and another former Bureau official. The pardon signaled that the handcuffs were coming off the FBI.

But in the eyes of administration officials and the members of Denton's Senate subcommittee, the Bureau was dragging its heels. It wasn't spending much of its budget on counterterrorism. With the exception of the New York Field Office, the Bureau didn't seem particularly aggressive in pursuing terrorism cases. Maybe it was the hated Levi Guidelines; members of Denton's committee complained about them endlessly. Maybe the Bureau had simply failed to comprehend the threat posed by America's homegrown bombers and their support networks. Or maybe the FBI as an institution was gun shy when it came to investigating terrorists.

Before long, the FBI would double down on leftist terror, but not because of congressional moaning or administration prodding.

The botched Brinks job caught the FBI off guard. It hadn't been staying current on the activities of the ultraleft—as far as the Bureau knew, that kind of extremism had disappeared with the Weather Underground. But the extreme violence and ensuing headlines instantly put the Family on the FBI's radar, and special agents immediately started investigating.

Specters from America's recent radical past had managed to reanimate themselves. The Brinks investigation, which the FBI called

"NYROB," began uncovering "a sophisticated and clandestine national network of domestic terrorists," said Kenneth Maxwell, the FBI's top man on the case.[31] With Brinks, "the FBI's inhibitions regarding domestic terrorism evaporated," wrote one former Bureau historian.[32]

There was no need for the FBI to be concerned about being seen as "political." The Brinks perpetrators had committed serious crimes, including armed robbery, conspiracy, and murder. They were cop killers. Nobody was being investigated for his or her political beliefs: this was a straight-up, coast-to-coast criminal investigation.

With that, FBI director William Webster made counterterrorism a top-tier priority, right up there with catching foreign spies and locking up mafiosi. Webster said that the Bureau wasn't going to be outgunned by terrorists, or by any other criminals for that matter. He created the Hostage Rescue Team, or HRT, an elite unit of antiterror action men. The HRT, he said, had "a whole range of skills that other agents would not be readily trained for and could be more effective in a problem that was bigger than the local SWAT [special weapons and tactics team] could handle."[33]

Webster wanted more law enforcement cooperation. Bureau men and state and local police had worked together in the past, but it had been on an ad hoc, case-by-case basis. One crime, one investigation, and then they'd part ways. And when they were forced to work together, there was serious tension between the FBI and its state and local counterparts. Cops often regarded the Bureau as self-aggrandizing, and some FBI officials saw state and local police as unprofessional, failing to meet their own high standards. But Webster ordered his agents to start treating state and local police as colleagues. Henceforth, they were to be the Bureau's partners in the fight against terrorism.

In 1979, the FBI and NYPD created a standing task force to investigate the string of bank robberies that had plagued the greater New York area. A year later, they set up the first Joint Terrorism Task Force, or JTTF, with eleven cops and eleven FBI agents. Instead of squabbling among themselves, they'd pool information and work together on terror cases. NYPD members became federal marshals; that way they could get security clearances. The model has endured; today, JTTFs all over the country handle terrorism investigations.

NYROB was the JTTF's first big case. And NYROB would lead the Bureau to May 19th.

Members of the Family had left behind a significant paper trail. In the Barker Avenue safe house in the Bronx, the FBI and NYPD found the floor plans of New York and Brooklyn police station houses and the Family's "hit lists" of police officers being considered for assassination.[34] During the searches, they also found tape recordings. "It was a gold mine," an investigator said. "When these people are underground, one of them invariably thinks he or she is going to write the new Das Kapital. So they write every damn thing down, and sometimes they tape it all. You'd think they would have learned from Nixon."[35]

What's more, the cops were on to Mtayari "Sonny" Sundiata, whose car had been seen circling the block outside 590 East Third Street not long after the robbery and shoot-out. On October 23, 1981, the NYPD spotted a car in Queens. The license plates matched those of the car seen in Mount Vernon. Sonny was in the car, along with Odinga.

A wild twenty-minute car chase ensued. Abandoning their vehicle in the Ozone Park neighborhood, the two men opened fire on the cops. Sonny climbed a fence, but not quickly enough to avoid the police gunfire that killed him. Odinga's pistol jammed, and he opted to surrender.

Odinga would serve thirty-three years for the Queens shoot-out and his role in the Brinks conspiracy. After he was let out of prison in November 2014, a longtime supporter said, "I think you can compare it to Nelson Mandela being released." The FBI's lead Brinks investigator, Ken Maxwell, had a different take: "Comparing Odinga, a hard-core felon, to Nelson Mandela is the theater of the absurd and an insult to the legacy of Mandela. If you think this lifelong domestic terrorist, self-proclaimed revolutionary and convicted cop-killer is going to be a contributor to the betterment of society, you are delusional."[36]

Investigators also discovered that Eve Rosahn was the owner of the Honda, and witnesses said she was the woman who had rented the red Chevy van. On October 27, she was arrested without incident for criminal facilitation.[37] The police also found a set of Linda's prints on a map inside the Honda's glove compartment.[38] The hunt for the Brinks conspirators led the FBI to discover that May 19th was an extremist group distinct from the Family.

10

IF NOT US, WHO?

May 19th tried to salvage something from the upstate debacle. An aboveground member, Dana Biberman, offered a public defense of the Brinks operation and the killing of the cops and a Brinks guard: "People who defend imperialism do so from their own choice. That is a choice that they must live—or die—with."[1]

Under the name "Revolutionary Armed Task Force," they issued a communiqué announcing that "Black revolutionary freedom fighters" and "North American anti-imperialists" had joined forces. Brinks wasn't a robbery—it was an "appropriation" to raise funds to fight the "fascist approach to genocide" waged by the white ruling class. The struggle would continue, the Task Force vowed.

The communiqué didn't seem to win anyone over to the cause. Nor did the on-air performance that May 19th aboveground members Mary Patten and Donna Borup gave later on WBAI, New York's venerable left-wing radio station. "What happened on October 20th was not a robbery, it was not a criminal act," Patten said. When asked about the Brinks victims, Patten argued that they'd had it coming: "To choose to be a cop . . . at this time in the history of the United States there is a very clear position about whose interests you are defending . . . there is a war situation in this country and the police . . . have a very particular side in that war." It was inevitable that the war would escalate, Patten said, and as it did, "there are going to be more cops who are killed." [2]

A month after Brinks, some Family members pulled a stickup job at a Navy Federal Credit Union in Arlington, Virginia, that netted a mere $1,900. But the alliance between the May 19th women and Shakur and his crew was over.

Four days after Brinks, the New Jersey State Police hit the safe house Marilyn had rented at 223 Prospect Street in East Orange. Nobody was home, but the cops discovered a semiautomatic rifle, a pistol, and other weapons, makeup, wigs, and fake mustaches, insurance documents for Marilyn's white Oldsmobile, and diagrams and paraphernalia for building bombs. [3]

The cops found something else: a photo of a woman named Betty Jean Abramson. It turned out she was in custody in New York awaiting extradition back to California to face murder charges. Her alleged victim: Rosanne Goustin, shot in the head on June 2, 1980, in remote Honeydew, California, while trying to escape the Tribal Thumb compound. Another Tribal Thumb communard, Wendy Sue Heaton, was arrested later in New Orleans in connection with the Goustin killing. Witnesses said she'd been around town with Marilyn.

There was another strange link with Marilyn. During their search of the Bronx safe house, investigators came across a radio base station. In those days you had to register such equipment with the Federal Communications Commission. The cops placed a call to Washington and learned that the gear belonged to Tribal Thumb.

Marilyn may have met Abramson and Heaton back in the Bay Area—they ran in overlapping far-left circles—and kept in touch. Or perhaps they linked up later through the BLA or other underground networks. Marilyn had a steel-trap mind, so she probably remembered that she had kept the photo at 223 Prospect. If so, she had to be worried that it would help the cops get closer to her and her comrades.

• • •

The media couldn't get enough of the Brinks story. It had it all: M16-wielding gunmen, dead policemen, sacks of stolen cash, angry revolutionaries, and glassy-eyed relics from the Weather Underground.

The *New York Post*, particularly, feasted. The paper most likely learned about May 19th from sources inside the NYROB investigation, and early in 1982, the paper published a richly lurid, multipart series on the group. The articles, written by a Guy Hawtin, a seasoned veteran of London's Fleet Street, described in titillating detail life inside the May 19th collectives. In one article, Hawtin called the group "a hardnosed matriarchy dominated by lesbians," with round-the-clock criticism/self-criticism sessions designed to expose ideological deviants. The collectives were "sexual slaughterhouses" for men, who were required to be celibate, he said, and straight women, too, were subject to sexual repression: "Women who look as though they may be getting together with a man are told: 'Stay away from him or you'll be hurting your politics. He's politically bad for you.'"[4]

May 19th members read the stories, and complained about them in their own publications: it was a pack of racist, sexist, and imperialist lies designed to discredit freedom fighters, they said. But some elements of the stories must have worried May 19th. The *Post* got some things right—they knew that Moncada was linked to May 19th, that May 19th was tight-knit and next to impossible to infiltrate, and that they'd been involved in armed robberies. And if the *Post* knew that, so did the police.

Months after the incident there was still plenty of post-Brinks heat. Every cop in the country had heard about what happened in Rockland County. Police rousted anybody with a Weather or BLA connection and hauled them in for questioning. Federal prosecutors decided to deploy a fearsome weapon, one usually reserved for mobsters: the Racketeer Influenced and Corrupt Organizations Act, or RICO.

In New York, the FBI was working wiretaps, snapping surveillance photos, and planting bugs. By then the Bureau had BAAANA and one of Shakur's apartments—85 Barrow Street, apartment 2L, in Greenwich Village—wired.

On March 8, 1982, Doc and a criminal crony were in the Barrow Street safe house. They had a long, rambling conversation about everything under the sun: women, dope, robberies, killing. They spilled on the various doings of "Cakes," "Flame," and "Maroon," and about "crackers," "sniff," and "smoke."[5] Not long afterward, the FBI and NYPD raided BAAANA and a couple of safe houses, looking for Doc. But he managed to slip away.

• • •

Pre-Brinks, the Bureau knew next to nothing about May 19th, but as the NYROB investigation continued, the name kept coming up again and again. Who were those people? Agents working the case picked up all kinds of interesting tips about the group: there were thirty to forty "hard-core" members in and around New York City, many of them had been in the Weather Underground, and the majority of May 19th members were "women who followed a lesbian lifestyle," as one report put it.[6]

FBI special agents discovered a network of groups they believed were affiliated with May 19th, including the John Brown Anti-Klan Committee. Agents in the Bureau's Chicago office speculated that May 19th had created the committee "in order to attract people who might otherwise be 'turned off' by a group having the word 'communist' in its name."[7] In addition to public activities such as leafleting, meetings, and demonstrations, May 19th had a clandestine presence—FBI sources revealed that "certain May 19 members operate in both underground and 'surface support' capacity."[8]

The Brinks investigation revealed that radical remnants of the Weather Underground and the BLA were working together and had done a string of pre-Brinks armored truck jobs in New York, New Jersey, and Connecticut, as well as the breakouts of Morales and Chesimard.[9] Marilyn, Judy, and Doc Shakur were all part of some sort of conspiracy, which was somehow linked to BAAANA and the Madame Binh collective. It was starting to connect up in the minds of investigators: cop-killing African American revolutionaries, angry lesbians, maybe even pro-Castro Puerto Ricans—it looked like a witch's brew of violent extremism.

The Bureau had been to see Alan, and he'd been hauled in front of a federal grand jury in the Southern District of New York investigating the Brinks crimes. He refused to talk, a federal judge said he was in contempt, and on May 26, 1982, he was sentenced to seven months at the Metropolitan Correctional Center in Lower Manhattan.[10] Not long after he got out, the Feds indicted him as an accessory (after the fact) for having treated Marilyn's gunshot wound—purportedly the first such indictment of a physician since 1865, when Dr. Samuel Mudd was charged with setting the fractured leg of John Wilkes Booth, the fugitive assassin of President Abraham Lincoln.

Alan scraped together $25,000 and made bail; then, almost immediately, he was subpoenaed to give hair samples. He calculated his odds and reckoned he was facing ten years, minimum. After visiting Barbara and little Sarah in Chicago, he decided to go underground.[11]

He forfeited the $25,000 bail, and as of February 3, 1983, he was a federal fugitive.

. . .

Meanwhile, the May 19th women were lying low, hoping to avoid the dragnet—if they kept cool and didn't make any stupid mistakes, maybe they could ride it out. The cops couldn't keep this up forever, could they?

Then Silvia was grabbed. Cops had found her prints inside one of the Brinks getaway cars. On November 9, 1982, FBI special agents picked her up outside her West 95th Street apartment. Tyrone Rison played a big part in the arrest; he'd been cooperating with the FBI in the hopes of getting a slot in the federal witness protection program.* Later, in court, he spilled his guts about the botched operation, including the pre-robbery training session he'd done with "Louise" (Marilyn) and other May 19th members.[12] It was payback time; he couldn't stand the woman, he told investigators. Silvia didn't care for him, either; she regarded him as a trigger-happy psycho.

Investigators tore through Silvia's place, spending hours inside. They left with seven cartons of papers, including May 19th documents. Also in the haul: evidence linking Brinks participants to the FALN, a carbon copy of an original FALN communiqué, folders marked "FALN" and "Morales escape," and a pre-explosion snap of Willie Morales.[13] The papers were loaded with latent prints, including those of Linda Evans and Betty Ann Duke.

The FBI thought Silvia knew about Fraunces Tavern and other FALN bombings around the country.[14] It also suspected she'd been a

---

* Rison's wish would come true. He pled guilty to felony murder, bank robbery, and Racketeer Influenced and Corrupt Organizations (RICO) conspiracy, and in exchange for his testimony, he disappeared into the witness protection program.

part of the Chesimard breakout. In custody, Silvia was unflappable, but although detectives grilled her at length, they came up with nothing. Federal prosecutors unleashed a grand jury and summoned her to testify about the FALN. Silvia told them to go to hell and got three years for criminal contempt.

The FBI tried to interview Linda in Austin, but they couldn't find her. A confidential source told them that when she'd heard the Bureau was looking for her, she had left town, presumably gone underground.[15]

. . .

"Repression has taken a toll on our movement," two May 19th women, "Marcy" and "Mary," concluded in an undated paper that appraised the current state of revolutionary anti-imperialism. Their assessment: Reagan and his reactionary clique were on a right-wing rampage, the noose of capitalism and imperialism was tightening, and the fascist hirelings in Congress and the media were pumping out lies about the triumphs of the unfolding Reagan Revolution.

After the Brinks fiasco and fallout, it would have made sense for May 19th to disband completely. There was no longer the Family to support, and many of their once secret activities were now known to the police and the media. And some aboveground supporters of May 19th did drop away. But the inner core of the group went in the other direction and become more hardened and committed. Supporting the national liberation movements that shared their beliefs was paramount, according to May 19th's analysis. It had to synch up with what those freedom fighters were doing on the ground. "We need to be able to respond to the offensives of Third World struggles by an offensive of our own," read one of its manifestos.[16]

They were under the leadership of the Third World brothers and

sisters. May 19th members believed that they had special obliga-
tions—they'd had middle-class backgrounds, they were white, privileged, and living in the belly of the American beast. If their black and
brown comrades were fighting and dying, so would they. But first,
they'd have to build what they called a "military capability." Michael
"Bommi" Baumann, a founder of 2 June Movement, a West German
militant anarchist group active during the 1970s, articulated a similar
approach: "What's needed is a vanguard in the metropolis that de-
clares its solidarity with the liberation movements of the Third World.
Since it lives in the head of the monster, it can do the greatest damage
there."[17]

The women weren't going to let anybody dismiss them as "just a
handful of leftovers from the sixties that are soon going to be out of
sight, out of mind," as Betty Ann said.[18]

"If not us, who? . . . If not now, when?" May 19th asked.[19]

In years past, the women had been relegated to the secondary
teams during the Family's robberies and jailbreaks. They were the
backups, always there to do the secondary work for the male urban
guerrillas.

May 19th concluded that it needed to change course. Most of those
guys were dead or in jail. While Marilyn and Alan were fugitives and
Silvia was locked up, the core had a lot more room for maneuvering
than Doc Shakur. He was on the FBI's Ten Most Wanted Fugitives list
and running from a motivated police force that wanted to bring him
to justice for killing fellow cops.

Using the alias "Donnell Jackson," Doc hid out in Washington, DC,
where he caroused at after-hours hot spots such as Ladies, Inc., and
Club Delight. He and a longtime companion, Cheri Laverne Dalton
(the aforementioned "Flame"), relocated to the West Coast, where
they lived for years as "David and Claudia Bryant."

The FBI eventually tracked them to Los Angeles, and on the morning of February 11, 1986, Special Agent David Mitchell, a member of the New York JTTF, arrested Shakur on an LA street. "I'm not going to talk," he told Mitchell, and he never did.[20]

On March 7, Doc was back in New York, where he faced federal charges in connection with Brinks and other armed robberies, as well as violation of the RICO statute. The ever-defiant Doc told his supporters in the courtroom that he was a "prisoner of war." "I wish to apologize for being caught," he said.[21]

Shakur was convicted on all counts in May 1988 and drew a sixty-year sentence. Turned down for early release in 2016 and 2018, he's scheduled to appear again before the parole board in 2020. Cheri Dalton managed to elude capture and went the way of Chesimard and Morales—she lived in Cuba and established herself as the "godmother" of Cuban hip-hop, according to press accounts. She died in January 2019.

The May 19th women decided on a new direction. "Because [Brinks] was in the media, because the [government] was investigating, it was the aftermath of that, and that was a terrible, awful, heinous thing that happened," Susan said. "If [we were] going to do anything for change it couldn't be in any way shape or form that kind of activity."[22]

To put it in more straightforward terms: though armed expropriations weren't wrong, they brought too much attention.

So May 19th had to look for another way. Something dramatic, something that made their political points, something that struck at the imperialist monster without inviting even more savage state repression.

．　．　．

After Linda and Betty Ann, there was another post-Brinks addition to the May 19th lineup. She brought all the right credentials: SDS, women's movement, the Weather Underground, the John Brown Anti-Klan Committee, and the Madame Binh Graphics Collective. She'd even crossed paths with Linda back in Chicago, when they had been part of the school invasion in the suburbs.

Laura Jane Whitehorn was born in Brooklyn on April 16, 1945, into a politically progressive family. Various aunts and uncles were ardent socialists. Her paternal grandfather was a Socialist Party member of the New York state legislature. Laura's father, Nathaniel, was a lawyer, and her mother, Lenore, a social worker. The Whitehorns certainly weren't rich, but they were comfortably middle class.

After World War II, the Whitehorns, like millions of other Americans, decamped from Brooklyn for a piece of the American dream in the New York suburbs. They bought a place in New Rochelle, an archetypal bedroom community.

Laura was politically aware early on. Even out in tranquil Westchester County, the Whitehorns felt the sting of McCarthy-era anticommunism—a number of friends and relatives lost their jobs because of their political ties. And even as a child, Laura hated racism. "As a Jewish kid born in 1945, I was raised to hate prejudice," she said.[23] She recounted an incident at a family gathering: a relative who had uttered a racist epithet was banished permanently from the Whitehorn household. On family excursions into the city, she saw relative depravation. "I would go into Harlem and see that people didn't have the same opportunities that people in white communities had," she recalled in 1999. "It was just as plain as that."[24]

Family photos show a rambunctious, fun-loving adolescent with a megawatt smile. But Laura realized she was different from the other young people. "When I was a kid, knowing that I was a lesbian, [and] feeling that I was a lesbian, made me feel I wasn't included in any recognized group," she told an interviewer in a 2000 documentary.[25] Her sexual orientation shaped her politics, she said. "Being a lesbian . . . made me more open to feeling some kind of link to other people who were despised by the system."[26]

An academic star, Laura went on to Radcliffe. She hadn't come out and continued operating under society's heterosexual norms and worked to meet its expectations. In 1966, she married a Harvard Law School–educated lawyer, Donald J. Stang, who had been an undergrad at the university and a contemporary of Laura's back at New Rochelle High School.

In Cambridge, she was swept up in the civil rights and antiwar movements, and her political rage was mounting. In the South, redneck cops were using cattle prods, dogs, and fire hoses on peaceful protesters. In the North, National Guard troops were patrolling riot-torn ghettos with fixed bayonets. In Vietnam, American jets were napalming hapless villagers, B-52 bombers were dropping massive explosive loads on both civilian and military targets, and UH-1 choppers were ferrying grunts into the swaying elephant grass. Grotesque phrases such as "free-fire zone" and "search and destroy" entered the American vernacular.

Before long, Laura's activism took on a harder edge. Like many others in the antiwar movement, she concluded that it was time to move "from protest to resistance," as the slogan went. She became infatuated with the Black Panther Party, which was a step too far in the eyes of her parents. Although politically progressive, they freaked out when they discovered that their daughter was consorting with the shotgun-wielding Black Power advocates.

She joined the Students for a Democratic Society and, as SDS fractured, the Weathermen. The FBI kept track of her along with her

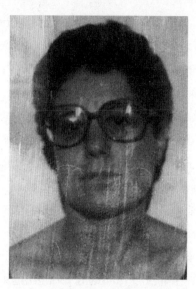

Laura Whitehorn: "My lesbianism makes me a better anti-imperialist."

Weather comrades, and a 1975 U.S. Senate report on the group item-ized her offenses: disorderly conduct, malicious mischief, and even "malicious prowling."

Laura was also part of Weather's Days of Rage demonstration in Chicago in October 1969. The theme: "Bring the War Home." In the run-up to the event, a poster declared "Hot Town—Pigs in the Streets . . . But the Streets Belong to the People. Dig It?" During the three-day rampage, hundreds of jacked-up young insurrectionists, wielding pipes and chains, their heads protected with football helmets, trashed cars and shops along the city's moneyed Gold Coast. Sirens screamed day and night, cops cracked heads, and paddy wagons bulged with scruffy radicals. President Nixon called the Weather hordes "thugs and hoodlums who have always plagued the good people." Less predict-ably, the Black Panthers denounced the Days of Rage as "opportunis-tic" and "child's play."

By that point, Laura considered herself a committed communist and revolutionary. "It was the high tide of national liberation around the world," she said in 1979.[27] "My lesbianism makes me a better anti-imperialist," she said. "I left graduate school, left my husband, and joined a Weather collective, and wound up eating noodles with garlic butter on them every night for a month and then oatmeal with nothing on it for three months."[28]

First lesbianism, now Leninism: a terrifying sexual-political combination as far as most of midcentury America was concerned.

. . .

Just as Laura Whitehorn got serious about her involvement, Weather started waging an armed campaign. On March 6, 1970, a nail-studded bomb, intended for a noncommissioned officers' dance at Fort Dix, New Jersey, accidentally detonated at 18 West 11th Street in Greenwich Village. The town house pancaked and burned. Neighbors, including the actor Dustin Hoffman, looked on as the mess smoldered and rescue workers recovered the bodies of three Weatherpeople: Terry Robbins, Ted Gold, and Diana Oughton. Oughton's corpse didn't have a head.

The incident didn't stop Weather from going on to carry out dozens of bombings, including dynamite attacks on the Pentagon, the State Department, and the U.S. Capitol. Other operations were more farcical—"insurgent mischief," former Weather Underground leader Bill Ayers called them.[29] One notable example: In September 1970, hippie icon and LSD guru Timothy Leary was at the low-security California Men's Colony prison, serving time for pot possession. Leary, a self-described "psychonaut," promoted LSD and other psychedelic drugs as a gateway to spiritual enlightenment and as a pathway to

God himself.* On September 15, during a routine bed check, prison guards discovered that Leary was gone. They found a note under his mattress in which the guru compared himself to Socrates, Jesus Christ, and the 6 million Jews murdered in the Holocaust.[30]

Leary, whom Ronald Reagan, while California governor, had called a "Robespierre on acid, a kingpin hell-bent on unraveling the normal order," had climbed over the prison's chain-link fence.† Weatherpeople picked him up, hid him in safe houses, gave him a doctored passport, and helped get him out of the country. They got $20,000 for the job. Dr. Tim made it all the way to Algeria, where exiled Black Panther Party minister of information Eldridge Cleaver took him in.‡ Newspaper photos showed a grinning, Lenin cap–wearing Leary strolling through Algiers at Cleaver's side.§

Leary's acid taking and merrymaking continued unabated, much to Cleaver's annoyance. Cleaver's concerns were well founded: the Algerian regime was politically radical but socially conservative, and soon it hustled Leary out of the country. Like an acid-addled Scarlet Pimpernel, he bounced from country to country, eventually winding

---

* Moreover, the former Harvard psychology lecturer insisted that psychedelics could cure an array of sexual disorders, including impotence and frigidity, "both of which, like homosexuality, are symbolic screw-ups," he told *Playboy* magazine in 1966.

† Leary's fawning followers referred to him as "Dr. Tim." Nixon fumed and fulminated about the Pied Piper of the counterculture, reportedly labeling him "the most dangerous man in America."

‡ The Algerian regime, which was sympathetic to many Third World anticolonial movements, had given Cleaver and his wife, Kathleen, the use of what the *New York Times* called "a drab, unheated apartment in the tacky suburb of Pointe Pescade." Cleaver was warned not to attract too much attention to himself. Joining his entourage was another Panther, Sekou Odinga.

§ In 1975, Cleaver's career took a new direction: he designed and marketed codpiece-fronted trousers. He told the *Harvard Crimson* that "in a conventional pair of pants the penis gets tucked behind the pants, you know? . . . But in these pants, the penis is held in a sheath of cloth that sticks outside of the pants. . . . What's wrong with getting an erection and letting people know about it?"

up in Kabul, Afghanistan, a stop along the so-called hippie trail. The FBI nabbed him at the airport.

. . .

Laura's ideological commitments grew stronger even as the Vietnam War wound down and the antiwar movement all but disappeared. Laura valorized the United States' enemies in Southeast Asia, who'd outfought and outlasted what she saw as an imperialist monster. She revered the women of Vietnam, particularly those who had served in combat roles fighting the Americans.

In July 1975, just months after Vietnam had fallen to the communists, she got a chance for a firsthand look at the country. The pilgrimage, which included Laura and three other female anti-imperialist activists, was organized by the Vietnam Women's Union, founded in 1930 to contribute to "anti-feudalism and anti-imperialism movements led by the Communist Party to struggle for the power of the people."[31] At the request of their hosts, the American activists evaded the U.S. embargo on material aid to Vietnam and smuggled in injectable Valium and other medicines.

One of Laura's traveling companions, the writer Tori Cade Bambara, wrote a short story about the trip. Laura disapproved of the tale on ideological grounds; "It conferred some unflattering attributes on some of the Vietnamese characters," she said. But eventually she rethought her political rigidity: Bambara's tale "was not the single-mindedly heroic portrait my narrow ideology needed, of women planting rice then rushing fearlessly to shoot down American planes using outdated weapons."[32]

During the late 1970s, living in New York, Laura continued her radical activism. She joined Madame Binh Graphics Collective,

May 19th's printmaking affiliate. Soon May 19th women reached out to her: Would she like to do more than just make posters and attend the occasional street demonstration?

The women told her there was a secret formation fighting racism and imperialism, and that this group wasn't afraid to use physical force. It wasn't male-dominated like the Weather Underground; women organized and led the group. Laura's obvious commitment to revolutionary anti-imperialism, her intelligence, and her real-life Weather experience would be invaluable. Laura liked what she heard and joined their formation. Now she was part of what May 19th called the "armed clandestine movement."

Bombings were intended to be percussive wake-up calls for the imperialists, warmongers, colonialists, and fascists. Every bomb that went off would signal to the world that they were still in the game and that they still mattered. It was proof that an underground army was at work. And, as May 19th discovered, bombing could be morale enhancing: reconnaissance, target selection, emplacement, detonation; tension and release, and a *frisson* of excitement. Like many other radicals who came of age in the 1960s and '70s, the women of May 19th were inspired by the writings of Frantz Fanon, the Martinique-born psychiatrist and author of *The Wretched of the Earth*, a powerful anti-colonial polemic. "At the level of individuals," Fanon wrote, "violence is a cleansing force. It frees the native from his inferiority complex and from his despair and inaction; it makes him fearless and restores his self-respect."[33]

The women experimented with various explosive concoctions and devices. It was on-the-job training, research, and development aimed at finding the right tools and creating the biggest bang for the buck, while keeping faces and fingers intact. They used Café Bustelo coffee cans to build firebombs brewed with granulated sugar, potassium chlorate, and hot water and poured into molds to set. The result was a semihard, whitish material called "firefudge." It resembled the confection, but, as a U.S. Army field manual warned, "it is poisonous and must not be eaten."[34] They set off the firefudge with a simple time-delay mechanism: Ping-Pong balls or Trojan condoms filled with concentrated sulfuric acid. The corrosive liquid ate through its container, giving the firebomber plenty of time to flee. May 19th discovered a way to amp up the firefudge by adding a material whose use by the U.S. military during the Vietnam War had earned international condemnation: jellied gasoline, better known as napalm.

The women built IEDs—improvised explosive devices. The raw ingredients were cheap and readily available. They'd load an inch-wide, foot-long pipe with half a pound of smokeless powder, then seal the ends. It could pack a wallop.

But they wanted something with a bigger punch.

Thanks to the dynamite theft in Austin back in 1980, May 19th had plenty of high-explosive ingredients, including dynamite, blasting caps, and det cord. *The Anarchist Cookbook*, assorted military manuals, and DuPont's *Blaster's Handbook: Practical Methods of Using Explosives for Various Purposes* offered basic bomb-making information. Though they didn't have the internet, the texts were easily accessed at libraries, bookshops, and army-navy stores.

But building and emplacing an explosive device took talent, technique, and tradecraft. They'd have to learn the art and the science. It was dangerous work. A bomb-maker could lose her hands, her face, or even her life. How could they forget poor Willie Morales or the three Weatherpeople atomized in the town house explosion on West 11th Street? Hands-on instruction from an expert would be invaluable. Essential, in fact.

Laura and Linda had been in the Weather Underground. They weren't experienced bombers, but they knew people who were. Cathy

Wilkerson, whose father owned the West 11th Street town house, had been in the building during the accidental explosion and had managed to flee from the wreckage. She went on to become a Weather bomb-maker.[35] She was living in New York, as was Weather's master bomb builder, Ron Fliegelman. They might be willing to give some guidance.

The post-Brinks law enforcement pressure was heavy. But the May 19th women weren't going to wait around forever.

11

WE ARE THE REVOLUTIONARY FIGHTING GROUP

We need to be able to respond to the offensives of Third World struggles by an offensive of our own. The rules of attack, like all rules of war, need to be learned, and the armed clandestine is the best place to learn them.

—UNDATED MAY 19TH PAPER, "SOME STRATEGIC
PREMISES AND POLITICAL CHANGES"

NEW YORK, JANUARY 1983

May 19th members figured that their first attack should be relatively low key, something local, in or around the city—a sharpener, a practice run to get their operational skills into shape. No casualties, just a big bang. Post-attack, they'd use a ferocious-sounding nom de guerre to scare the fascists and imperialists.

Up front in the New York City telephone directory, there were blue pages listing federal, state, and local government offices. The FBI's

167

New York Field Office was in a forty-one-story, slablike building downtown at 26 Federal Plaza.

By that time, FBI offices in places such as Chicago, Los Angeles, and New York were locked down tight. Laura, Susan, Linda, Marilyn, and their friends knew this; they'd tangled with the FBI in the past, when they'd been involved in SDS, Weather Underground, and the BLA. During the Bureau's frantic but ultimately unsuccessful coast-to-coast hunt for Weather fugitives during the 1970s, left-wing agitators of all kinds had been hauled in for questioning.

One particular incident in 1971 had pushed the FBI toward increasing security: on a night in March, antiwar activists crowbarred their way into a tiny, two-man satellite office in Media, Pennsylvania. The burglars had successfully counted on the fact that the office would be empty because it was the night of the Muhammad Ali–Joe Frazier "Fight of the Century," and most Americans would be at home, glued to their TV sets or radios.

The thieves made off with reams of Bureau files that documented the FBI's decades of snooping and disinformation directed against the New Left, black radicals, communists, and the Ku Klux Klan, known collectively as COINTELPRO, the Bureau abbreviation for Counterintelligence Program. COINTELPRO was all about penetration and disruption—just like operations against adversary intelligence services. The Media activists shared their COINTELPRO gleanings with reporters.

It was preinternet WikiLeaks. A wave of public protest followed, with most of the abuse falling on the head of J. Edgar Hoover, the FBI's aging and increasingly legacy-conscious director. Hoping to tighten things up, Hoover shuttered many of the Bureau's small "resident agencies"—but not all of them.

The New York phone book listed another FBI office, tucked away in a federal building at 45 Bay Street in the St. George section of Staten Island. An added bonus: it also housed navy and air force recruiting stations.

May 19th did a little reconnaissance. They strolled right in; the place was a real sleepy hollow. The FBI office was on the second floor. They noted the women's bathroom conveniently located just across the hall. The setting seemed ideal for their plans.

On January 28, 1983, a woman and a man walked into the building at 45 Bay Street. Witnesses later told the FBI that she was about thirty-five, roughly five feet, five inches tall, with a medium complexion. He was described as a white male, twenty-five years old, five feet, nine inches tall, with dirty blond hair, a mustache, and a slim build.

The bomb they'd built was a little bulky, but it didn't seem to draw any attention. The woman found a hiding spot in the upstairs bathroom, and then the pair slipped out of the building.

At 10:30 that night, the thing went off: a huge blast, followed by burst pipes and cascading water. At 9:10 the next morning, the news desk at United Press International received a call. It was a taped message: "We bombed the F.B.I. office on Staten Island. They are the political police. They are responsible for attacks in the United States and around the world. Death to traitors. Free political prisoners. We are the Revolutionary Fighting Group."[1]

Everything went exactly according to plan. May 19th started mapping out fresh attacks. It considered a new theater of operations—maybe somewhere closer to the heart of the "Amerikkkan" state.

• • •

Part of the fallout from the Brinks job was that every public May 19th meeting, rally, and gathering seemed to draw law enforcement scrutiny. Men in windbreakers and bucket hats standing around outside, trying to look inconspicuous. Strange hissing noises and clicking sounds came through on the telephone. Lots of wrong numbers—it seemed as though somebody wanted to find out whether they were at home.

It was obvious that the cops had Madame Binh under surveillance. Suspicions were confirmed on January 3, 1983, when cops hit the studio on Taaffe Place in Brooklyn and said they were looking for Donna Borup, who'd been on the run ever since she'd jumped bail after the JFK fracas. The FBI men tossed the place and hauled off loads of leftist literature and artwork but found no traces of their peripatetic target.[2]

Madame Binh looked for a new home, someplace less well known to the authorities. The women found one across the Hudson River at 665 Newark Street in Jersey City. A woman Judy Clark had lived with on West 98th Street in Manhattan ran the collective's day-to-day operations. They continued to crank out agitprop artwork supporting their favorite causes, including Puerto Rican revolution.

It didn't take much time for the Bureau to discover Madame Binh's new home, and before long, heavy law-enforcement surveillance was under way. Revolving teams of agents with mustaches, sideburns, and tight trousers clocked their comings and goings. Black wall–tired surveillance sedans abounded. And there was nighttime rummaging in the garbage cans outside, either the cops or the FBI or both, doing what they called "trash runs."

Government probes weren't confined to the New York area: May 19th members in Chicago reported that cops were snapping photos at demonstrations, showing up at public meetings, and writing down license plate numbers—just as the Bureau and the Chicago police force's antiradical Red Squad had done in the 1960s and early '70s.

May 19th concluded that if they were going to survive and continue the armed struggle, there was only one way forward. They'd have to go on a wartime footing: disappear from sight, pick new identities, cut off contact with friends, family, loved ones, and political comrades. It would be like living the life of a fugitive.

But although Marilyn, Susan, and Alan were on the wanted list, they certainly didn't see themselves as criminals. Ordinary crooks were in the *underworld*. Marilyn, Susan, and Alan were in the *underground*. Linda, Betty Ann, and Tim now had no choice but to join them.

Writing in 1943, two former members of the anti-Nazi resistance in Germany described the power of the all-seeing "scientific surveillance of a modern police state." You couldn't hide from it, they said, but you could deceive it. And the best way to do that was to live as ordinary a life as possible. "The more you resemble a normal everyday citizen in every respect," they wrote, "the less apt you are to be suspected. And as long as you do not arouse suspicion and scrupulously observe a long series of rules of caution, you may be able to carry on underground work for years on end. Once you are suspected, even catacombs will not help."[3]

There was more: "Maintain in all circumstances the appearance that you are the same as other people, that you have an ordinary job," the former resistance members advised. This turned out to be excellent advice.

May 19th hid in plain sight, attired in pants suits, dad jeans, flannel shirts, momma skirts over aqua-colored panties, purple scarves, corduroy jackets. They held down ordinary jobs, working as printers, technicians, and office clerks[4]—work that was mainstream and anonymous and not particularly well paid, but enough to scratch out a living. Typically the gigs had well-defined, regular hours, which made it easier to allocate time for the armed struggle.

Grinding it out underground was a major challenge. The subterranean diet was pretty terrible. Ex-Weatherwoman Cathy Wilkerson described her intake during the 1970s: "oatmeal, candy, doughnuts, coffee, the occasional egg or grilled cheese sandwich, and red wine and bourbon," as well as endless cigarettes.[5]

The most important requirement of underground life was security; without it, an operative would end up dead or in jail. When asked about her subterranean years, Marilyn kept her mouth shut, telling one interviewer only, "It is hard to say very much without getting specific, and that I can not do. I suspect that is something the state repressive apparatus would read with great interest."[6]

But good security was cumbersome and laborious, and it came at a cost. The underground lifestyle was anything but glamorous. Everything one took for granted aboveground needed to be acquired with risky, painstaking effort.[7]

There were disguises: Mrs. Doubtfire–style glasses, wigs, dye jobs. Sometimes Susan dressed like an old woman. "We laughed when the first time we dyed our hair it turned orange, a long-honored tradition of underground participants around the world," she said. "The color was called 'underground orange' because it would take several attempts to get the color right."[8]

The May 19th cells built a complex security infrastructure: multiple information relay points, false identification, code names, and frequent relocation. "In clandestine work," noted the anonymous author of one internal May 19th paper, "sloppiness, laziness, and inattention to detail are all forms of opportunism and are dangerous." At all times, the author insisted, "science and seriousness must be applied to developing correct methodology."[9]

They typed out handbooks—meticulous, exhaustive, even obsessive, just like everything else May 19th did. Intellectuals hunched over typewriters, writing and rewriting, peer reviewing, critiquing. Members relied on a document called "Rules of Security and Operations" for in-depth advice, guidance, and regulations for preventing the "fatal blows" that had doomed other, unspecified "revolutionary organizations of the continent." [10] It was essential to "protect the Organization, its combatants, its secrets, documents, arms, and other instruments of work." May 19th's ability to carry out operations hinged on the group's ability to safeguard itself. Without such measures, its members would end up like those of the BLA or the FALN—dead or behind bars.

A central tenet: secrecy. No blabbing to outsiders, of course. It was essential to "maintain the most rigorous silence." Everything was on a compartmentalized, need-to-know basis. No mingling with outsiders.[11] Another principle was being punctual—and never missing a meeting, as they were hard enough to arrange. But don't show up early. And if somebody fails to appear within ten minutes of the scheduled time, call off the meeting. Always think about a line of retreat ahead of time. And if the cops show up, you might have to undertake "armed maneuvers" in order to get out of there.

Always assume the authorities are listening. If you need to talk inside, crank up the radio. The phones are probably tapped, so try to use a pay phone. May 19th had inventories of public phone numbers and locations all over town. There was a cluster of fifteen on the East Side alone. Each phone was assigned a name, such as "Agnes's" (87th Street and Second Avenue, southeast corner, 534-9574), "Bernie's" (79th and Second, southeast corner, 744-9824), "Carol's" (74th and Second, southeast corner, 650-1302), "Doug's" (70th and Second, southwest corner, 650-1289), and so on.

If Marilyn wanted to talk to Judy securely, they might make arrangements for "Agnes" to call "Carol" at a certain time and date. If they didn't connect, the protocol was that they were to try again an hour later, this time using the next name on the list. Marilyn would move on to "Bernie's" at 79th and 2nd, and Judy would go to "Doug's." The system was clunky and time-consuming, but it reduced the chance of government eavesdropping. It was like "Moscow Rules," novelist John le Carré's fictional tradecraft for spies: Never forget you're operating in hostile territory.

Everybody had aliases and noms de guerre, memorable but not too distinctive: "Bess J. Lunderman," "Loretta Polo" (Betty Ann); "Barbara Grodin," "Susan Knoll" (Susan); "Milagros Matese" (Laura); "Louise Harmon," "Eve Mancusco," "Dee" (Marilyn); "Alex" (Judy); "Christine Porter," "Louise Robinett," "Katherine Orloff" (Linda); "Leonard Cohen," "William Lunderman," "Kenneth Abrams" (Alan); and "William Bassler," "William J. Hammond" (Tim).[12]

It was good OPSEC to rotate aliases from time to time. But it took discipline and practice to remember to use the right name.

May 19th needed identification documents, the most essential tools for surviving in the underground. Library cards were a start, but much more important were Social Security cards, "anchor documents" that they could use as the foundation for a phony persona. With a Social Security card, you could get credit cards and a driver's license, rent an apartment, even land a passport.

How to get one? There was the "dead baby" method. Record keeping was less digitized and much more lax back in the early 1980s—Social Security cards weren't issued at birth the way they are today. You'd look at old obituaries or gravestones and find somebody who was born around the time you were but had died young, before he or she applied for a Social Security card. Then you'd get a copy of the birth certificate—a public record. With the right gear and skills, you could even make your own.

Or you could skip the whole process and print some phony Social Security cards. You'd have to make up the numbers, of course, but unless a suspicious clerk at the Department of Motor Vehicles or some other place where you were applying for something went through the arduous process of verifying them, you were free and clear.

Life underground was draining, and moreover, it was tedious—being constantly on guard, doing countersurveillance, being under-employed in a crappy job. An Italian terrorist, "Giorgio," spoke of the grinding boredom of his subterranean existence: "I imagine that few wars or guerrilla campaigns or armed uprisings, call it what you like, have required the level of drudge work, routine, or rat race that is so much a part of ours."[13]

WASHINGTON, DC, AUGUST 17–18, 1983

Built in 1799, the Washington Navy Yard, in DC's gritty southeast quadrant, is one of the country's oldest military installations. During its heyday, personnel at the site built naval guns, repaired ships, did scientific research, and even made the massive gears for the Panama Canal. Some of the original laborers there were enslaved Africans.

In the decades after the Second World War, the yard evolved into a largely administrative center, including back-office activities such as the Naval Command Systems Support Activity. In the early 1980s, computers with any real power were massive contraptions, and the navy had Regional Data Automation Centers in nine places around the country to do data processing.

The one at the Navy Yard was in Building 196, a hulking, four-story factory-like brick structure.[14] Hundreds of people, both civilian and military, worked inside.[15] Just as at Fort McNair and the FBI office on Staten Island, security at the Navy Yard was light: gates and guards and fences, but at most nothing more than an ID check. It wasn't hard to wander in and out—not like the Pentagon, where you needed a badge or a visitor's pass.

May 19th thought the center did computing for the Naval War College up in Newport, Rhode Island. Newport was where the navy ran big war games, simulating massive battles, and practicing to sacrifice the lives of millions on behalf of the ruling class. May 19th believed they could do some significant sabotage against the imperialist enterprise with an attack on the Navy Yard.

May 19th rigged up a device: a DuPont electric blasting cap, a couple of nine-volt batteries, two pocket watches to serve as timers, pin socket connecters, blue, orange, and red wires linking the parts, and the key ingredient, dynamite, wrapped in black plastic tape.

The bomb had what the U.S. military called a "dual firing circuit," that is, "two independent firing systems, both electric or both non-electric, so that the firing of either system will detonate all charges." [16] In other words, there was less chance of its being a dud. On August 17, May 19th members carried it into the Navy Yard in a blue duffel bag and placed it beside the air-conditioning unit next to Building 196.

A Navy duty officer got a call at 11:56 p.m. A tape recording of a middle-aged man's voice came over the line: "Clear out, there's a bomb inside the computer center." At 12:04 a.m., there was a loud blast. The explosion rocked the building and created a huge mess. [17] A worker was knocked out of his chair, but nobody was killed or wounded. [18]

At 12:15 a.m., reporters at the *Washington Post* and United Press International received phone calls: another prerecorded message, the voice of a middle-aged man announcing that there'd been an attack. Later, there was a communiqué: "BUILD A REVOLUTIONARY RESISTANCE MOVEMENT! FIGHT U.S. IMPERIALISM!" [19]

CONNECTICUT, SEPTEMBER 1983

Keeping on the move is good security hygiene, and May 19th decided to relocate. It took time, money, and effort, but its members knew they'd be safer if they didn't linger in a place for more than a few months. There were hazards, entanglements, and potential pitfalls everywhere: nosy neighbors, suspicious bodega clerks, eager-beaver citizens, busybodies who might do a friendly drop-in and see, hear, or smell something suspicious, and call the cops.

They clustered in Connecticut. Most went to New Haven. It certainly wasn't as interesting as the Upper West Side or Morningside Heights, but for May 19th, it had considerable appeal. The city had a pretty transient population, so nobody was going to pay any particular attention to new arrivals. Rents were relatively low. The scruffy environs of Yale University seemed just about right—they could easily pass as grad students, as postcollegiate bohemians, as harmless off-campus kooks. New Haven was a small city but just big enough to hide in.

Marilyn, Susan, and Tim moved into the Cambridge Apartments, unit 57 at 66 Norton Street, in September 1983. Linda signed the lease, using the name "Katherine Orloff." [20] The rent was $430 a month. Linda kept her distance, no doubt for security reasons; four adults shacking up in one apartment might have attracted unwanted attention, even in New Haven. She was six miles up the road in Hamden, renting a weathered clapboard bungalow at 135 Cherry Ann Street under the name "Christine Porter." [21] Using yet another alias, "Christine Johnson," she got a job at Printing Plus in North Haven and started bringing in a little income for cash-strapped May 19th. Alan was farther from the scene, lodging in a place twenty miles down the Connecticut Turnpike, somewhere in Bridgeport.

There were a lot of potential military targets for May 19th to consider. Defense plants were scattered around the state: General Dynamics built submarines in Groton, and Sikorsky Aircraft made attack helicopters in Stratford. May 19th carried out thorough surveillance and reconnaissance, and the group's files bulged with photos, drawings, and trade journal articles.

· · ·

Alan wasn't too happy underground. He felt cut off—his comrades weren't too far away, but living alone in Bridgeport, a disintegrating, postindustrial urban void, didn't enhance his morale. He missed his wife, Barbara. It was too dangerous for him to travel all the way to Chicago again, but she managed to get back east from time to time, sometimes bringing young Sarah. The family reunions required code phrases, calls to pay phones, and meticulous planning. They were surely emotionally gratifying, but they were also resource draining and a threat to the security of the whole group.

Paranoia started to creep in. As Susan pointed out, altering one's hair color could be tricky. Alan botched his hair-dying job, rendering his black hair a lurid shade of orange, which didn't help his emotional state. "I looked like a clown," he said.[22] Out at the movies one night, he was convinced that people were staring at him. They probably were.

Alan wasn't the only May 19th member under psychological stress. Susan recalled the loneliness and anxiety she felt as a denizen of the subterranean world: "It was hard to let down the wall we had constructed between our past and present lives." Although she was a hardened revolutionary, she missed her parents.

Marilyn, too, felt the absence of the family members she hadn't spoken to in years. "It is difficult and personally heart-wrenching to be separated from one's family, friends and one's political cohorts," she said.[23] She wanted to have kids, but that was tough on the run.[24] She ended up forgoing children to devote herself to the armed struggle.

Being underground can mess with your mind and screw you up emotionally. Humans are of course social animals, and it goes against our nature to cut ourselves off from others. One ex-member of the Red Brigades described it this way:

> When you remove yourself from society, even from the most ordinary things, ordinary ways of relaxing, you no longer share even the most basic emotions. You become abstracted, removed. In the long run you actually begin to feel different. Why? Because you are different. You become closed off, become sad, because a whole area of life is missing, because you are aware that life is more than politics and political work.[25]

But ultimately, despite the dangers, physical and mental, some May 19th members relished the subterranean life. They had the cause, the comradeship, and the ingrained habits of conspiracy. Susan confessed that her secret existence jacked her up and gave her "a feeling of power."[26] "I loved being underground," she said.[27]

There was certainly a strange glamour associated with their high-risk enterprise: the guns, the bombs, the atmosphere of secrecy, and of course the excitement when one of their creations detonated according to plan. They were the rightful heirs to the BLA and the fearsome FALN. They radiated North American anti-imperialist danger, and they were proud of their revolutionary aura.

They'd done some very solid military actions, and they'd kept their cool before, during, and after the attacks. They had the psychological disposition that one Italian terrorist said was essential to success: "Tense but not nervous, calm but not relaxed, decisive but not foolhardy, careful but not fearful."[28]

• • •

May 19th hoped to expand and bring in more members. In addition to being morale boosting, it would help with their growing plans.

They considered a new process to "develop aboveground members," who would go on to form their own secret cells. These formations would "engage in limited military work (fire bombs, stin[k] bombs, rock throwing, tire slashing, et cetera)."[29] It would be a sort of farm-team system for May 19th: see who was promising, who was a high performer, pluck out the most talented and committed, and bring them into the secret group.

It sounded plausible, but then they considered some practical matters. The aboveground pool of potential recruits was shrinking. It had never been all that big to begin with—a couple of hundred people at most, if you included May 19th's largest affiliated group, the John Brown Anti-Klan Committee. People were tired of all the hassle from the cops, tired of the endless meetings, pointless demonstrations, and the ideological fanaticism. In *The Sophie Horowitz Story* (1984), the eponymous heroine of the novel described the arduous and exhausting life of women who were part of a tiny extremist political sect not unlike May 19th:

> *when most of us started readjusting our lives to match a different reality, going back to school, raising families, these women kept at it. They kept at the tiny demonstrations, the long boring leaflets, educational after educational. They were afraid to go on with their lives.*[30]

Considering how far they'd gone underground, meeting *anybody* outside their little formation—cadres, spouses, kids—was dangerous. Getting new people in would require the outlay of a lot of time and resources—resources that might be better spent carrying out armed actions.

They ultimately decided to shelve the expansion idea. May 19th's violent inner circle—Marilyn, Susan, Linda, Laura, Betty Ann, Alan, and Tim—would continue on as the foot soldiers.

The members of May 19th had gained some real bomb-building skills by this time. They even codified their best practices in a typewritten manual, "Sessions of Training, Building of Timing Circuits, Session on Explosives, Final Assembly, Packaging." [31] The goal: to "perfect our weapon for its primary purpose of carrying out guerrilla attack against the enemy" while ensuring "maximum safety, maximum simplicity, maximum security." They wanted everybody in the group to learn how to build a device and maintain the raw materials: "This is not the province of an explosives expert."

May 19th needed plenty of room for its matériel. Susan rented a self-storage space in New Jersey, a quiet place to keep the dynamite and the blasting agent off-site. It was also her responsibility to rotate the sticks every thirty days so there wouldn't be a dangerous buildup of nitroglycerin.

They planned to put their bomb-making skills to use at a choice target three hundred miles away.

12

TONIGHT WE BOMBED
THE U.S. CAPITOL

Two of the May 19th women arrived in DC on the night of November 6, 1983. They drove an Oldsmobile with Connecticut tags. It was Marilyn's car, registered under her "Louise Harmon" alias. For added security, they switched out the original plates.

Using the name "Ana Stackliff," one of the women registered at the Master Hosts Inn at 1917 Bladensburg Road, in the northeast section of the city. It wasn't too far from their target, the gleaming, slave-built domed structure that dominates the DC skyline.

At 10:48 p.m. on the seventh, a call came in to the Capitol switchboard. "Listen carefully, I'm only going to tell you one time," a male caller told the operator. "There is a bomb in the Capitol building. It will go off in five minutes. Evacuate the building." Then he hung up.[1]

At 10:58, a blast went off on the second floor of the structure's north wing. The explosive load blew doors off their hinges, shattered chandeliers, ripped into a stately portrait of Daniel Webster, and sent a shower of pulverized glass, brick, and plaster into the Republican cloakroom.[2] Security guards gagged on the dust and smoke. The shock wave from the bomb was reported to have sounded like a sonic boom. A jogger outside on the Capitol grounds heard the blast: "It was loud enough to make my ears hurt," she said. "It kept echoing and echoing—boom, boom."[3]

The blast left a fifteen-foot-wide crater in a wall. It also shredded a portrait of John C. Calhoun, the nineteenth-century senator from South Carolina, former U.S. vice president, Yale man, and political theorist. The South's most articulate defender of states rights and slavery, Calhoun has been called "the Marx of the master class."[4] Wiping out his filthy image was an unintended but welcome consequence of the operation for the group.

National Public Radio received a message from the Armed Resistance Unit: "Tonight we bombed the U.S. Capitol."[5]

The message continued with denunciations of U.S. imperialism and aggression against the people of Grenada, El Salvador, Lebanon, and Nicaragua.

The communiqué also included a new message. The bombers made it clear that they had contemplated lethal action: "We purposely aimed our attack at the institutions of imperialist rule rather than at individual members of the ruling class and government. We did not choose to kill any of them this time. But their lives are not sacred and their hands are stained with the blood of millions."[6]

· · ·

Nobody was killed or wounded in the attack, but that did little to soothe frazzled congressional nerves. There was a million dollars' worth of damage, according to one estimate.

Senator Denton denounced the bombing as "an attack that strikes at the heart of our constitutional democracy." He pointed fingers at the

November 7, 1983: "Tonight we bombed the U.S. Capitol"

news media, which he said had failed to heed the alarms sounded by his Subcommittee on Security and Terrorism. "It takes incidents such as the attack on our Marines in Lebanon or a bomb going off in the Capitol to obtain the attention that could have and should have been accorded to the problem earlier," he said.[7]

Senate minority leader Robert Byrd—an ex-Klansman, legendary bloviator, and incorrigible pork-barrel spender—said he had had a premonition. "I told my staff yesterday something like this was going to happen," the West Virginia Democrat said to reporters. "I was sort of anticipating something, especially in light of other occurrences that have taken place around the world recently."[8]

The FBI announced that an investigation had begun. It brought in the DC cops and the Bureau of Alcohol, Tobacco, and Firearms. Dozens of people answered questions about what they had witnessed in or around the Capitol building, and one person said he had seen a "Middle Eastern–type male" lurking around the Senate Reception Room.[9] Somebody else mentioned the "strange" behavior of a stocky Hispanic male with a "hooked nose."[10] Another person said he'd seen a mustachioed man in a navy blue windbreaker and old sneakers—an "Iranian-Turkish type," the guy called him.[11]

A Capitol employee remembered a white male who had checked a Puma sports bag around 11:00 a.m. on the day of the bombing. "The bag seemed rather heavy for the type of bag it was," the employee said.[12] A security guard reported that he'd seen a jittery white guy up on the second floor sometime between 6:00 and 6:30 p.m. He said the guy had had some kind of sports bag with him, and he saw him again, right around 7:00 p.m. That time he didn't have a bag.

It was the third "ARU" DC attack that year. With public opposition to the Reagan administration's wars in Central America running high, some in Congress and law enforcement speculated that a leading antiwar group, Committee in Solidarity with the People of El Salvador, or CISPES, might be involved with the bombings. One senior Bureau man suggested that CISPES "action cells" were involved.[13]

For May 19th, it was good news that the dogs were on the wrong trail. Obviously, the FBI hadn't figured out yet who was behind the nonexistent Armed Resistance Unit or that the same people had been responsible for the Staten Island attack.

May 19th felt that its security systems were solid. Yes, there was surveillance, but not enough to keep its members from carrying out military operations. Silvia had been lifted, but there hadn't been any other recent arrests. And May 19th was almost certain that it wasn't facing every underground movement's most lethal adversary: the informer, the enemy within. They'd all known and trusted one another for years. Plus there were the communal living, the marathon criticism/self-criticism sessions, the lack of privacy—the cops would never be able to get anyone on the inside.

Still, there was no time for complacency. It was time to examine the past, consider the present, and plan for the future. New targets were everywhere.

NEW YORK, APRIL 1984

Laura kept a small spiral-bound notebook. The margins of the gridded paper were dotted with doodles: a cat, a flower, the space shuttle. In her notes, she provided an assessment: they would have to step up the pace of their operations, hit harder—the enemy needed more frequent reminders of "what the wrath of the people will do," she wrote.[14]

So far, May 19th's targets had been limited to institutions of U.S. global domination—the FBI, the navy, Congress. Now, its members decided, it was time to broaden the list and pay attention to the United States' international co-conspirators. They also felt it was time to retire the ARU name. As they had learned with their constantly changing code names, a new nom de guerre for the group would help keep their enemies guessing and fearful that other formations had joined the armed struggle against imperialism.

Israel, according to May 19th, was a fascist "white settler" entity, a racist ethnostate that was relentless in its persecution of the Palestinians, and a U.S. client to boot. May 19th insisted on inserting quotation marks around the country's name to signify its questionable legitimacy, and it always used a lowercase "z" when writing about Zionism. In an undated typewritten paper, May 19th declared that "'Israel' and South Africa are major sub-imperialist [*sic*] powers that attempt to economically, politically, and militarily dominate entire regions while colonizing the Palestinian and Azanian [South African] people." [15]

They had notes on possible targets in New York, including the government-owned Israel Aircraft Industries, or IAI, which had an office at 50 West 23rd Street. The women learned that IAI made airborne radar, electronic warfare systems, and the Gabriel sea-launched missile for the Israel Defense Forces, as well as the export market, and they discovered that IAI had supplied the U.S.-backed dictatorship in Guatemala and upgraded South African military aircraft.

The women clocked the comings and goings at the West 23rd Street building. There wasn't much security to speak of; the building was a "soft" target. Laura kept track in her notebook. Collectively, they decided to officially retire the Armed Resistance Unit moniker. From then on, they called themselves the Red Guerrilla Resistance, or RGR.* The women put their graphics skills to use and came up with a striking new logo: a red star emblazoned with a silhouette of a female fighter toting an AK-47 assault rifle—the weapon of choice for revolutionary insurrectionists the world over.

On April 5, 1984, they put the IED fashioned from a pocket watch, a Radio Shack 9-volt battery, a Hercules Millidet blasting cap, 23-gauge wires, and of course dynamite, the sticks wrapped tightly with black

---

* European terrorist groups during the 1970s and 1980s also adopted militarized names, the Red Army Faction and the Red Brigades being among the most notorious. In Italy, scores of other violent formations operated during the blood-drenched *anni di piombo* ("years of lead"), including Nuclei Comunisti Combattenti (Nuclei of Combatant Communists); Nuclei Territoriali Antimperialisti (Anti-imperialist Territorial Nuclei); and Squadre Armate per la Lotta di Liberazione Comunista (Armed Squads for the Communist Liberation Struggle). Neofascist terrorist groups took similarly ferocious names. Nuclei Armati Rivoluzionari (Armed Revolutionary Nuclei) was responsible for the worst terrorist attack in postwar Italy, the August 2, 1980, bombing of Bologna's central railway station, which killed eighty-five people and wounded two hundred more.

plastic tape into a cardboard box, and hid it in a third-floor stairwell in the IAI building. At 1:40 a.m., a security guard answered the phone. A prerecorded male voice said a bomb would go off soon. Then the United Press International news desk received a call and heard a recording. It was a man's voice: a bomb was about to detonate, and Red Guerrilla Resistance was responsible.

At 1:45, there was an explosion in the stairwell of the AIA offices. Walls cracked, plaster and debris rained down. Nothing terribly dramatic, but they had made a point. A subsequent communiqué laid out May 19th's grievances. They blasted right-wing figures such as Richard Nixon, Ronald Reagan, and the Reverend Jerry Falwell, the fundamentalist founder of the Moral Majority. Ed Koch also got a drubbing. They said the mayor's "virulent hatred of Palestinian and Arab people was matched only by his racism toward Black and Latin people." [16]

• • •

A large-scale U.S. military exercise, Ocean Venture 84, was scheduled to kick off on April 20, 1984, and it would include an aircraft carrier, other surface ships, an amphibious assault unit, and paratroopers. Ocean Venture 84, according to the *New York Times*, "was intended to be a form of psychological warfare intended, as one official put it, to intimidate the Salvadoran guerrillas and their Nicaraguan backers." [17]

May 19th considered Ocean Venture 84 a rehearsal for a full-on U.S. invasion of Central America. First Grenada, now Nicaragua and El Salvador. It was naked aggression, and it was not going to go unanswered.

The Officers Club at the Washington Navy Yard was a venerable spot more than a century old. It was another soft target picked by May 19th for its lax security and obvious connection to the war machine.

In the early morning of April 20, the news desk at United Press International received another call with a prerecorded message: a man with a raspy voice. The person who picked up the phone reported the message as being about a "guerrilla resistance" that had "bombed at 2 a.m. the officer's club at the Washington Naval [*sic*] Yard . . . in protest of current war games" and the "'imperial war' against the people of Central America and the Caribbean."[18] The club was closed at the time, and no one was hurt, but the building "was torn up pretty good," according to a navy spokesman.[19]

The newly minted Red Guerrilla Resistance issued a communiqué about why they had planted the bomb at the officers' club. "Genocide is a ladder to success for these men," said RGR. It couldn't be business as usual for those killers. Members of the military should start worrying about their own safety. "We need to rob them of the security of a home base and make them know that they are the enemy wherever they go," according to the communiqué. "Their officers' club is gone— let them hide in their homes."[20]

April 20, 1984: "Their officers' club is gone—let them hide in their homes."

. . .

The Bureau by this point had been able to piece together that the Revolutionary Fighting Group, the Armed Resistance Unit, and Red Guerrilla Resistance were all related. A close analysis of the communiqués revealed common turns of phrase, themes, and messages. And there was something important in the physical evidence: after each attack, agents had combed the bomb sites and gathered up bits and pieces of what had turned out to be fragments of explosive devices. According to one special agent, "Every bomb-maker has a unique signature because they make them in certain fashions."[21] The DC and New York bombs used similar timing devices, detonating cord, wires, and batteries.

The FBI concluded that a single group was responsible but still didn't have enough clues to identify its members.

PART THREE

ENDGAME, 1984–1985

13

THIS WILL BLOW A HOLE IN YOU

CONNECTICUT, SUMMER 1984

Rich radicals, sympathizers with extra rooms and cars, and the odd trust fund and family money kept the Weather Underground financially afloat. May 19th didn't have those resources. Well-heeled leftists had moved on to other causes years before, and the aboveground support apparatus was withering under constant FBI, police, and grand jury harassment.

By 1984, funds were running low, and desperation was creeping in. If they wanted to keep going, May 19th would have to do some high-risk fund-raising and revolutionary expropriations. But not Family style—killing was still deemed too politically risky.

The women found an enticing soft target: a Stop & Shop supermarket at 195 West Street in Cromwell, just off the interstate near Hartford and a quick drive from their southern Connecticut safe houses. Cromwell was strictly small town, nice and quiet. The potential for any serious law enforcement interference seemed minimal.

Marilyn did additional reconnaissance in late August. At the Stop & Shop service desk, she asked a clerk to cash an out-of-state personal check, using an out-of-state driver's license as ID. The clerk refused, and Marilyn made a stink—let me speak to the manager, she demanded. The manager didn't cash the check, but Marilyn got what she had really come for—an eyeful of the supermarket's service area and offices. She learned where the money was kept.

With that, May 19th hatched a plan. Using their well-honed printing skills, the women ran up an official-looking Form AO 93, a federal search warrant. There were cocaine, marijuana, Quaaludes, and other controlled substances on the premises, and the warrant demanded access. The women also made a couple of credible-looking U.S. government IDs.[1]

Alan and Tim would pose as Drug Enforcement Administration agents. They'd make their search sometime over the upcoming Labor Day weekend. Cromwellians would no doubt be stocking up on hot dogs, burger meat, and beer for the holiday, and the Stop & Shop's safes should be bulging with cash. Alan and Tim would walk out with the money, with everything looking nice and legal, and nobody raising a fuss.

On August 31, Alan and Tim went up to Cromwell. They clocked the Stop & Shop for a day or two and decided that the evening of Monday, September 2, would be the ideal time for the operation. The armored car that serviced the supermarket wasn't likely to make a pickup on Monday, when banks were shut for the federal holiday. All the cash should be there.

At eight o'clock, just before closing time, Alan and Tim walked into the supermarket. Dressed in suits and wearing horn-rimmed glasses, fake mustaches and wigs, and toting attaché cases, they went to the service desk and asked for the manager. Donald P. Corrigan came out from the office, and Alan and Tim badged him with their ersatz IDs.

The three of them went into Corrigan's office, and Alan and Tim got down to business. The would-be DEA men announced that they were looking for dope. Alan waved the phony warrant in the manager's face and insisted that there were loads of illegal drugs inside the supermarket's safes. They needed the safes open.

Corrigan balked; something didn't seem quite right. He told the suited duo that he needed official confirmation from the Cromwell police department before he'd let them have a look inside the safes. "Let me make a quick call."

Time for plan B: Alan whipped out a black revolver and said to Corrigan, "This will blow a hole in you." Nobody moved, so Alan pulled out a second weapon—a nasty looking semiautomatic handgun, silencer equipped. "This one will blow an even bigger one in you," he told the manager.[2] Get the cash *now*, he demanded.

At that point Corrigan stopped resisting. He led the two men downstairs to the cash room, where the supermarket's weekend profits were held. He dialed open a safe. There were stacks of money inside, piled high on the shelves.

There was also a second safe, and Alan told Corrigan to open it, too. The manager inserted the safe's special key, but it needed an additional one that only the armored car service had. Later it was reported that there had been $70,000 in the safe.

Alan and Tim didn't press the point. They jammed a rag into Corrigan's mouth, pushed him to the floor, cuffed him, and trussed him up like a Christmas turkey. With the cash stashed in their briefcases, they left the Stop & Shop and drove off in separate cars.

The $21,480 Alan and Tim netted couldn't compare with the big scores from the Family days, but it was enough to keep May 19th in ramen noodles, wigs, and ammunition. Though the money wasn't near what the Family had brought it, the stickup must have weighed on May 19th members as reducing them to garden-variety criminals and not living like true revolutionaries avoiding possessions belonging to the people.

. . .

After the Cromwell job Marilyn got spooked and decided they needed to relocate again. Maybe it was her revolutionary tradecraft, her years of experience, her well-honed underground discipline. Or perhaps she was a little paranoid—after all, she'd been on the run for five years, enough to rattle anyone. In any case, there had been some worrying stories in the bourgeois press; the FBI had told reporters that the four Washington bombings might have been linked.[3]

On September 19, 1984, Tim rolled up to the Norton Street apartment house in a rented U-Haul van. He and Alan loaded it up, they hit the road, and by 1:00 p.m. they reached the bungalow on Cherry Ann Lane in Hamden. And just like that, Linda had a new roommate. Later, when the landlord asked about the extra woman bunking on the premises, Linda said it was her cousin who was going through a painful divorce and needed a place to stay. She and Marilyn shared a mattress on the floor. Susan was into and out of the place on a regular basis. But the living arrangement lasted just a few months.

NEW YORK, SEPTEMBER 1984

They continued to press on with the armed campaign. They considered bombing a New York Telephone central switching office. "If a stick of dynamite is strapped to the cable and lit, the whole central office will blow up putting out most of Manhattan" according to one unsigned May 19th document.[4] But they scrapped the idea, concluding that an infrastructure attack would send a politically confusing message. They decided instead to plant the next bomb at the South

African Consulate at 425 Park Avenue in Midtown, the Apartheid regime's New York outpost.

The women studied the comings and goings at the building's entrance: deliverymen, mailmen, plenty of white people in suits. They
noted the police presence and the hourly rounds made by security
personnel. They cased the lobby. They dressed unobtrusively and
didn't do anything to draw attention to themselves. They made a dual-
firing bomb for the occasion, designed to produce a hell of a blast, and
planted it in a stairwell on the twelfth floor.

A couple dozen people were working inside the consulate during
the early-morning hours of September 26, 1984. At 12:07, a security
guard answered the phone. It was a warning call to get everyone out.
At 12:23, May 19th's device went off.

The blast was May 19th's most powerful yet—the explosion took a
steel fire door off its hinges and sent it flying thirty feet. It blew holes
in the walls, destroyed a bank of elevators, and damaged six floors.

At 12:36 a.m., there was a call to the Associated Press, a taped
message from a man with a vaguely Spanish accent: "We bombed the
South African Consulate in New York in solidarity with resistance to
South African human rights violations. Down with apartheid. Victory
to the freedom fighters. Defeat U.S. imperialism. Guerrilla Resistance."[5]

Twenty months, five attacks.

14

PUT OUT THE FUCKING CIGARETTE

We have to be qualitatively better guerrillas than we are—especially now that the state can focus on capturing us in their efforts to smash armed resistance. This [has] proved to be very difficult because of failures to adhere to our rules of clandestine procedure, lack of combativity, and accepting low standards of conduct. We are in the midst of a struggle to try to resolve this.

—UNDATED MAY 19TH LETTER, "GREETINGS COMRADES"[1]

CHERRY HILL, NOVEMBER 29, 1984

Susan and Tim were loading boxes into a blue Oldsmobile Cutlass sedan and U-Haul trailer that was parked at a self-storage facility in Cherry Hill, New Jersey, not far from Philadelphia. The boxes were heavy, so despite the autumn-night chill and the wind, they were working up a sweat. Tim was wearing an ill-fitting wig that he barely managed to keep on his head. Both of them wore glasses as part of their disguises.

An FBI wanted poster called Susan armed and extremely dangerous, and the Bureau wasn't wrong. On the front seat of the Olds, purses held semiautomatic pistols: an Interarms Walther PPK .38-caliber and a Browning Hi-Power 9mm.[2] They were fully loaded, with chambered rounds. "Hi-Power" wasn't an exaggeration—the pistol could put a bullet through a wall or a car. The Walther was loaded with Glaser Safety Slugs, so-called frangible rounds filled with tiny metal shot.[3] The slugs would mushroom and shred on impact—they were meant for human targets.

A Cherry Hill policeman, Mark DeFrancisco, pulled up at 5:52 p.m.[4] The night manager had called. Moving toward Susan and Tim, the policeman demanded to see ID. Tim's driver's license said he was William J. Hammond. Susan handed over hers, and DeFrancisco asked her what her birth date was. Her answer didn't match the date on the license.

Officer DeFrancisco asked her if she had any other identification. Maybe it was just a simple mistake. Susan told him she could go back to the Olds and get another ID. DeFrancisco declined. "Something told me I'd better not let her get to the car," he recalled later on.[5]

Officer Craig Martin arrived as backup. Looking inside the trailer and locker, the patrolmen found what the press would call a "terror arsenal"[6]: an Action Arms 9mm semiautomatic Uzi, complete with replacement barrels; hundreds of rounds of ammo; sawed-off shotguns; rifles; a Sturm Ruger .357 magnum revolver with its serial number filed off.[7] And lots of paper: weapons manuals, hundreds of fake FBI, DEA, and state police IDs, a New York Police Department Major Case Squad business card, and 10,250 phony Social Security card blanks.

Before long, Tim and Susan were in handcuffs.

A cop lit up a smoke. "Put out the fucking cigarette," Susan said.[8] The patrolman quickly got the point. Susan and Tim had been trying to move 740 pounds of explosives, including 199 sticks of Hercules Unigel Tamptite dynamite and 110 cartridges of DuPont Tovex 210 water-gel explosives, plus electric blasting caps, detonating cord, and Hercules Slurry Hp-374, a blasting agent. Susan and Tim called it "combat material."[9]

The dynamite was in horrible shape. The sticks were meant to be rotated every thirty days to prevent a dangerous buildup of nitroglycerin, but somebody hadn't been doing his or her job. The dynamite was breaking down. Nitroglycerin was oozing—"weeping"—from the cylinders. That made the contents of the car extremely dangerous: a stray spark could have set off a terrifying blast.

Bureau of Alcohol, Tobacco, and Firearms agents and cops from the Philadelphia bomb squad were called in to recover the stuff. They piled up the dynamite and materials but realized they would have to divide it up before hauling it over the Benjamin Franklin Bridge to the bomb disposal site in Philadelphia. The explosives were unstable, and if they moved it all together, it could have detonated and dropped the bridge or taken out a city block.

• • •

On the way to the Cherry Hill police station, Susan was in the back seat of the cruiser, cuffed and glowering. DeFrancisco turned to her. "I really appreciate your not blowing me away tonight," he said. Like a film noir femme fatale, Susan replied, "I guess this is your lucky day."[10]

The station house had an "armed camp atmosphere," Susan said. "Machine guns were constantly aimed at us." She claimed an FBI agent had looked toward her and said, "I can always tell a kike. At least now we know it's the kikes, the ones with the niggers."[11]

Susan kept up her hardened revolutionary facade. "We're caught, but we're not defeated. Long live the armed struggle!" she shouted on the way to her arraignment.

Tim couldn't get over how easily he had allowed himself to be arrested. In a document titled "Self-criticism," he pummeled himself. Face-to-face with the Cherry Hill police, he had "given up, punked out, refused to fight." The cop "was fairly low key, [he] hadn't drawn his gun, & didn't seem to be onto who we were. This was our chance. I just froze. I wasn't confident I could take out the cop unarmed." [12]

Later in the document he sounded like an "enemy of the people" confessing to the Red Guard during the Chinese Cultural Revolution: "I completely understand that my membership is profoundly in question. I have shown none of the character required of a guerrilla." [13]

But Susan was also to blame for the Cherry Hill shambles. She'd rented the storage space on November 3, 1984, under the name "Barbara Grodin," written down a Social Security number, listed ABC News as her most recent employer, and given a home address. Then there was some kind of paperwork problem, and the facility's manager needed to get in contact with Ms. Grodin. He called ABC in New York. Nobody had ever heard of her.

But he was persistent and wrote a letter, asking her to get in touch. The real Barbara Grodin called him and asked what was going on. She'd never been in Cherry Hill, much less rented a self-storage space, but somebody had stolen her wallet while she had been in New Jersey a year earlier.

Daniel phoned the Cherry Hill cops. The police told him to call if anyone using the name Barbara Grodin showed up on the premises. He asked his staff to be on the lookout.

It was that string that led the manager to call the police when Susan arrived at the front gate on the night of the twenty-ninth.

The FBI made quite a haul in Cherry Hill: weapons, explosives, fake IDs. They got Tim; however, the Bureau concluded that he wasn't any kind of terrorist mastermind but "just a gofer," said retired FBI Special

Agent Donald R. Wofford.[14] Susan, a Brinks fugitive and Chesimard breakout suspect, was the bigger catch.

There was more. The Bureau found Alan's prints on one of the manuals and Linda's on a phony ID card. It also learned that two of the recovered weapons, a Ruger Mini-14 rifle and a Hi-Power pistol, had been bought in Norco, Louisiana, by "Louise Robinett." They knew that was Linda's gun-buying nom de guerre.[15]

The Olds towing the U-Haul was registered to somebody in Orange, Connecticut, named Louise Harmon.[16] On suspicion that it could be one of Marilyn Buck's aliases, special agents from nearby New Haven were dispatched to check it out. The address on the registration was phony, but they kept at it. Special agents showed mug shots to area mechanics and got a match to Marilyn's from a guy who fixed cars at the Exxon station at 284 Whalley Avenue in New Haven. He said she had called herself Ms. Harmon.

Up until that point the FBI's focus on May 19th had been Chesimard and NYROB related. After Cherry Hill, the FBI began widening its investigative aperture and started to get a clear picture of how much destruction the organization was responsible for.

Meanwhile, behind bars, Susan penned a lengthy letter. "Dear Friends," she wrote. "The pigs seized on all the Fed ID & were going to pursue it with a vengeance. Also they were going to comb all storage places. . . . We hope you can vacate both CT and Ph[iladelphia] ASAP."[17]

• • •

Donald Corrigan read the front-page story in the *Hartford Courant* about terrorists on the loose in Connecticut: bombings, armed robberies, rifles. He looked at the people in the accompanying photos and immediately recognized a woman from the photo: Marilyn Buck looked like the woman who had raised the check-cashing ruckus at the Stop & Shop in August. And a man named in the piece as Alan Berkman was definitely one of the two who had robbed him in September. At 2:30 a.m., Corrigan called the Cromwell Police Department with the tip.

The local cops called the FBI. The robbers had worn black latex gloves when they had pulled the cash from the safe. But one of the thieves had been barehanded in the manager's office, and there was a set of prints all over the phony warrant. The FBI's crime lab identified them as Alan Berkman's: federal fugitive, bail jumper, accessory to murder, and now armed robber.

• • •

On March 17, 1985, a federal jury found Susan and Tim guilty on eight counts involving explosives, weapons, and fake IDs. At their sentencing, Judge Frederick B. Lacey compared the explosive potential of their storage locker load to the October 1983 truck bomb in Beirut that had flattened a four-story military barracks, killing 220 U.S. marines. Boisterous supporters of Susan and Tim were in the courtroom—"New York weirdos came out of the woodwork for the event," Officer DeFrancisco remembered.[18]

But arrest and prosecution hadn't cooled their revolutionary ardor. Tim insisted that he and Susan were "captured combatants" who had worked to become "the best guerrillas we could be" in their struggle against a "diseased and terroristic system." They told the court that they'd been trying to live up to Cuban comandante Che Guevara's injunction to revolutionaries to combine "perfect love and perfect hate."[19]

"It's not a crime to build revolutionary resistance against the single greatest enemy of the people of the world," Susan told the judge.[20]

Judge Lacey wasn't persuaded. He gave each of them fifty-eight years in prison. One of Susan's appeals would be heard by a federal judge in Philadelphia, Maryanne Trump Barry, an older sister of Donald Trump. During the 2016 Republican presidential primaries, Senator Ted Cruz described Barry as a "Bill Clinton–appointed federal appellate judge who is a radical pro-abortion extremist." [21]

15

REALITÄTSVERLUST

Execution is the killing of a foreign spy, of an agent of the dictatorship, of a police torturer, of a dictatorial personality in the government involved in crimes and persecutions against patriots, of a stool pigeon, informer, police agent or police provocateur.

—CARLOS MARIGHELLA,
MINI-MANUAL OF THE URBAN GUERRILLA (1969)[1]

BALTIMORE, FEBRUARY 1985

In "A Wink at a Homely Girl," a *Sports Illustrated* piece published in 1966, Mark Kram described his hometown as "an anonymous city even to those who live there, a city that draws a laugh even from Philadelphia, a sneer from Washington, with a hundred tag lines that draw neither smile nor sneer from the city. Baltimore: Nickel Town, Washington's Brooklyn, A Loser's Town, The Last Frontier, Yesterday Town."[2]

A decade later, Baltimore still had an image problem. A small group of Baltimore bigwigs, ad men, and city boosters came up with a snappy new nickname, one they thought might help transform the city's reputation as a crime-ridden backwater. Their choice: "Charm City."

The ploy didn't work, of course. Call it whatever you want, the city remained a national punching bag through much of the twentieth century. But Baltimore was perfect for May 19th. It was like New Haven: a town anchored by a major university with a transient population, cheap housing, excellent lines of communication, and an easy hop to Washington or New York.

Marilyn, Laura, and Linda moved into the Yorkewood Apartments, located in the city's northeastern Hamilton neighborhood.[3] It was easy rent with lots of entrances and exits, making it ideal in terms of countersurveillance.

Marilyn was now one of America's most wanted. Her FBI poster hung in post offices from coast to coast—she was "extremely dangerous and may kill without provocation or warning," it said.[4] It was obvious that the Bureau knew plenty about her—the same poster mentioned her pronounced limp, her skill with disguises, and even her dietary habits—the FBI said that she was a "health food user," apparently a distinguishing characteristic for a federal fugitive in the 1980s.[5] Linda, too, had to keep low. She knew that the Cherry Hill bust would lead the Bureau to her; hence her rapid departure from Hamden.

Laura, on the other hand, was relatively clean. There was nothing that tied her to Brinks or to any of the stuff seized in New Jersey. So she handled the rental arrangements. Using the name "Anne Morrison," Laura signed the Yorkewood lease, and on February 1, 1985, the women moved into 5714 The Alameda, apartment D.

They furnished the place in full grad school style: a rabbit-eared TV atop a two-drawer filing cabinet; a swing-arm lamp stood on a milk crate; thrift shop and hand-me-down furniture, including a rocker, a stool, and a patio chair. Spider plants to provide a little greenery. A few tracts, such as *Triumph of the People: The Sandinista Revolution in Nicaragua*, as well as some lighter fare, including a Robert Ludlum spy thriller.

A cassette player provided additional in-home entertainment, with the Spinners' *Grand Slam* album in heavy rotation. Knitting helped Marilyn relieve a little of the stress of underground life.

As in their previous relocations, they needed new IDs, and they got to work concocting them. As a first step, they got cards from the Enoch Pratt Free Library in Baltimore. Then Linda applied for a printing job at Graphic Expressions, at 5418 Harford Road. She used a new alias, "Kate Johnson," and came up with a backstory for the owner, Jerome A. Casciero—she was from Chicago, and she lived at the Dunhill Apartments on Belair Road in Baltimore with her sister, who had a kid with severe medical problems.

In the preinternet age, it was harder to check out someone's credentials. It required phone calls, letters, paperwork, all kinds of hassle. Linda was personable and professional, and she certainly knew her way around a printing press. She got the gig. She netted less than $200 a week—small change even back in 1985, but it was something.[6]

Alan and Betty Ann followed. Alan was almost as hot as Marilyn, but as far as anyone in May 19th knew, the FBI wasn't on Betty Ann's tail. And they were right—the Bureau had snapped some photos of her at John Brown Anti-Klan Committee events, but they weren't paying much attention to her. Betty Ann signed the lease for apartment D-2 at 101 East 25th Street using the alias "Janice Adams," and she and Alan moved in.

What was left of May 19th's violent inner circle was all in Baltimore now.

. . .

Underground man: An assortment of Alan's phony IDs

The RAND Corporation's Konrad Kellen had made some dubious claims about links between lesbianism and terrorism, but the erudite refugee from Nazi Germany did have some useful insights about the stresses and strains, psychological and otherwise, that came with the terrorist underground lifestyle.

Kellen's observations were general, but they applied to what was happening inside May 19th. "According to those who have been part of the terrorist scene," Kellen wrote in 1982, "almost anything [they] do produces great pressures on them, be it risky action or nerve-racking nonaction; constant hiding out in 'safe' houses; ideological controversies; . . . disputes over tactics and strategies; or any kind of group interaction."[7]

And there was something else going on inside May 19th. The Germans have a word for it: *Realitätsverlust*—the loss of a sense of reality. It was a by-product of living in a small, isolated group.

All information emanating from the outside passed through the group's ideological filters. Members were totally dependent on one another for physical and mental survival. Individualism was a liability, a threat to be struggled against—for the greater good. In the close-knit hothouse atmosphere, sound judgment becomes difficult, if not impossible. Everything confirmed preexisting beliefs. The ability to make good decisions eroded.

Leaving the group meant abandoning the people you'd sacrificed for and who'd sacrificed for you. Departure meant that all you had done had been in vain. As one Italian former terrorist put it, "after having already paid such a price, to quit meant to admit that all we had done had been useless."[8] It was a psychological prison; you'd invested too much to quit. In the bloodless language of microeconomics, it was the fallacy of sunk costs.

May 19th members had a bad case of *Realitätsverlust*. They saw themselves as warriors, combatants in the "armed clandestine movement," the ACM. In reality, the ACM didn't extend much beyond May 19th's formation. They were locked into their own private war.

They pounded out tracts for circulation among themselves. They went on at considerable length about the armed struggle, the depredations of imperialism, and the ideological requirements for making revolution. May 19th's writings were rambling, sclerotic, and virtually impenetrable to outsiders. "We need to accumulate forces and to do so in a principled fashion," a member wrote in a single-spaced, twenty-two pager dedicated to the noted Puerto Rican *independista*, Juan Antonio Corretjer. "We cannot be satisfied with being a sect that parasitically gains legitimacy from its relationship to Third World struggle; we cannot exist in a self-contained mini-environment that we call 'the movement.' Perhaps paradoxically, going underground may have brought us more into contact with the dominant society than we had been during our years in the public movement."[9] They were writing the stuff for themselves, and they couldn't speak in any language other than their own.

May 19th was coming to resemble a cult. In "How Cults Can Produce Killers," the political scientist Dennis Tourish wrote that members of cults "spend more and more time talking only to each other. They engage in rituals designed to reinforce the dominant belief system. Language degenerates into a series of thought-stifling clichés which encourages other actions that are consistent with the ideology of the cult."[10]

Their prose revealed their near-total detachment from Reagan-era political reality. Living in an ideological cul de sac, they didn't have any contact with the dominant society. They were cut off from everybody on the political left, too. May 19th routinely excoriated fellow radicals who ignored the armed clandestine movement. And, to the extent that anybody outside May 19th thought about them at all, they considered them a bunch of crazy dead-enders.[11]

. . .

Marilyn, Linda, Laura, Betty Ann, and Alan had their backs to the wall. Susan, Silvia, and Tim were locked up in prisons, resources were thin, and the forces of repression were stronger than ever. In these dark times, the writings of Mao Zedong could offer comfort and inspiration. In 1930, suffering setback after setback, the Chinese communists were growing pessimistic. Would the revolution never come? The Great Helmsman told his comrades not to despair—after all, he said, "a single spark can start a prairie fire." Nineteen years later, the communists were in power. And don't forget the slogan of the Cuban Revolution: "*Socialismo o muerte.*" Socialism or death.

The now greatly reduced May 19th pushed ahead. They kept planning, kept plotting, and started working on bombs, right there inside Apartment D.[12] They kept looking for targets. The women cased the U.S. Naval Academy in Annapolis, Maryland. The officers' club looked promising. They picked up a flyer advertising a St. Patrick's Day lunch: "Leprechauns Not Invited," the handbill read.

They studied Fort Meade, Maryland, home of the supersecret National Security Agency. The women scoped out the U.S. Army's Aberdeen Proving Grounds in the northeastern part of the state. Down in Virginia, they considered Fort Belvoir and the Marine Corps Air Station in Quantico. And they surveilled the Naval Research Laboratory way out in southeast Washington near Bolling Air Force Base.

And there was another prime target right in the heart of the nation's capital. The Old Executive Office Building, a flamboyant nineteenth-century structure built in the French Second Empire style, housed much of the president's staff, including the National Security Council. Vice President George H. W. Bush had offices in the building. And the structure was next door to the West Wing of the White House, the epicenter of the American empire.

May 19th got it all down on paper. A file marked "In Progress" bulged with surveillance notes, diagrams, exposed film, and photographs.[13]

. . .

The use of deadly force by New York cops was making headlines around the world. For years, the press, community groups, and politicians had been calling attention to civilian deaths at the hands of the NYPD. Among the most notorious cases was the fatal beating by police of an African American graffiti artist, Michael Stewart. Arrested in a Manhattan subway station in the early-morning hours of September 15, 1983, cops delivered him hog-tied and bloodied to Bellevue Hospital, where he died thirteen days later.[14]

Then there was the case of Eleanor Bumpurs, a sixty-six-year-old African American. She was four months behind on her $98.65 monthly rent payments and facing eviction from her apartment in city-run public housing at 1551 University Avenue in the Morris Heights neighborhood in the Bronx. On October 29, 1984, the Metropolitan Housing Authority called the NYPD—the Bumpurs woman's deranged and dangerous, they said, and the marshals needed help getting her out. The department sent in the Emergency Services Unit, a highly trained, heavily armed force specializing in forced entry, raids, and other high-risk missions.

The six-man ESU squad found a half-naked, 270-pound old lady brandishing a ten-inch kitchen knife. Cops said she had lunged at them. Officer Stephen Sullivan fired two shots with his 12-gauge pump. Mrs. Bumpurs died twenty minutes later at the entrance to Lincoln Hospital.[15] The Patrolmen's Benevolent Association called it self-defense. Civil rights activists called it murder.*

May 19th had long raged against what the group called "the front-line enforcers of a system of colonization of Black, Puerto Rican, Mexicano-Chicano, and Native American peoples."[16] It was the police versus the people, and like the American Communist Party back in the day, May 19th was automatically for the people. "After the murder of Eleanor Bumpurs," Linda said in a statement from prison, "what Black person doesn't need to defend their home and their life?"[17]

---

* Sullivan was charged with second-degree manslaughter and criminally negligent homicide. Five thousand city cops marched in protest after the indictment. A judge acquitted Sullivan in a nonjury trial in 1987.

A group created by May 19th, the Clifford Glover Contingent, was named after a ten-year-old African American who was shot in the back and killed by a white police officer in Queens on April 28, 1973. The kid was armed with nothing more than an Afro pick. May 19th created the group to help children "learn new values" and "grow into young revolutionary women and men."[18] A Clifford Glover Contingent coloring book explained that Assata Shakur was a freedom fighter struggling "to free other Black people" from the underground. It urged children to "Fight the Klan and Free the Land."[19] At a May 19th gathering at the Ukrainian Labor Home at 85 East 4th Street on April 7, 1983, the young people entertained their elders with a play about the destruction of Puerto Rico's environment by U.S. mining interests.

After Mrs. Bumpur's death, May 19th vowed to retaliate against "killer cops" and "white supremacist pigs."[20] The target: PBA headquarters at 250 Broadway, just across the street from City Hall in lower Manhattan. Reconnaissance, surveillance—despite the fact that the place housed the police union, there was not much in the way of security. It was another soft target.

They made a couple of IEDs in the Alameda apartment and brought them up to New York.[21] They slipped into 250 Broadway, took the elevator up to the twenty-first floor, walked into the women's bathroom, and planted the bombs above the ceiling tiles and under the sink.

On February 23, 1985, at 1:03 a.m., the IEDs went off. The detonations caused heavy damage. "It was a good shot," said a police union spokesman. Two maintenance workers in the building sustained minor injuries.

Just after the attack, somebody called the Associated Press and played a taped message: "Tonight we bombed the offices of the PBA, which promotes racist murder and killer cops. The 10,000 racists are not worth one hair on the heads of Eleanor Bumpurs, Michael

Stewart . . .".[22] "That target, it was correct and it was just," Laura said years later.[23]

. . .

Inside May 19th, frustration and rage were mounting. They'd sacrificed everything, but nothing had changed. Imperialism wasn't in retreat. Quite the contrary—under Reagan, it seemed to have a new vitality, energizing the agents arrayed against the forces of liberation in Central America, the Middle East, and Africa. Black and brown people were being terrorized and victimized on a worldwide basis.

Back in the 1970s, while Weather leaders had been agonizing over bourgeois moral niceties, the BLA had been attacking police who were waging "counterinsurgency" operations in the nation's ghettos and the FALN had been taking out Wall Street capitalists. In southern Africa, the Middle East, and Southeast Asia, national liberation forces had been going toe to toe with First World military forces. And in Europe, the RAF, the Irish National Liberation Army, and the Red Brigades weren't bombing empty office buildings—they were using deadly force against soldiers, politicians, informants, and collaborators.

Why should May 19th restrict itself?

Freedom fighters aren't afraid to kill.

May 19th members had been mulling over targeting questions for some time. They had considered the option of lethal force during the planning of the U.S. Capitol bombing. They were open to new tactics: maybe they should start sticking it to federal prosecutors, grand jurors, and other "agents of imperialist strategy"; go after them in their own neighborhoods and workplaces in a way that "holds them accountable for the impact of their actions";[24] go harder, start counterpunching, and build "the skills necessary to take offensive armed action against the State and its agents."[25]

Alan had put some thoughts down on paper. They'd all had martial arts and small-arms training. He said it was time "to transform ourselves from target shooters to combat shooters." He continued, "Investigative work showed the possibility of doing an action that could possibly eradicate several high ranking officers."[26]

Eradicate—an interesting choice of word. One eradicates pests, vermin, undesirables, subhuman creatures. This kind of mental preparation makes it easier, even necessary, to snuff out human life—what psychologists call the process of "moral disengagement." According to the psychologist Albert Bandura, this process includes the use of euphemism (referring to bombings as "actions"), dehumanizing language (calling police "pigs"), and the depiction of enemies as boundlessly evil (thereby making the use of violence to defeat them morally justifiable). Collective decision making can also contribute to moral disengagement, wrote Bandura: "Group decision making is another common bureaucratic practice that enables otherwise considerate people to behave inhumanely, because no single person feels responsible for policies arrived at collectively. When everyone is responsible, no one is really responsible."[27]

There's "ordinary" murder, the by-product of a drug- or alcohol-induced frenzy; or maybe someone's double-crossed you; or the classic *crime passionnel*. But May 19th was not going to commit those kinds of crimes. Its goals were strictly political. It was an armed clandestine military formation.

Alan added, "We believe that selective assassination of very clear targets is on the agenda now. We believe retaliatory actions . . . are on the agenda now. We believe that guards may die during an attempt to liberate POWs, now."[28]

In case anyone had forgotten, this was war.

16

NONCONSENSUAL ENTRY

We must assume we are being followed and plan on do-ing a series of maneuvers. . . . None of this is foolproof, and now we know even better that they are professionals and we are amateurs.

—MAY 19TH, "PRELIMINARY NOTES
ON 'LARGE TEAM' SURVEILLANCE"[1]

The FBI special agents learned a lot nosing around New Haven after the Stop & Shop heist. Marilyn had definitely been in the city, and Linda had been nearby. Interview subjects told the Bureau that the two women had decamped for Baltimore. And there was another nugget of information: somebody matching Linda's description and using the name "Chris Johnson" had dropped off a guitar for repair at the Youngblood Music Workshop in nearby Guilford.

The Bureau got the permission of the owner to listen in on telephone calls to the shop—what police and prosecutors call "consensual monitoring."[2] In early May, Johnson called the repair shop to check on the guitar. Agents did a "trap and trace" that recorded the numbers of all incoming calls—an early version of what we now call metadata. There was one to the shop from 301-254-9831, a pay phone at 5432 Hartford Road in Baltimore.[3] They were convinced it was Linda.

The Baltimore Field Office deployed seven men in seven surveillance vehicles. Instead of finding Linda, they snapped a photo of somebody who looked a lot like Marilyn outside the Hasslinger Athletic Association. Rather than make an arrest, they decided to keep watching her—maybe she'd lead them to Linda or Doc Shakur or Joanne Chesimard.

The FBI team also kept an eye on the Hartford Road pay phone. On Thursday, May 9, a woman in a red wig, plaid shirt, and mom jeans used the phone. No question—it was Linda Sue Evans.

At 7:15, she used the phone again. A few minutes later, a nut-brown 1979 Toyota with New York plates, tag number 7731-AXS, rolled up. A guy who matched Alan's description was behind the wheel, sporting an Afro, probably a wig. Linda got in, and they drove off. The special agents followed them to 1134 East Belvedere—one of the entrances to the Yorkewood Apartments. Alan street parked, and he and Linda entered the sprawling complex separately. The Bureau men watched the place all night.

The next morning, at around 10:00, Linda and Marilyn left the complex and drove off in the Toyota, heading north along I-95, through Wilmington, past Philadelphia, and into New York. FBI teams watched them all along the way.

At 1:00 a.m. on the eleventh, the women checked into a room at the Inn Town Motel on Route 9A in Ardsley, in Westchester County, about fifteen miles north of midtown Manhattan.

It took the women fifteen hours to travel the 185 miles from Baltimore to Ardsley. They made lots of stops, including a one-hour visit to apartment 12L at 3451 Giles Place in the Kingsbridge Heights

*Running on empty: Linda and Marilyn in disguise
and under surveillance, Baltimore, May 1985*

neighborhood in the Bronx, where they changed their clothes. A neighbor later told the Bureau that she'd seen a few of women coming and going from the apartment a few times a year or so earlier. One was tall, the other one was short, and they sometimes wore turbans.

Why this lengthy and circuitous route? It was obvious to the FBI that Marilyn and Linda were doing everything possible to make sure they weren't being followed. It was classic countersurveillance.[4]

The brown Toyota was parked right outside the motel. It was the perfect chance to gather more evidence. The FBI filed an emergency Title III surveillance request with a federal judge, and got approval to plant a bug inside the car.

At 9:30 the next morning, Marilyn and Linda left the Inn Town and headed west on Route 9A. The JTTF couldn't hold out much longer—it wasn't going to let those dangerous fugitives roam around forever. A couple of miles down the road, in Dobbs Ferry, the Toyota pulled into the parking lot of the Mayflower Diner.

Ten unmarked cars converged on the Toyota. Linda tried to escape on foot but didn't get far. Cops cuffed her and looked inside her bag. There was ID in the name "Joanne Roth," and a fully loaded 9mm pistol. Marilyn, wearing one of her signature wigs, stood motionless. In her purse: ID cards for an "Eve Mancuso," and there was something heavy wrapped in a towel—a .38-caliber revolver.[5]

Later, as she was paraded past reporters, Marilyn turned to them and said, "Long live the anti-imperialists!" Tip Tipograph, the stalwart May 19th lawyer, represented the women at their arraignment at the Southern District courthouse in lower Manhattan. Supporters in the gallery shouted the RNA slogan, "Free the Land." With a wan Mona Lisa smile on her face, Marilyn told Judge Kevin Duffy that she was "a captured anti-imperialist freedom fighter."[6] Then she turned her back on Duffy.

On November 14th, Rudolph Giuliani, then the U.S. attorney for the Southern District of New York, offered an explanation for the women's car trip from Baltimore to Westchester. They had been on a job, Giuliani said, surveilling the supermarket at the Goldens Bridge Shopping Center, a strip mall about twenty-five miles northeast of Ardsley. Agents had seized a camera during their arrest, and on the film were images of the supermarket.[7] Shades of Cromwell and the Stop & Shop stickup.

· · ·

Back in Baltimore on the afternoon of May 11, special agents H. Thomas Moore, Roger Kuhlman, and Michael A. Garrett II went to the sprawling Yorkewood complex. There was no question that Linda and Marilyn had lived there, but in which apartment?

Agent Moore talked to the building manager, Otis Watts, and to a secretary, Maria Twig, who said that an Anne Morrison had rented apartment D in Building 5714 the previous February. The manager handed over a passkey. Moore also questioned the maintenance supervisor, William Preston, and showed him photos of Marilyn and Linda. He confirmed that the two lived in apartment D. He remembered that the taller one had frosted hair.

The three special agents headed over to Building 5714. Garrett stood watch outside apartment D while Moore and Kuhlman questioned building residents.

Sharon A. Glass told the agents about an upstairs neighbor lady: she was "a very distant individual [who] would never say anything, but occasionally would nod her head hello only when spoken to." And there was something else: the lady had "a limp and found it necessary to straighten her leg and pull it up as she went up the stairs."[8] She looked at a stack of nine photos and identified Marilyn, Linda, and somebody named Anne as the occupants of apartment D.

Garrett interrupted the interview. He told Moore that he'd just seen "caucasian feet" between the bottom of the front door and the threshold. Who could that be? Maybe it was Alan, the federal fugitive, described in Bureau bulletins as armed and dangerous. The FBI had seen him enter the complex on the ninth, but nobody had seen him leave.

The three agents went to their squad cars for sidearms and bulletproof vests. They returned to the apartment, and Moore rapped on the door.

"Who's there?" a woman asked.

"It's the FBI, open up, please."

"No."

"We have a warrant for the arrest of Dr. Berkman, open the door."

"No."[9]

The Bureau men began what they called a "non-consensual entry."[10] They tried the passkey—no good, the occupants had probably changed the lock. Then they started breaking the door down. It was three inches thick and took the agents five minutes to break through. Inside they found a barefooted woman standing in the entryway. Moore told her she was under arrest for harboring a fugitive and asked her if she'd like a pair of shoes.

"Fuck you, pig," Laura said.[11]

Moore put cuffs on her and took her out of the building. The agents had a quick look around the apartment—no Berkman. They'd do a more extensive search later. In the meantime, Garrett would keep an eye on the place.

Laura didn't go quietly. She struggled with Special Agent Gerald Dougher as he tried to get her into the back of a squad car. During the trip to the Baltimore Field Office, she managed to undo her seat belt and unlock the door, and she fought like a wildcat, kicking Dougher as he tried to subdue her. Later in Baltimore, while riding with U.S. marshals, she slipped out of her handcuffs and opened the door as the vehicle slowed down to take a curve. A marshal grabbed her waist chain before she could get out.[12]

• • •

When the bomb technicians did a sweep of apartment D, they picked up dynamite traces and lots of other suspicious materials; the place was like a terrorist Aladdin's cave. Agents found timing devices, theatrical makeup, $10,000 in cash, Marilyn's FBI wanted poster, U.S. Army and Air Force uniforms, an Uzi, and an aerial photo of what looked like the Bedford Hills Correctional Facility for Women in Westchester County, New York, where Judy was serving her Brinks-related sentences. They also found notes that described apparent lapses in security procedures at the prison.[13] Investigators wondered: Was May 19th planning to spring Judy?

There was a large blue filing cabinet crammed with incriminating papers, including a hanging folder labeled "Kidnapping," homemade bomb-building manuals, and a notebook chockablock with assorted aliases, including "Milagrose H. Matese," "Jane Bortner," "Loretta Polo," "Mary Androvett," "Leonard Cohen," and "Sheila Levine." Documents were also found with the latent prints of Alan, Betty Ann, Laura, Susan, Donna, Marilyn, and Linda, as well as schematic diagrams for IEDs.[14]

They found a document titled "RAF Session." May 19th had apparently at some point had a face-to-face session with the notorious West German terrorist group where they discussed politics, ideology, and revolution.[15] Maybe the terror network notion wasn't so far-fetched after all.

There was a folder marked "In Progress," filled with detailed notes and surveillance photos of prime targets, including the Aberdeen Proving Ground, the Naval Academy, and the Old Executive Office Building.

• • •

At 6:00 p.m. on May 12, the phone in apartment D rang. A special agent picked up the receiver. There was a man on the other end of the line.

Hi, this is David, is Anne Morrison there?

No, she isn't, who's calling, please?

The caller hung up.[16]

The FBI agents concluded that the caller was probably Berkman trying to find out if the place had been raided.

The FBI lugged ten thousand pieces of evidence out of the apartment. It took months to comb through it, but years of loose ends were coming together to form a clearer picture. Investigators knew from

Cherry Hill that Linda, Susan, Alan, and Tim were part of a conspiracy involving guns and bombs. Up in New Haven, agents found out that Marilyn was in on it, too. From apartment D, they discovered that Laura was involved and that the group had been planning a whole series of operations in DC.

The matériel seized in apartment D revealed something else as well. The Bureau now knew what it had suspected all along: that the Washington and New York bombings had been done by the same people. The drilling on the timing mechanisms recovered at the Capitol and elsewhere had proved that. But who those terrorists were was, before the apartment D raid, still an open question.

The lab techs had a look at the watches agents had removed from the apartment. They were timing devices, no question, and there was drilling on the back. It was the same drilling they'd found on the mechanisms used in the DC and New York attacks.[17] It was a forensic jackpot.

• • •

Special Agent Moore got a call at home on the evening of May 22. An agent had information on Betty Ann's whereabouts—she'd been spotted in a yellow Hertz rental truck parked on 24th Street in Baltimore, and she'd been seen going into an apartment building on 25th Street.

Moore went to the neighborhood, and sure enough, there was the yellow truck. He showed some pictures around the neighborhood, and a Mr. Schucthalter positively identified her as "Janice Adams" living at 101 East 25th.

FBI agents were also closing in on Betty Ann and Alan, who they assumed were hiding out together. They were on the lookout for a brown Toyota.

17

PUT YOUR GODDAMN HANDS UP WHERE WE CAN SEE THEM

Always take advantage of cover and have the gun in hand before the shooting starts if a gunfight is in the offing. If you shoot a man, keep shooting until he is unconscious, disarmed or so torn apart that he can't function.

—MAY 19TH MANUAL ON SMALL-ARMS TACTICS [1]

The law enforcement net continued to tighten. "Our underground organization had unraveled in the past few weeks," Alan wrote in his unfinished memoirs. "All that remained now was the bust." [2] There was still a handful of public, aboveground members, but after the Dobbs Ferry bust, they stopped using the May 19th name. None of them were going to be able to help.

Betty Ann and Alan were professional revolutionaries, so they didn't panic. But they were "numbed and exhausted," Alan said. [3] They decided their only option was to try to flee the country.

Cuba seemed like the ideal destination. The Castro regime was a sanctuary for fugitive American radicals. Maybe they could meet up with Willie Morales and Assata Shakur. Morales remained one of Alan's biggest fans. As he wrote later, "Alan, your [*sic*] my hero, and above all you will be my brother no matter what the damn consequences are."[4]

They'd planned a layover at a bungalow they had rented in the Poconos Mountains in northeastern Pennsylvania, where they'd have a chance to rest and regroup.

MAY 23, 1985

Alan was driving a blue Toyota, registered to someone called "Frances Marshall" in New Jersey, and carrying a driver's license in the name of "William Lunderman." He was wearing a red wig and had a white plastic shopping bag, inside of which was a fully loaded Walther PPK .38-caliber pistol. Betty Ann rode in the passenger seat. Inside her tan purse, there was May 19th's favorite sidearm—a Browning Hi-Power 9mm pistol, fully loaded, with a round in the chamber.

They headed up Route 611 toward their Poconos hideaway. Seventeen miles outside Philadelphia, they decided to take a break. Driving through Horsham, Pennsylvania, they saw a Friendly's Restaurant and pulled into the parking lot. Betty Ann took her purse, and Alan grabbed his plastic bag. They had hamburgers and coffee for supper, and fifty minutes later, they returned to the Toyota and headed north toward Doylestown.

Then their antennae started to twitch—something wasn't right. "We've got to get off this road and check it out," Alan said.[5]

At about 8:30 p.m., they pulled into the parking lot of a Doylestown Township elementary school. Their instincts were right. Unmarked cars cut them off, and FBI special agents pounced.

"Put your hands up," an FBI agent shouted. "Put your goddamn hands up where we can see them or I'll fuckin' kill you! Get your hands off that fuckin' wheel." [6]

The Bureau man grabbed Alan's hair, and the wig came off in his hand. Another agent got the drop on Betty Ann, who had her hand in her purse. Betty Ann and Alan were cuffed and taken away to the FBI's Philadelphia Field Office at 600 Arch Street.

Special agents searched the Toyota's passenger compartment. In addition to the pistols, they found a bottle labeled "sulphuric acid." They popped the trunk, and inside there was a miniarsenal: a 12-gauge sawed-off Mossberg pump, loaded; a silencer-equipped 9mm Beretta pistol, also loaded, with a round in the chamber. Sniffer dogs detected TNT traces.

"They both seemed stoical and hardly said a word when agents surrounded them," said FBI special agent James McIntosh. ". . . They offered no resistance." [7] During processing, Alan maintained his revolutionary discipline and kept his mouth shut. Betty Ann said nothing more than that she was not going to collaborate and demanded to speak to her lawyer.

The FBI found plenty of evidence to connect them to the New York and Washington bombings and to other May 19th members. There was a key in Betty Ann's handbag, and it turned out it was for a lock on a garage she'd rented at 1850-52 South Easton Road in Doylestown. The Bureau had a look and found loads of cash—between the garage and what Betty Ann and Alan had had on them when they were busted, about $15,000 was recovered. The garage was stuffed with DIY publications: "The Women's Gun Pamphlet," "The Poor Man's James Bond," "Blaster's Handbook," "Five Steps to Good Shooting," and "Full Auto Uzi."

The FBI men dusted the garage. Everybody's prints were there: Alan's, Betty Ann's, Linda's, Laura's, Susan's, Tim's, and Donna's. The agents found some spent shell casings, and the FBI lab determined that they had been fired from weapons used during Brinks.[8] There was also a substantial cache of weapons, explosives, and other materials, including semiautomatic rifles, ammunition, a silencer, bulletproof vests, fifteen to twenty pounds of Tovex, eighty-six pounds of dynamite, and ten pounds of Gelodyn.

The dynamite was in terrible shape, just like the stuff in Cherry Hill. "The nitroglycerin had begun to seep out of the tubes" and was crystallizing, making it extremely dangerous, Special Agent Michael Macys said. It could be set off easily—even by a vibration from a passing truck. "I wouldn't want to be anywhere near," he added.[9]

The Gelodyn had also deteriorated badly and was highly volatile. As with the dynamite, the nitroglycerin had wept out, and it had the consistency of honey—"and that makes the hair stand up. It's not very safe," Macys said.[10]

Betty Ann was arraigned on explosives and gun charges and for harboring a fugitive, namely Alan. And Alan had a full load of legal woes hanging over his head: conspiracy, possession of unregistered firearms, unlawful storage of explosives, bail jumping, the Stop & Shop heist, accessory to murder after the fact. And the authorities still suspected he had been part of the Morales breakout back in 1979.

• • •

United States District Court in the Eastern District of Pennsylvania, Judge Louis H. Pollak, presiding. Betty Ann told the judge that she was "fed up with the depravity of the system," and she vowed to continue to fight the forces of repression that were working against progressive forces.[11] She and Alan were "revolutionary anti-imperialists," she declared.[12] For many in the courtroom, it must have sounded a little odd—like when Patty Hearst had stated her occupation as "urban

guerrilla" or Watergate burglar Bernard Barker had said at his arraignment that his profession was "anticommunist."

"The charges against me are far less serious than those brought
against murderers, rapists who are frequently released on bail," Betty
Ann said. "People such as abortion bombers are granted bail while I
and other revolutionaries are held in preventive detention." [13]

The defense lawyers asked for bail. Pollak said no to Alan, a fugitive
and veteran bail jumper. But the judge was inclined to be more lenient
with Betty Ann. She'd never been in trouble with the law before; letters
to the judge from friends, loved ones, and the clergy attested to her
sterling character; and her two sisters down in Texas were willing to
put up their houses as collateral to cover the $300,000 bail.

The federal prosecutors didn't like the idea. They said that she
was facing decades in prison and that she had "no known legitimate
employment, no known legitimate source of income, no ties to this
district, had traveled in several districts within the last year in the
company of notorious fugitives [and] had acted to assist those fugitives while using disguises and false identification." And incendiary
rhetoric in the courtroom indicated that she intended "to flee and
continue the clandestine lifestyle." [14]

Judge Pollak remained unconvinced and on July 24 revoked Betty
Ann's detention order, and she was released. There were many conditions, though: she could have no credit cards, could carry no more
than ten dollars in cash at any given time, would have to live with her
sister Kathleen Weir Vale in San Antonio and work at the family business, Hope Medical Supply, and would have to check in with the federal Pretrial Services Agency twice a day. During the trial, she'd have
to travel back to the Eastern District courthouse in Philadelphia at her
own expense. And when she was in Philadelphia, she would have to
stay with a court-approved defense lawyer.

Maybe if ankle monitoring bracelets had been invented, the judge could have found the conditions to force Betty Ann to prove him right. Instead, while she was at the house of one of her approved lawyers, Judith Chomsky, on the night of Friday, October 13, 1985, she skipped bail. The next morning, Chomsky found a note from Betty Ann saying she was sorry, but she was leaving. On Monday morning, the court issued a warrant for her arrest.

AFTERMATH

Even behind bars, May 19th struggled to keep the armed clandestine campaign going.

Linda and Marilyn wrote long letters about their capture that described law enforcement tactics and procedures. The letters also included detailed information about items they believed investigators were likely to have recovered, such as lists of aliases, phony ID cards, keys—things that might lead the authorities to anyone connected with May 19th's underground operations. Susan had done something similar after her Cherry Hill bust.

"We feel that above all [it's] primary that you stay free," Linda wrote. "This probably means leaving the U.S. We support whatever it takes to keep you free to carry out our revolutionary work wherever it may be." [1]

According to Jay B. Stephens, the U.S. attorney for the District of Columbia, those communications were meant "to help unarrested co-conspirators evade apprehension and destroy and sever themselves from possible leads." [2] Betty Ann was an unarrested coconspirator, but were there others? Linda seemed to suggest there were, as did Marilyn. "From here we are going to carry on this struggle for transformation . . . and build an ACM [armed clandestine movement] that can fight to win," she wrote. "Others will have to come up to build outside but how many years will that be? I know you will make a maximal contrib[ution] to the war against imperialism wherever you are." [3]

But their armed clandestine movement didn't have legs. There were no May 19th bombings after February 23, 1985, when the group hit the PBA. Still, there were aftershocks.

. . .

Former FALN leader Oscar López Rivera was in the federal prison in Leavenworth, Kansas, serving fifty-five years for seditious conspiracy, firearms offenses, and other crimes. The FBI also suspected he'd masterminded the 1975 Fraunces Tavern attack in New York, but it couldn't prove it.

Like his comrade Willie Morales back in 1979, López had had enough and wanted out. He and some fellow cons hatched a plot. López was highly intelligent, meticulous, and a U.S. army combat veteran who'd won a Bronze Star in Vietnam. He did his homework and pored over aerial photos of the penitentiary, a surveyor's map, and a report about an escape attempt at the Marion penitentiary in Illinois.

In late 1984 and early 1985, the escape plan took shape: have a helicopter land in the prison yard, hold off the guards with smoke and gunfire, and fly off to freedom, where they'd continue to fight for Puerto Rican independence, financing the armed struggle with bank robberies. One of the plotters said he could line up a chopper. López drew up a shopping list: smoke grenades, automatic rifles, ammo, bulletproof vests, and fifty pounds of C-4, a plastic explosive. Another prisoner, George Lebosky, said he could get to an arms dealer in Louisiana who could supply everything on the list.

But Lebosky's nerves got the best of him, and he spilled his guts to a prison official, who called the FBI. The Bureau then set up a sting operation.

On the afternoon of May 4, 1985, undercover Special Agents Roger Rubrecht and James Judd were in the parking lot of a Baton Rouge motel. They were posing as arms dealers, and they were supposed to meet the guy who'd make the buy on behalf of López and his crew, a man named Claude Marks.

Marks bought thirty sticks of C-4. It was inert, of course. He and a companion, former Weather Underground member Donna Jean Willmott, took the ersatz C-4 to a storage site in Bloomington, California. The trip back was agony for Marks—he picked up a load of chiggers during his run down to Louisiana.

Marks and Willmott were part of a tiny, nameless terrorist cell whose formation had been inspired by the Joanne Chesimard jailbreak (during subsequent investigations, the Bureau referred to the group as the "SEQUEL SIX").[4] One member, Diana Block, explained that "we could no longer put off our own accountability to Third World forces that were committed to developing an armed clandestine capacity."[5] They moved in overlapping circles with May 19th—in fact, Block and Laura, Susan, and Silvia were old comrades, having worked together before the Prairie Fire East Coast–West Coast split in the 1970s.

On May 9, back home in Van Nuys, California, Marks discovered that somebody had planted a listening device in his car. No question— the FBI was onto him and his fellow terrorists. Everybody hit the road and vanished. Not long afterward, the Bureau searched Marks's house and discovered three footlockers packed with gunpowder and ammunition.

Marks and Willmott were charged with conspiracy in connection with the Leavenworth breakout plot, and both made it onto the FBI's Ten Most Wanted Fugitives list. Hiding out in Pittsburgh's middle-class Squirrel Hill neighborhood under the name "Greg Peters," and living with Diana Block, Marks coached Little League baseball and donated his homegrown tomatoes to a home for the mentally impaired. Willmott, who worked as a medical assistant, lived nearby under the name "Jo Eliot." In 1995, Marks and Willmott—the only two members of SEQUEL SIX wanted by the FBI—turned themselves in to federal authorities in Chicago. Marks drew a six-year prison sentence. Willmott was sentenced to three years. "They were very nice neighbors, caring and compassionate," said a Squirrel Hill neighbor. "If you picked anyone on the street you would think was a former terrorist, they'd be right at the bottom of the list."[6]

Back in 1985, the FBI had made a discovery, a cache in Santa Fe Springs, California: det cord, blasting caps, and dynamite—dynamite with the same date-shift code found on the sticks recovered in Cherry Hill, New Jersey, and Doylestown, Pennsylvania. It had all been robbed from the same place, the Bland Construction Company in Austin, Texas, in March 1980.

On June 27 and 28, back in Leavenworth, López had a visit from his mother-in-law, a paralegal. They communicated—not orally, only in writing, on a legal pad, passing pages back and forth. A quiet fellow inmate sat in on the sessions: Tim Blunk.

Escape planning continued into the following year. Then came the federal indictments and arrests. López was immediately shipped off to the penitentiary in Marion, Illinois, an early "supermax" prison built after the closure of Alcatraz Federal Penitentiary in 1963. López drew an additional fifteen years for conspiracy to escape, to transport of explosives with the intent to kill and injure people, and for destroying government buildings and property.*

In 1999, López turned down a clemency offer from President Bill Clinton—he didn't like the preconditions, his lawyer said. Eighteen years later, López got a better deal. President Barack Obama com-

---

* Prosecutors said the plot seemed to have been drawn from a forgettable Charles Bronson movie, *Breakout.*

muted his sentence, no strings attached, and López walked free after thirty-five years behind bars.

Tim didn't face any charges in connection with the escape plot. But the Leavenworth authorities decided he needed a stricter prison regime and moved him to Marion.

He was in solitary confinement for much of his sentence. He said that while he was underground he was living "24 hours a day as an enemy of the state."[7] Being buried alive in the bowels of the maximum-security prison extracted a psychic toll. In 1992, he told ABC News that the prison was "forcing me to dive deeper into myself. It's like you dig a trench in your heart and you keep your own humanity from slipping through your fingers."[8]

Released after serving twelve years, Tim has traveled a long way from the terrorist underground. Today, he's a New Jersey florist.

.   .   .

In 1988, Laura, Linda, Marilyn, Susan, Tim, Alan, and Betty Ann were indicted for the Washington and New York bombings. With the exception of Betty Ann, who remained at large, all of them were already serving long sentences for other crimes, including participation in the Brinks robbery.

Nobody went to trial, though. In September 1990, the defendants reached an agreement with federal prosecutors in Washington: Laura, Linda, and Marilyn would plead guilty in exchange for the government dropping charges against Susan, Tim, and Alan.* Laura drew twenty years; Linda, who was serving thirty-five years for illegally buying guns, got an extra five years; and Marilyn, who was serving fifty years for

---

* According to the *New York Times*, the plea agreement filed by the government said that the disposition of the bombing case was "in the interest of justice" but gave no reason for the government's agreeing to settle the case.

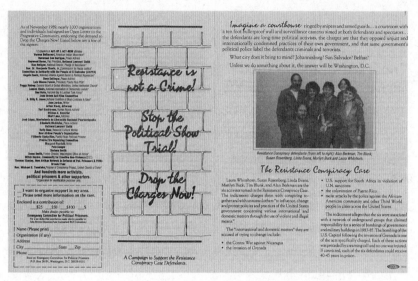

*All together now: Alan, Tim, Susan, Linda, Marilyn,
and Laura, locked up in Washington, DC*

Brinks and the Chesimard breakout, got an additional ten-year sentence.*

What was left of May 19th's aboveground structure dissolved in the aftermath of the arrests and trials. But though the group no longer formally existed, former members were active in groups such as the Committee to Fight Repression and the Washington Committee for Political Prisoners' Rights, which continued to agitate on behalf of imprisoned North American anti-imperialists, including Laura, Marilyn, Linda, Susan, Tim, and Alan.

Valerie Barr, a member of one May 19th affiliate, the Women's Committee Against Genocide, would go on to become a professor of

---

* Marilyn, together with Shakur, was charged with conspiracy to violate the RICO Act, participation in a racketeering enterprise, bank robbery, armed bank robbery, and bank robbery murder. On May 11, 1988, they were convicted on all charges in the Southern District of New York court.

computer science at Union College in Schenectady, New York. In 2013, she took leave to work at the National Science Foundation, or NSF. The following year, the NSF fired her after the Office of Personnel Management concluded that she had misrepresented her affiliations with "subgroups of M19CO—a known terrorist organization."[9] Although Barr later acknowledged that she had known Judy Clark and Kuwasi Balagoon casually, she denied that she had had any firsthand knowledge of the Brinks robbery and murders.

The Bureau continued to review and assess information it had collected on May 19th. The New York Field Office reported to FBI headquarters in 1991 that back in 1986 May 19th had "played host" to five members of the Red Army Faction: "These members met with M19CO attorney [name redacted] and attended pretrial hearings in the SDNY [Southern District of New York] for M19CO member MARILYN JEAN BUCK and former FBI Top Ten fugitive and RNA member [name redacted]."*

·   ·   ·

Silvia had drawn a forty-year RICO sentence for her participation in May 19th's criminal operations, including Brinks. She spent part of her time in the High Security Unit in the federal penitentiary in Lexington, Kentucky, a women-only underground prison within a prison. It was a strict regime—no mingling with the general population, walls painted white, routine strip searches, cavity probes, and strictly rationed communications with the outside world.

Susan was a fellow prisoner—Federal Bureau of Prisons officials argued that harsh control measures were necessary for any "inmates

---

* The Bureau typically redacts the names of living people before it releases documents requested under the Freedom of Information Act, but it's obvious that the "former fugitive" was Mutulu Shakur.

who may be subject to rescue attempts by outside groups."[10] Amnesty International reported in August 1988 that the work opportunities for Silvia and Susan, despite their being highly educated, were limited to folding army shorts for six hours a day in a cramped, stuffy former utility closet.[11] The Soviet Union claimed that the two women were among the thousands of people kept behind bars in the United States for political crimes. During the 1980s, the Reagan administration worked aggressively to counter Soviet disinformation, forgery, and deception operations, such as Moscow's claim that the Central Intelligence Agency had created AIDS as a biological weapon. *Trud*, a leading government organization, said that "There is no doubt that methods of exerting psychological pressure aimed at breaking the will of prisoners are being mastered there. . . . This is a kind of experiment that the FBI is making on them."[12]

Silvia was an Italian national, and under the terms of an international treaty governing extradition and rehabilitation, she was entitled to serve out her U.S. sentence on Italian soil.[13] Italian politicians, journalists, and friends and family members agitated for Silvia's repatriation. As her mother told the *Washington Post*, Silvia was "a nice girl . . . it's only her politics that is bad."[14] Washington and Rome came to terms in 1999, and after sixteen years behind bars, Silvia was returned to Italy, where she spent time under house arrest. By 2006, she was a free woman.[15]

．　．　．

On January 20, 1981, his last day in office, Bill Clinton dispensed pardons to an assortment of tarnished figures, including Marc Rich, the fugitive tax evader, racketeer, and rogue commodities trader; Roger Clinton, the president's coke-dealing half-brother; and Patty Hearst, the ex–Symbionese Liberation Army member who had wielded a carbine under the nom de guerre "Tanya."

That same day, Clinton issued two noteworthy commutations, one for Susan and one for Linda. In the waning months of the Clinton presidency, celebrity lawyer Alan M. Dershowitz and Congressman Jerrold Nadler had lobbied White House Counsel Bruce Lindsey, pleading for presidential mercy for Susan. Susan had been indicted in 1982 for her role in Brinks and the Chesimard escape. In 1985, then-U.S. Attorney Rudolph Giuliani dropped the case, citing the fact that she was already serving fifty-eight years in connection with the Cherry Hill conviction. For her part, she has long denied any involvement in Brinks. "I am not guilty of those charges," Susan said in 1999.[16] A letter from Nobel Laureate Elie Wiesel was part of the package that went to Lindsey.

After twenty-seven years in prison for Susan and twenty-five for Linda, their sentences were commuted and they were released. Who pushed for Linda's commutation, and why Clinton decided to grant her clemency, remains unclear. The decision-making surrounding presidential pardons is typically veiled in secrecy, and in the judgment of most constitutional scholars, the president's powers are essentially unlimited. As U.S. Senator Jeff Sessions said at a 2001 hearing on the Clinton pardons, "this is an unfettered power, a power given with no review whatsoever, contrary to almost everything else in our Constitution that has checks and balances."[17]

. . .

On August 6, 1999, having served her sentence, Laura walked out of Federal Correctional Institution Dublin in northern California. A reception committee of activists awaited her at the front gate. Her prison pallor aside, she didn't look too bad, considering that she had been locked up in one jail or another for the past fourteen years. She's spent much of her time since her release working as an HIV/AIDS activist and on behalf of prisoners she considers "political."

Laura in prison

Today Laura speaks elliptically about her life underground. She's been the subject of a documentary and has made many public appearances, but she's never offered any revelations about May 19th. She's no longer a terrorist, but she maintains the discipline of the underground. She has no public regrets for the violence, nor is there any indication that she's had second thoughts about devoting most of her adult life to revolution.

. . .

Behind bars, Marilyn devoted herself to caring for other inmates, promoting prisoner rights, and writing poetry. PEN, the writer's group, gave her multiple awards for her jailhouse verse. In "Clandestine Kisses," a poem she wrote in 1990, she described the love that was forbidden behind bars as a form of political resistance: "A crime wave of kisses . . . flouting women-hating satraps/in their prison fiefdoms/ furious that love can not be arrested." [18]

Her family never approved of her politics or her revolutionary escapades, but kinfolk visited her often. If the photos taken at the time are any indication, she had a loving relationship with them. Like Laura, Marilyn stayed on message, never renouncing her past actions or spilling any real information about May 19th operations.

In 2010, Marilyn was paroled after serving twenty-six years. Gravely ill with aggressive uterine cancer, she died in Brooklyn three weeks after her release. What remains of the extreme Left still reveres her as an all-American icon of violent rebellion. Recalling "Marilyn Buck the guerrilla" and "Marilyn Buck the artist," one admiring academic insisted that "fugitive freedom was her avocation, and it remains her legacy." [19]

·   ·   ·

Sentenced to ten years, Alan served his time in Marion and in Philadelphia's Holmesburg Prison, a grim nineteenth-century penal fortress. Alan told reporters that he didn't care for the "cheap, heavy meats" dished out in the chow hall.[20] Screaming inmates kept him up at night, he said, and he didn't like his jailors' mocking serenades—their patriotic repertoire, which included "America the Beautiful" and "Ballad of the Green Berets," got on his nerves. A fanatically anticommunist Cuban shared his cell block. The decidedly pro-Castro Alan worried about taking a shiv. "I have to keep my eyes open," he scribbled in his prison journal.[21]

But Alan spoke of his jailhouse hardships without a trace of self-pity. He had moved along a trajectory from Eagle Scout to medical doctor to professional revolutionary; from gentle healer to armed robber to convicted terrorist. Prison time was a rite of passage for any insurrectionist as committed as he was.

Interviews with Alan during his first years behind bars revealed a man who hadn't wavered in his political commitments. When asked how he felt about the cops who were murdered during "revolutionary appropriations," he gave a chilling response: "I know policemen have families. But that's not your sole definition in life. Maybe Adolf Hitler was nice to Eva Braun. I don't know." [22]

One jailhouse informer told the FBI that prisoners knew Alan was doing time for Brinks and other serious crimes, "which they consider a big deal and they are aware of his politics and they respect him for fighting for their cause, as well as the fact that he is a doctor which gains him respect." [23] His fellow inmates nicknamed him "Brother Doc." [24]

But Alan's revolutionary ardor cooled over time. During his prison stretch, he finally put aside his dreams of violent revolution and made no more calls for "selective assassination."

He got out in 1992 after serving eight years. On the outside, he became a prominent AIDS activist and vice chairman of the epidemiology department at Columbia University's Mailman School of Public Health. He lived modestly in a railroad apartment in Greenwich Village, his flat decorated with political posters and Indian throw pillows that gave it a distinctly 1970s feel. [25] Hodgkin's disease killed him in June 2009.

· · ·

Judy was convicted on second-degree murder and robbery charges in connection with Brinks, and since 1983 she's been behind bars in the maximum-security Bedford Hills Correctional Facility for Women in Westchester County, New York: "an old con in her late fifties," as she once described herself. [26] She's been reported to be a model prisoner and has reestablished a relationship with her long-estranged parents and rediscovered Judaism. [27] She's said that she's no longer the person she was back in 1981, "a single-minded fanatic who considered myself 'at war' with America." [28]

Politicians, members of the clergy, Hollywood notables, and Broadway luvvies like Glenn Close, Steve Buscemi, and Kevin Kline lobbied for her release. But given her sentences, there was only one way that Judy could expect to get out of Bedford Hills alive: clemency from the New York governor, which would make her eligible for an early parole. For decades, a gubernatorial commutation seemed far-fetched.

But one evening in September 2016, Judy received a special visitor: New York governor Andrew M. Cuomo, who spent an hour with her. She told the governor how her ideological extremism had led her into a moral cul-de-sac. "Groupthink and zealotry and internalized loyalty had sapped me of my own moral compass," she said during their meeting.[29]

Cuomo was impressed. He told reporters, "When you meet her you get a sense of her soul." He said his session with Judy had helped him understand her motivations: "You're fighting for good versus evil. That's what sends young men into war with guns to kill other people."[30]

In late December 2016, Cuomo commuted her sentence, and she became eligible for parole the following spring. Judy's friends, supporters, and family were naturally ecstatic. As one supporter told the *Daily News*, "She's been able to analyze what she did wrong and will certainly be an asset to the world if she is released."[31]

The families of the Brinks victims, prosecutors, police, and FBI agents who had investigated NYROB were outraged. Rockland County executive Ed Day, a former NYPD detective, said, "Commutation of Judith Clark's sentence is a vicious slap in the face to every member of law enforcement, the victim's families and every person who was touched by the brutal and cowardly 1981 Brinks robbery in Rockland County that she chose to take part in."[32] Hundreds of letters opposing her release flooded into the New York State parole board and opponents of Judy's release held public rallies in Rockland and Albany.

But most people on both sides thought her release was practically inevitable; nobody could recall the last time in New York that a commutation from the governor hadn't resulted in parole.

The board issued a unanimous ruling on April 21, 2017. It told Judy that letting her out "would deprecate the seriousness of your crimes as to undermine respect for the law. You are still a symbol of a violent and terroristic crime."[33]

"I want her to stay there for the rest of her life," Josephine Paige, the widow of Peter Paige, the Brinks employee murdered during the botched robbery, said after the decision. "My husband is in the ground and she's going to get out? She doesn't deserve it."[34]

Judy's daughter, Harriet, said that her mother "did not kill anyone and it's hard for me to understand who is served by making her die in prison, which is what decisions like this eventually amount to."[35] In April 2019, seven months shy of her seventieth birthday, Judy faced the parole board again, and in a 2–1 decision, they voted to release her after thirty-seven years behind bars. Supporters were jubilant. New York Mayor Bill de Blasio said that Judy had "atoned for and taken full responsibility for her part in the heinous crime. . . . Her rehabilitation and release should be a model for detainees to strive to emulate."[36] Others blasted the board's decision. "Judith Clark is a murderer and a terrorist," said the New York Police Benevolent Association. "This is not justice."[37] Clark's lawyers said she planned to live in New York City and work for a nonprofit group that helps incarcerated women and their children.

● ● ●

Thirty-four years after jumping bail in Philadelphia, Betty Ann's still on the run.

She's near eighty if she is still alive, but she's still armed and dangerous according to the FBI, which is offering a $50,000 reward for information leading to her arrest and conviction. In 1995, the Bureau speculated that unspecified May 19th remnants in central Texas might be part of a support network for Betty Ann.[38] Obama-hating "birthers" claimed that Betty Ann is the forty-fourth president's real mother. Martha Trowbridge, the hostess of *Terrible Truths*, an online radio show, insists that Betty Ann's purported "son" is a Manchurian Candidate–like stooge, a golem in a "U.S. Government Overthrow" plot that's been spooling out for decades.[39]

· · ·

And thirty-seven years after she failed to appear in court to face charges in connection with the antiapartheid protest at JFK airport, Donna's still at large. Back in 2013, the FBI reportedly picked up some fresh leads and thought it might be closing in on her. Allegedly, she was traveling with Betty Ann—they were a couple of real-life "Thelma and Louise" style fugitives, the press said.[40]

Donna's on an Interpol wanted list, she's been profiled on the CNN series *The Hunt with John Walsh*, and the Bureau's offering a $100,000 reward for information leading to her arrest.[41] It's been one of the longest fugitive hunts in New York history, according to the Port Authority of New York and New Jersey. "The Port Authority will not let this go until Borup is brought to justice," said a spokesman.[42]

· · ·

The far-left terrorist project that began with the Weathermen in 1969 and 1970 and continued into the mid-1980s with May 19th ended in abject failure. Former May 19th member Mary Patten concluded that "our larger project of revolutionary 'war in amerikkka' could not have been more ambitious, or more delusional." May 19th, she wrote, was always "on the margins of the margins, the periphery of the periphery."[43]

Writing about the world of Soviet espionage inhabited by members of the Communist Party USA during the 1930s, the journalist Daniel Oppenheimer described a similar atmosphere of isolation and futility: "the accumulated tedium of years of underground work, and how little there was to show for it [and] the sappingly antisocial patterns of underground life [and] all the dislocations and secrecy and lying."[44]

With the fall of the Berlin Wall in 1989, the dissolution of the Soviet Union in 1991, and China's vigorous embrace of authoritarian capitalism, whatever prospects of Marxist-Leninist revolution that had existed disappeared. Ideological inspirations such as Castro's Cuba and Mugabe's Zimbabwe descended into despotism and deprivation, and the prospects for Palestinian liberation have only diminished over time. That said, the passionate anti-Zionism of at least some former May 19th members hasn't waned. In 2016, Laura was part of the U.S. Prisoner, Labor and Academic Solidarity Delegation to Palestine. In a statement after the trip, the delegation reported that the "Palestinians we spoke to insisted on framing the roots of current-day problems in the historical context of Israel's settler-colonial apartheid regime." The group included two former Black Panthers, as well as Diana Block and Claude Marks, the members of the cell connected to the attempted López breakout.[45]

As sociologists such as Donatella della Porta have concluded, leftist terrorism emerged in the West as mass protest movements (including those against the Vietnam War) entered a period of terminal decline. The prospect for the emergence of the kind of large-scale left-wing radicalism such as the United States experienced in the late 1960s and early 1970s seems remote. Despite claims by Fox News and others that antifa activists are "terrorists," their street brawling and harassment of right-wing extremists hardly rise to the level of the left-wing political violence of the 1960s, '70s, and '80s.[46]

The same cannot be said about neo-Nazi and white supremacist violence. The historian Kathleen Belew argues that the Vietnam War bred a generation of "White Power" extremism that culminated in the horrific attack in Oklahoma City in 1995.[47] That movement, never far below the surface of American life, was reenergized by the election of Barack Obama—and Donald Trump—and remains committed to the use of deadly violence against perceived "enemies": African Americans, Jews, assorted "race traitors," and members of other minority groups. That terrorism includes incidents such as the Charlottesville, Virginia, protests in August 2017, when a right-wing extremist drove his car into a crowd of counterprotestors, killing one person and injuring thirty-five others; the June 2015 murder by a white supremacist of nine African American parishioners at the Emanuel African Methodist Episcopal Church in Charleston, South Carolina; and the October 2018 massacre of eleven worshippers and the wounding of seven others at the Tree of Life synagogue in Pittsburgh. The White Power terrorists responsible for those crimes were not isolated "lone wolves" but members of a wider movement. "They're reading the same websites, talking to each other, and killing the same targets," says the journalist David M. Perry. "The lone wolves are actually a pack."[48]

In some important respects, however, today's White Power extremists—and indeed violent Islamic jihadists—share many of the attributes of the earlier generation of terrorists that ended with May 19th. Of course, their ideological agendas are far different: the creation of an all-white "homeland" in the United States, the establishment of a new caliphate, communist revolution. But white supremacists and jihadists draw on some of the same impulses, beliefs, and emotions that motivated their far-left counterparts: a burning hatred of the United States; a yearning for a kind of utopia and a heaven on Earth; a sense that they are "soldiers" engaged in a "war"; the demonization and dehumanization of their perceived enemies; and the conviction that the bomb and the gun are essential instruments for creating a new order.

In a speech delivered not long after the attacks of September 11, 2001, President George W. Bush described an aggressive global campaign that would become known as the "Global War on Terror," or GWOT. Bush said, "We wage a war to save civilization, itself. . . . This is a different war from any our nation has ever faced, a war on many fronts, against terrorists who operate in more than 60 different countries. And this is a war that must be fought not only overseas, but also here at home."[49] The GWOT immediately assumed a highly militarized character, with the wars in Afghanistan and Iraq justified (at least in part in the case of the latter) as key responses to the threat posed by terrorists capable of what the Bush administration termed "global reach." The Obama administration dropped the term GWOT, but what has become the "war with no name" ground on, as it does today under Trump.

The demise of May 19th suggests that a militarized approach to counterterrorism is not the only model, or the most effective one. Lacking any outside support, even within the ultraleft, May 19th (like their European counterparts the RAF and the Red Brigades) never had any real prospects for success. But countermeasures also played a large part in May 19th's downfall. Although the Reagan administration and congressional hard-liners tried to position May 19th and other left-wing terrorists inside a global "terror network" controlled from Moscow, the FBI took a persistent but low-key approach. Patient investigative work, surveillance, and aggressive prosecution—all done within the confines of the law—as well as some lucky breaks brought the group down. Ultimately, the United States never waged a domestic "war on terror."

ACKNOWLEDGMENTS

I couldn't have written this book without the support of friends, family members, and colleagues, including Don Brown; Peter N.G. Schwartz; Sean McFate; Will McCants; Afshon Ostovar; William N. H. Rosenau; Chip Rodgers; Lynn Goldberg; Bob Moskin; Peter Bergen; Dan Byman; Chung Min Lee; Celie Rosenau; Gail Ginsburgh; Randy Blake; Russ Gershon; Bob Swartz; Zack Davis; Ben Bahney; Jon Schroden; Linette Neal; Ralph Espach; Joanna Philpotts; Mark Rosen; Tim Beres; Kate Hammerberg; Bob Gabriel; Johnny Rice; Terry Hyman; Sara Daly; Bruce Hoffman; Steve Simon; Freda Vittone; Doug Sosnick; Shelley Rodgers; Debbie Windsor; Ryan Evans; and the members of the Air Power Policy Seminar. Many thanks to all of you, and to everyone else who helped me along the way.

I'd also like to thank the following individuals and organizations: Kenneth Maxwell; Dr. Jim Wilson; Don Wofford; Guy Hawtin; Dave Mitchell; Bob Daley; Doug Wolfe; Richard Conte; the Society of Former Special Agents of the FBI; the U.S. District Court, District of Columbia; the U.S. District Court, Southern District of New York; the Sophia Smith Collection of Women's History, Smith College; the Brooklyn Public Library's Brooklyn Collection; the New York Public Library; the National Archives at New York City; the Boston Federal Records Center; the Philadelphia Federal Records Center; and the Archives & Special Collections, Columbia University Health Sciences Library.

I want to acknowledge my agent, Roger Freet at Foundry Literary + Media, for believing in this project and working so tirelessly on my behalf. It was an absolute pleasure to work with Matthew Benjamin at Simon & Schuster—an editor of talent and vision. Special thanks also to Simon & Schuster's Haley Weaver; Sara Kitchen; Lynn Anderson; Susan Bishansky; Jonathan Evans; Tina Peckham; and Shida Carr.

Most of all, I'd like to thank Annie Rosenau for her guidance, love, unwavering support, and near-limitless patience.

NOTES

PROLOGUE

1. Committee to Fight Repression, *"Build a Revolutionary Resistance Movement": Communiqués from the North American Armed Clandestine Movement, 1982–1985* (New York: Committee to Fight Repression, 1985), 6.
2. Joseph E. Bouchard, "Explosive 'Noise' Shakes Building at Navy Yard," *Washington Post*, August 18, 1983, https://www.washingtonpost.com/archive/local/1983/08/18/explosive-noise-shakes-building-at-navy-yard/a1288f6d-b66a-4f85-bd3c-81c362fd1f7b/?utm_term=.fc5bd41d26bb.

INTRODUCTION

1. Jeffrey Toobin, "Patty Hearst and the Era of Televised Terror," *Wall Street Journal*, July 29, 2016, https://www.wsj.com/articles/patty-hearst-and-the-era-of-televised-terror-1469806518.
2. "You Don't Need a Weatherman to Know Which Way the Wind Blows" (1969), in *Sing a Battle Song: The Revolutionary Poetry, Statements, and Communiqués of the Weather Underground, 1970–1974*, eds. Bernardine Dohrn, Bill Ayers, and Jeff Jones (New York: Seven Stories Press, 2006), 68.
3. Quoted in Ellen Frankfort, *Kathy Boudin and the Dance of Death* (New York: Stein and Day, 1983), 66.
4. Mark Rudd, *Underground: My Life with SDS and the Weathermen* (New York: HarperCollins, 2009), 164.
5. Quoted in Cyrana B. Wyker, "Women in Wargasm: The Politics of Women's Liberation in the Weather Underground Organization," master's thesis, University of South Florida, 2009, https://scholarcommons.usf.edu/cgi/viewcontent.cgi?referer=https://www.google.com/&httpsredir=1&article=1092&context=etd.
6. Ehud Sprinzak, "The Psychological Formation of Extreme Left Terrorism in a

Democracy: The Case of the Weathermen," in *Origins of Terrorism: Psychologies, Ideologies, Theologies, States of Mind*, ed. Walter Reich (Washington, DC: Woodrow Wilson Center Press, 1990), 69.

7. Bryan Burrough, *Days of Rage: America's Radical Underground, the FBI, and the Forgotten Age of Revolutionary Violence* (New York: Penguin Press, 2015), 370.

8. Gilda Zwerman, "The Identity Vulnerable Activist and the Emergence of Post-New Left Armed, Underground Organizations in the United States," Center for Studies of Social Change Working Paper Series, New School for Social Research, Working Paper no. 218, September 1995.

9. Gregory Sholette, "Afterword (Leftists Like Us)," in Mary Patten, *Revolution as an Eternal Dream: The Exemplary Failure of the Madame Binh Graphics Collective* (Chicago: Half Letter Press, 2011), 66.

10. "An Exclusive Interview with Susan Rosenberg After President Clinton Granted Her Clemency," *Democracy Now!*, January 23, 2001, https://www.democracynow.org/2001/1/23/an_exclusive_interview_with_susan_rosenberg.

11. Susan Rosenberg, *An American Radical: A Political Prisoner in My Own Country* (New York: Citadel Press, 2011), 12.

12. Bruce Hoffman, "Putting German Terrorism in Perspective: An American Response," *GHI Bulletin* 43 (Fall 2008): 60, https://www.ghi-dc.org/fileadmin/user_upload/GHI_Washington/Publications/Bulletin43/59.pdf.

13. Kati Marton, *True Believer: Stalin's Last American Spy* (New York: Simon & Schuster, 2016), 1.

14. Quoted in Lillian Faderman, *Odd Girls and Twilight Lovers: A History of Lesbian Life in Twentieth-Century America* (New York: Columbia University Press, 1991), 237.

15. Quoted in Tamsin Wilson, *Lesbian Studies: Setting and Agenda* (London: Routledge, 1995), 98.

16. Ariel Levy, "Lesbian Nation: When Gay Women Took to the Road," *New Yorker*, March 2, 2009, https://www.newyorker.com/magazine/2009/03/02/lesbian-nation.

17. "The Pop-up Museum of Queer History," http://queermuseum.tumblr.com/post/23670469348/a-lesbian-is-the-rage-of-all-women-condensed-to.

18. Sarah Irving, *Leila Khaled: Icon of Palestinian Liberation*, https://www.jstor.org/stable/j.ctt183p7fm.

19. Leila Khaled, *My People Shall Live: The Autobiography of a Revolutionary*, ed. G. Hajjar (London: Hodder and Stoughton, 1973), 126.

20. Marion Banzhaf, ACTUP Oral History Project, April 18, 2007, http://fds.lib
.harvard.edu/fds/deliver/417792845/wid00003c00070.pdf

21. Quoted in Angela Chen, "Mail Bombs Don't Need to Explode to be Destructive,"
Verge, October 26, 2018, https://www.theverge.com/2018/10/26/18026592
/mail-bombs-soros-clinton-trump-politics-john-horgan-terrorism-psy
chology.

22. Bill Ayers, *Fugitive Days: A Memoir* (Boston: Beacon Press, 2001), 256.

23. Charles Nicholl, *The Reckoning: The Murder of Christopher Marlowe* (Chicago:
University of Chicago Press, 1994), 3.

24. Jerome P. Bjelopera, "Sifting Domestic Terrorism from Hate Crime and
Homegrown Violent Extremism," Congressional Research Service, August
14, 2017, https://fas.org/sgp/crs/terror/IN10299.pdf.

25. Peter Bergen, "The Real Terror Threat in America is Homegrown," CNN,
June 13, 2016, https://www.cnn.com/2016/06/12/opinions/orlando-home
grown-terror-bergen/index.html.

1. KEEPERS OF THE FLAME

1. Susan Rosenberg, "Compañera," (Fall 1986), in *Conspiracy of Voices: Poetry,
Writings and Art by the Women of the Resistance Conspiracy Case* (Washing-
ton, DC: Emergency Committee to Defend the Human and Legal Rights of
Political Prisoners, 1990), 37.

2. "Principles of Unity of the May 19th Communist Organization," https://issuu
.com/randalljaykay/docs/principlesofunityofthem19co053.

3. Ibid.

4. Arm the Spirit, *Enemies of the State: An Interview with Anti-imperialist Political
Prisoners* (Montreal: Abraham Guillen Press, 2002), 52.

5. *Conspiracy of Voices: Poetry, Writing and Art by the Women of the Resistance
Conspiracy Case* (Washington, DC: Emergency Committee to Defend the
Human and Legal Rights of Political Prisoners, 1990), xvi.

6. Mao Tse-tung, "Report on an Investigation of the Peasant Movement in
Hunan" (March 1927), in *Selected Works of Mao Tse-tung*, vol. 1, https://www
.marxists.org/reference/archive/mao/selected-works/index.htm.

7. Laura Whitehorn, "Fighting to Get Them Out," *Social Justice* 30, no. 2
(2003): 51.

8. May 19th Communist Organization, "War in Amerika, 1981: Fight White
Supremacy, Support the Black Liberation Army," http://freedomarchives.org
/Documents/Finder/DOC37_scans/37.May19.WarinAmerikaaa.pdf.

9. Mary Patten, *Revolution as an Eternal Dream: The Exemplary Failure of the Madame Binh Graphics Collective* (Chicago: Half Letter Press, 2011), 45.

10. Quoted in John E. Haynes and Harvey Klehr, "Note: 'Moscow Gold,' Confirmed at Last?," *Labor History* 33, no. 2 (1992): 293.

11. Federal Bureau of Investigation, "Purge Victims of the Communist Party, USA," undated, https://archive.org/stream/foia_FBI_MONOGRAPH-Purge_Victims_of_CPUSA/FBI_MONOGRAPH-Purge_Victims_of_CPUSA_djvu.txt.

12. Gilda Zwerman, "Mothering on the Lam: Politics, Gender Fantasies and Maternal Thinking in Women Associated with Armed, Clandestine Organizations in the United States," *Feminist Review*, no. 47 (Summer 1994): 39, https://doi.org/10.2307/1395252.

13. Ibid., 40.

14. Ibid.

15. Tom Robbins, "Judith Clark's Radical Transformation," *New York Times Magazine*, January 12, 2012, http://www.nytimes.com/2012/01/15/magazine/judith-clarks-radical-transformation.html.

16. Joseph Clark, "Thus Spake Fidel Castro," *Dissent*, January–February 1970, 38.

17. Judy Clark, "So Here I Am," in *Red Diapers: Growing Up in the Communist Left*, eds. Judith Kaplan and Lynn Shapiro (Urbana and Chicago: University of Illinois Press, 1998), 305.

18. Zwerman, "Mothering on the Lam," 40.

19. Robbins, "Judith Clark's Radical Transformation."

20. Clark, "So Here I Am," 306.

21. Paul Berman, "Fanaticism and the New York State Parole Board," *Tablet*, April 25, 2017, https://www.tabletmag.com/jewish-news-and-politics/231041/judith-clark-communism.

22. New York State Department of Corrections and Community Supervision, "Parole Board Hearing in the Matter of Judith Clark," April 5, 2017, 9.

23. Alan Berkman, "A Modest Supposal," in Tim Blunk and Raymond Luc Levasseur, eds., *Hauling Up the Morning: Writings and Art by Political Prisoners and Prisoners of War in the U.S.* (Trenton, New Jersey: Red Sea Press, 1990), 115.

24. Quoted in Alice Echols, *Daring to Be Bad: Radical Feminism in America 1967–1975* (Minneapolis: University of Minnesota Press, 1989), 97.

25. Quoted in ibid., 322.

26. Western Goals, *Outlaws of Amerika: The Weather Underground Organization* (1982), https://www.usasurvival.org/home/docs/Outlaws_Of_Amerika.pdf.

27. Merle Hoffman, "America's Most Dangerous Woman?" *On the Issues* 13 (1989), http://www.ontheissuesmagazine.com/1989vol13/rosenberg.php.

28. Douglas Martin, "Walden School, at 73, Files for Bankruptcy," *New York Times*, June 23, 1987, http://www.nytimes.com/1987/06/23/nyregion/walden -school-at-73-files-for-bankruptcy.html?mcubz=0.

29. Susan Rosenberg, "The Family: English," Susan Rosenberg Papers, Sophia Smith Collection, Smith College.

30. *Through the Wire* (documentary), directed by Nina Rosenblum, Daedalus Productions Inc., 1990.

31. Darrel Enck-Wanzer, ed., *The Young Lords: A Reader* (New York: New York University Press, 2010), https://www.marxists.org/history/erol/ncm-1/ylp -reader.pdf.

32. Midge Decter, *Liberal Parents, Radical Children* (New York: Coward, McCann & Geoghegan, 1975).

33. Quoted in Susie Day, "Political Prisoners: Guilty Until Proven Innocent," in *Let Freedom Ring: A Collection of Documents from the Movements to Free U.S. Political Prisoners*, Matt Meyer, ed., (Oakland, CA: PM Press, 2008), 60.

34. Hoffman, "America's Most Dangerous Woman?"

35. Queers United in Support of Political Prisoners (QUISP), "Dykes and Fags Want to Know . . . : A Written Interview with Lesbian Political Prisoners Laura Whitehorn, Linda Evans and Susan Rosenberg," 1991, *Arm the Spirit— for Revolutionary Resistance* (blog), https://armthespiritforrevolutionary resistance.wordpress.com/2017/08/30/dykes-and-fags-want-to-know/.

36. Michael Kazin, "Cuba, Que Linda Es Cuba? Notes on a Revolutionary Sojourn, 1969," *Dissent*, August 17, 2015, https://www.dissentmagazine.org /blog/cuba-first-venceremos-brigade-michael-kazin-memoir-1969.

37. Molly Porzig, "Lincoln Detox Center: The People's Drug Program," *Abolitionist*, March 15, 2013, https://abolitionistpaper.wordpress.com/2013/03/15 /lincoln-detox-center-the-peoples-drug-program/.

38. Dan Berger, "'The Malcolm X Doctrine': The Republic of New Afrika and National Liberation on U.S. Soil," in *New World Coming: The Sixties and the Shaping of Global Consciousness*, eds. Karen Dubinsky, Catherine Krull, Susan Lord, et al. (Toronto: Between the Lines, 2009), https://www.academia .edu/3758873/The_Malcolm_X_Doctrine_The_Republic_of_New_Afrika _and_National_Liberation_on_U.S._Soil.

39. Akinyele Omowale Umoja, *We Will Shoot Back: Armed Resistance in the Mis-*

sissippi Freedom Movement (New York: New York University Press, 2013), 173.

40. FBI, New York Field Office, "Jeral Wayne Williams," March 12, 1970, 1 (FBI FOIA release).

41. "People's Doctor Murdered!" *White Lightning: A Revolutionary Organization Dedicated to Serving the People*, no. 27, November–December 1974, https:// freedomarchives.org/Documents/Finder/DOC58_scans/58.White.Light ning.N27.NovDec.1974.pdf.

42. "Speech by Susan Rautenberg, New York Material Aid Campaign for ZANU, Evening in Solidarity with ZANU," September 29, 1978, http://freedomar chives.org/Documents/Finder/DOC52_scans/52.SusanRautenberg.tran script.Sept.1978.pdf.

43. Paul L. Montgomery, "How a Radical-Left Group Moved Toward Savagery," *New York Times*, January 20, 1974, 51, http://laroucheplanet.info/pmwiki /pmwiki.php?n=Library.PressArticles85.

44. Dennis King, *Lyndon LaRouche and the New American Fascism* (New York: Doubleday, 1989), 34.

45. U.S. Labor Party, "Zombie Killers Out of Control," http://www.lyndonla rouche.org/larouche-zombie-killers.pdf.

46. Brett Sokol, "Exiled in Havana," *Miami New Times*, September 7, 2000, http:// www.miaminewtimes.com/news/exiled-in-havana-6354908.

2. CRACK THE FACADE

1. *Freeing Silvia Baraldini* (documentary), directed by Margo Pelletier and Lisa Thomas, Thin Edge Films, 2009.

2. Nancy M. Tracy, "Law Is Her Role in the Revolution," *Hartford Courant*, June 2, 1985, A6.

3. Ibid.

4. Bruce Rosen, "A Law 'Collective' for Radical Clients," *National Law Journal*, December 9, 1985, 13.

5. "*United States of America v. Rosenberg, Susan Lisa*, appeal of Susan Lisa Rosenberg, Appellant in 85-5360. United States of America v. Blunk, Timothy. Appeal of Timothy Blunk, Appellant in 85-5361, 806 F.2d 1169 (3d Cir. 1986)," December 31, 1986, Justia, https://law.justia.com/cases/federal/appellate -courts/F2/806/1169/45719/.

6. Matulu Shakur, "In Memory of Marilyn Jean Buck," in "In Her Spirit: A Commemorative Booklet for the Marilyn Buck Solidarity Fund for Political Pris-

oners," Docplayer.net, http://docplayer.net/35594394-Marilyn-buck-in-her -spirit-a-commemorative-booklet-for-the-marilyn-buck-solidarity-fund-for -political-prisoners-1.html.

7. Quoted in Aroline Booth Pinkston, "The Gospel of Justice: Community, Faith, and the Integration of St. Andrew's Episcopal School," master's thesis, University of Texas at Austin, 2014, 42.

8. FBI, "Marilyn Jean Buck: Identification Order 4893/Wanted Flyer 508/Bank Robbery-Conspiracy; Escaped Federal Prisoner," undated, 1 (photocopy in author's possession).

9. Quoted in W. Gardner Selby, "A Soldier's Story," *Third Coast*, October 1985, 58.

10. "Woman Is Jailed as a Gunrunner," *New York Times*, October 28, 1973, https:// www.nytimes.com/1973/10/28/archives/woman-is-jailed-as-a-gunrunner -says-she-changed-returned-to-texas.html.

11. Marilyn Buck, "Autobiographi," in "In Her Spirit: A Commemorative Booklet for the Marilyn Buck Solidarity Fund for Political Prisoners," Docplayer.net, http:// docplayer.net/35594394-Marilyn-buck-in-her-spirit-a-commemorative-book let-for-the-marilyn-buck-solidarity-fund-for-political-prisoners-1.html.

12. Ibid.

13. Robert Pardun, *Prairie Radical: A Journey Through the Sixties* (Los Gatos, California: Shire Press, 2001), 185–87.

14. Sundiata Acoli, "From Behind the Walls," in "In Her Spirit: A Commemorative Booklet for the Marilyn Buck Solidarity Fund for Political Prisoners," Docplayer.net, http://docplayer.net/35594394-Marilyn-buck-in-her-spirit-a -commemorative-booklet-for-the-marilyn-buck-solidarity-fund-for-political -prisoners-1.html.

15. Mariann G. Wizard, "Warrior-Poet Marilyn Buck: No Wall Too Tall," *Rag Blog*, May 19, 2010, http://theragblog.blogspot.com/2010/05/warrior-poet-marilyn -buck-no-wall-too.html.

16. Quoted in James E. Westheider, *The African American Experience in Vietnam: Brothers in Arms* (Lanham, MD: Rowman & Littlefield Publishers, 2007), 25.

17. FBI, "Marilyn Jean Buck: Identification Order 4893/Wanted Flyer 508/Bank Robbery-Conspiracy; Escaped Federal Prisoner," undated, 11 (photocopy in author's possession).

18. "In Her Spirit: A Commemorative Booklet for the Marilyn Buck Solidarity Fund for Political Prisoners," Docplayer.net, http://docplayer.net/35594394 -Marilyn-buck-in-her-spirit-a-commemorative-booklet-for-the-marilyn -buck-solidarity-fund-for-political-prisoners-1.html.

19. Norman Mailer, *The Armies of the Night: History as a Novel, the Novel as History* (New York: Penguin, 1994), 116.

20. Michael Renov, "Newsreel: Old and New—Towards an Historical Profile," UC Press E-Books Collection, 1982–2004, http://publishing.cdlib.org/ucpressebooks/view?docId=ft5h4nb36j&chunk.id=d0e6233&toc.depth=1&toc.id=d0e6198&brand=ucpress.

21. Norm Fruchter, "Newsreel on Newsreel," *Film Quarterly*, Winter 1968, https://www.twn.org/digihome/monograph/fruchter_ms.aspx.

22. J. Hoberman, *The Dream Life: Movies, Media, and the Mythology of the Sixties* (New York: New Press, 2005), 183.

23. Becky Thompson, *A Promise and a Way of Life: White Antiracist Activism* (Minneapolis, MN: University of Minnesota Press, 2002), 103.

24. Rick Riley, *The Thief on the Cross*, 2015, https://books.google.com/books?id=NqkbCgAAQBAJ&q=pussy#v=snippet&q=hot%20revolutionary&f=false.

25. "Terror Behind Bars: A Short History of the Black Liberation Army," 2003, http://www.newspress.com/terrorbehindbars/history.htm.

26. Quoted in Curtis J. Austin, *Up Against the Wall: Violence in the Making and Unmaking of the Black Panther Party* (Fayetteville: University of Arkansas Press, 2006), 99.

27. "In the Matter of the Application of the United States of America for an Order Authorizing the Interception of Wire Communications," 1987, 11, FBI Special Agent David Mitchell (draft) (photocopy in author's possession).

28. Robert K. Tannenbaum, *Badge of the Assassin* (New York: Pocket Books, 1979), 57.

29. Elizabeth Solomont, "New Arrests in a Decades-Old Slaying of Police Officers," *New York Sun*, January 24, 2007, http://www.nysun.com/new-york/new-arrests-in-a-decades-old-slaying-of-police/47292/.

30. Sundiata Acoli, "Brinks Trial Testimony," http://freedomarchives.org/Documents/Finder/DOC513_scans/Sundiata_Acoli/513.acoli.brinks.testimony.1983.pdf, 29.

31. William F. May, "Terrorism as Strategy and Ecstasy," *Social Research* 41, no. 2 (Summer 1974), https://www.jstor.org/stable/40970181?seq=1#page_scan_tab_contents.

32. Tannenbaum, *Badge of the Assassin*, 60.

33. FBI, memorandum from acting director to Special Agent in Charge, New York, "Black Liberation Army: Extremist Matters—Urban Guerrilla Warfare," October 16, 1972, 1, (FBI FOIA release).

34. FBI, memo from Moore to Miller, May 17, 1973, 1, (FBI FOIA release).

35. FBI, "Black Liberation Army," May 14, 1973, 3, (FBI FOIA release).

36. Thomas Tracy, "Cop-killer Herman Bell Denied Parole in Murder of Two NYPD Officers in 1971," *Daily News* (New York), February 25, 2014, http://www.nydailynews.com/new-york/nyc-crime/cop-killer-herman-bell-denied-parole-article-1.1701111.

37. Jim Dwyer, "Officers' Killer Took Aim at New York City of Today," *New York Times*, December 21, 2014, https://www.nytimes.com/2014/12/22/nyregion/officers-killer-took-aim-at-new-york-city-of-today.html?mcubz=0.

38. John Koopman, "2nd Guilty Plea in 1971 Killing of S.F. Officer," July 7, 2009, http://www.sfgate.com/bayarea/article/2nd-guilty-plea-in-1971-killing-of-S-F-officer-3226167.php.

39. FBI, "Marilyn Jean Buck: Identification Order 4893/Wanted Flyer 508/Bank Robbery-Conspiracy; Escaped Federal Prisoner," undated, 11 (photocopy in author's possession).

40. Al Baker, "Nearly 5 Decades Later, Man Who Killed New York Officers Wins Parole," *New York Times*, March 14, 2018, https://www.nytimes.com/2018/03/14/nyregion/herman-bell-nypd-parole.html.

41. FBI, Acting Director, FBI from SAC, San Francisco, airtel, "Marilyn Jean Buck: SM–RA (Extremist)," April 30, 1973, 2 (FBI FOIA release).

42. "Trends in Urban Guerilla Tactics," *FBI Law Enforcement Bulletin*, July 1973, 3.

43. FBI, "Marilyn Jean Buck," April 17, 1973, 2 (FBI FOIA release).

44. FBI, Director, FBI from Special Agent in Charge, San Francisco, airtel, "Changed: Marilyn Jean Buck," December 14, 1973, 2 (FBI FOIA release).

45. "White Member of Black Liberation Army Sentenced," *Phoenix Gazette*, March 3, 1974.

46. "Full Text of 'Fire to the Prisons #10—Winter 2010–2011,'" https://archive.org/stream/fttp10/fttp10_djvu.txt.

47. Thompson, *A Promise and a Way of Life*, 104.

48. FBI, "Marilyn Jean Buck: Identification Order 4893/Wanted Flyer 508/Bank Robbery-Conspiracy; Escaped Federal Prisoner," undated, (photocopy in author's possession).

3. THE WHITE EDGE

1. "Serve the People: The Urban Guerilla and Class Struggle," *The Red Army Faction: A Documentary History*, introductory texts and translation by J. Smith

and André Moncourt, vol. 1, *Projectiles for the People* (Montreal: Kersplebedeb Publishing and Distribution, 2009), https://theradical1970s.files.word press.com/2014/02/the-red-army-faction-a-documentary-history-vol-1.pdf.

2. New York State Department of Corrections and Community Supervision, "Parole Board Hearing in the Matter of Judith Clark," April 5, 2017, 31 (photocopy in author's possession).

3. FBI, "Black Liberation Army (BLA): Domestic Terrorism," October 25, 1982, 1 (FBI FOIA release).

4. *United States of America v. Marilyn Buck*, 84 Cr. 220 (CSH), "Government's Memorandum of Law in Opposition to Buck's Motion to Suppress Evidence Seized from Apartment D, Building 5714, The Alameda, Baltimore, Maryland," U.S. District Court, Southern District of New York, Daniel Patrick Moynihan Courthouse, September 8, 1987, 2.

5. John Castellucci, *The Big Dance: The Untold Story of Weatherman Kathy Boudin and the Terrorist Family That Committed the Brink's Robbery Murders* (New York: Dodd, Mead & Company, 1986), 67.

6. FBI, "May 19th Communist Organization: Domestic Security/Terrorism," April 21, 1987, 2, (FBI FOIA release).

7. David Gilbert, *Love & Struggle: My Life in SDS, the Weather Underground, and Beyond* (Oakland, CA: PM Press, 2012), 263.

8. Kuwasi Balagoon, *A Soldier's Story: Writings by a Revolutionary New Afrikan Anarchist* (Montreal: Kersplebedeb Publishing, 2003), 61.

9. Terry Bisson and Sally O'Brien, "For Mutulu Shakur, the Revolution Isn't Over," *City Sun* (Brooklyn), April 9–15, 1986, http://freedomarchives.org/Docu ments/Finder/DOC513_scans/Mutulu_Shakur/513.mutulu.shakur.article.pdf.

10. Quoted in *United States of America v. Linda Sue Evans*, Cr. N-85-36, FBI Special Agent Daniel B. Caylor, "Affidavit in Support of an Order Approving the Emergency Interception of Oral Communications," U.S. District Court, Southern District of New York, May 1985, in U.S. District Court, District of Connecticut, Boston Federal Records Center, 8–9.

11. Anna Quindlen, "About New York," *New York Times*, October 28, 1981, https:// www.nytimes.com/1981/10/28/nyregion/about-new-york.html.

12. *United States v. Shakur*, SSS 82 Cr. 0312, "Memorandum & Order," U.S. District Court, Southern District of New York, March 29, 1983.

4. HANDLESS TERRORIST ESCAPES

1. "Statement of Special Agent (Ret.) Donald R. Wofford Before the Senate Committee on the Judiciary Hearing on FALN Clemency," September 15, 1999, http://www.latinamericanstudies.org/puertorico/wofford.htm.

2. *United States of America v. Julio Rosado, Andres Rosado, Ricardo Romero, Steven Guerra, and Maria Cueto*, Cr. 83-0025, "Sentence Memorandum of the United States," U.S. District Court, Eastern District of New York, May 20, 1983, Docplayer.net, https://docplayer.net/57118026-Name-title-supervisory-archives-specialist-name-and-address-of-depository.html.

3. Quoted in Richard Esposito and Ted Gerstein, *Bomb Squad: A Year Inside the Nation's Most Exclusive Police Unit*, (New York: Hyperion, 2008), 82.

4. U.S. Senate, Committee on the Judiciary, "Hearings on Clemency for FALN Members."

5. *United States of America v. Linda Sue Evans*, Cr. N-85-36, FBI Special Agent Daniel B. Caylor, "Affidavit in Support of an Order Approving the Emergency Interception of Oral Communications," U.S. District Court, Southern District of New York, May 1985, in U.S. District Court, District of Connecticut, Boston Federal Records Center, 9.

6. Robert McG. Thomas, Jr., "16 in Correction Posts Accused of Negligence in Escape by Morales," *New York Times*, December 17, 1979, http://www.nytimes.com/1979/12/17/archives/16-in-correction-posts-accused-of-negligence-in-escape-by-morales.html?_r=1.

7. FBI, to Director FBI from SAC, Chicago, airtel, "May 19th Communist Organization," December 13, 1982, 19 (FBI FOIA release).

8. *United States of America v. Julio Rosado, Andres Rosado, Ricardo Romero, Steven Guerra, and Maria Cueto*, Cr. 83-0025, "Sentence Memorandum of the United States," U.S. District Court, Eastern District of New York, May 20, 1983, Docplayer.net, https://docplayer.net/57118026-Name-title-supervisory-archives-specialist-name-and-address-of-depository.html.

9. Joseph P. Fried, "Court Brief Implicates Lawyer in Escape by William Morales," *New York Times*, June 13, 1983, https://www.nytimes.com/1983/06/03/nyregion/court-brief-implicates-lawyer-in-escape-by-william-morales.html.

10. Quoted in Cerisse Anderson, "Lawyer Susan Tipograph Denied Allegations Thursday that She Smuggled . . ." UPI, June 9, 1983, https://www.upi.com/Archives/1983/06/09/Lawyer-Susan-Tipograph-denied-allegations-Thursday-that-she-smuggled/5049423979200/.

11. *United States of America v. Julio Rosado, Andres Rosado, Ricardo Romero, Ste-*

ven Guerra, and Maria Cueto, Cr. 83-0025, "Sentence Memorandum of the United States," USDC, Eastern District of New York (EDNY), May 20, 1983, Doc player.net, https://docplayer.net/57118026-Name-title-supervisory-archives -specialist-name-and-address-of-depository.html.

12. David Oshinsky, *Bellevue: Three Centuries of Medicine and Mayhem at America's Most Storied Hospital* (New York: Doubleday, 2016).

13. Robert D. McFadden, "Fugitive Puerto Rican Terrorist Arrested in Mexico," *New York Times*, May 28, 1983, http://www.nytimes.com/1983/05/28/nyre gion/fugitive-puerto-rican-terrorist-arrested-in-mexico.html?mcubz=0.

14. Photocopy of FBI special agent's notes in author's possession; District of Columbia Metropolitan Joint Terrorist Task Force (JTTF) to Herbert Rutherford, memorandum, U.S. Marshal for the District of Columbia, "Summary Background: *US v. Laura Whitehorn, et al.*," Cr. 88-145, May 26, 1988, U.S. District Court, District of Columbia, E. Barrett Prettyman U.S. Courthouse, 3.

15. Marie E. Colvin, "Jailed FALN Bombmaker William Morales Used Bolt Cutters Smuggled . . ." UPI, June 1, 1983, https://www.upi.com/Archives/1983/06/01 /Jailed-FALN-bombmaker-William-Morales-used-bolt-cutters-smuggled /3653423288000/.

16. Mike Kelley, "Suspected Mastermind of NYC Bombing That Killed Fair Lawn Man Keeps Low Profile in Cuba," Northjersey.com, October 4, 2015, https:// www.northjersey.com/story/news/2015/09/18/record-columnist-mike -kelly-in-cuba/94237410/.

17. Douglas Montero, "Puerto Rican Bomber Asks for Amnesty," *New York Post*, December 7, 1997, http://www.latinamericanstudies.org/puertorico/sep11.htm.

18. Alan Berkman, unpublished memoir/manuscript, undated, Alan Berkman Papers, Archives & Special Collections, Columbia University Health Sciences Library, 2.

19. Letter from Steven Berkman to U.S. Parole Commission, January 4, 1990, Susan Rosenberg Papers, Sophia Smith Collection, Smith College.

20. Transcript of Dick Polman (*Philadephia Enquirer*), interview with Alan Berkman, August 19, 1985, Berkman Papers, Archives & Special Collections, Columbia University Health Sciences Library, 1–4.

21. Ibid., 1–4.

22. Susan M. Reverby, "The Fielding H. Garrison Lecture: Enemy of the People/ Enemy of the State: Two Great(ly Infamous) Doctors, Passions, and the Judgment of History," *Bulletin of the History of Medicine* 88, no. 3 (2014): 403–30, https://muse.jhu.edu/article/556934.

23. Berkman, unpublished memoir/manuscript, undated, "Chapter 2—In the garbage underground," 1.

24. Emily Chertoff, "Occupy Wounded Knee: A 71-Day Siege and a Forgotten Civil Rights Movement," *Atlantic*, October 23, 2012, https://www.theatlantic .com/national/archive/2012/10/occupy-wounded-knee-a-71-day-siege-and -a-forgotten-civil-rights-movement/263998/.

25. Matt Meyer and Barbara Zeller, "Picking up the Work: Health Care in Prison: A Conversation with Dr. Barbara Zeller," in *Let Freedom Ring: A Collection of Documents from the Movements to Free U.S. Political Prisoners*, Matt Meyer, ed., (Oakland, CA: PM Press, 2008), 569–72.

26. Polman interview with Berkman, 3–1, Berkman Papers, Archives & Special Collections, Columbia University Health Sciences Library.

27. Ibid., 3–2.

28. Letter from Steven Berkman to U.S. Parole Commission, January 4, 1990, Susan Rosenberg Papers, Sophia Smith Collection, Smith College.

29. Dan Berger, *Outlaws of America: The Weather Underground and the Politics of Solidarity* (Oakland, CA: AK Press, 2006), 227.

30. Quoted in ibid., 237.

31. Laura Whitehorn, "Self-Criticisms from the National Committee," *A Single Spark: Internal Newsletter of the Prairie Fire Organizing Committee*, no. 1, May 1976, 18.

32. Fran Moira, "Judy Clark: 75 to Life, But Life Goes On," *off our backs*, December 31, 1984, 2–8.

33. Lesbian Health Information Project, "Artificial Insemination: An Alternative Conception for the Lesbian and Gay Community," 1979, 9 (photocopy in author's possession).

34. New York State Department of Corrections and Community Supervision, "Parole Board Hearing in the Matter of Judith Clark," April 5, 2017, 19, 32, (photocopy in author's possession).

35. Ibid., 32.

5. "AMERIKKKA IS TRYING TO LYNCH ME"

1. Robert Daley, *Target Blue: An Insider's View of the N.Y.P.D.* (New York: Dell, 1974), 467.

2. "Sundiata Convicted," Friends of Assata Shakur & Sundiata Acolie, undated leaflet, http://freedomarchives.org/Documents/Finder/DOC513_scans/Assata _Shakur/513.Assata.SundiataConvicted.pdf.

3. Lacey Fosburgh, "Patrolman Tells of 1971 Shooting," *New York Times*, No-

vember 7, 1972, http://www.nytimes.com/1972/11/07/archives/new-jersey
-pages-patrolman-tells-of-1971-shooting-testifies-at.html?mcubz=0&_r=0.

4. "Joanne Deborah Chesimard," Most Wanted Terrorists, FBI, https://www.fbi
.gov/wanted/wanted_terrorists/joanne-deborah-chesimard.

5. Assata Shakur, *Assata: An Autobiography* (Chicago: Lawrence Hill Books,
1988), 246.

6. "Free Assata Shakur," May 19 Communist Organization, Freedomarchives
.org, http://freedomarchives.org/Documents/Finder/DOC37_scans/37.May
19.FreeAssataShakur.flyer.pdf.

7. Ibid.

8. "In the Matter of the Application of the United States of America for an Order
Authorizing the Interception of Wire Communications," 1987, 11, FBI Special
Agent David Mitchell (draft) (photocopy in author's possession).

9. *United States of America v. Mutulu Shakur and Marilyn Buck*, SSS 82 Cr. 312 (CSH),
"Government's Memorandum of Law in Opposition to the Petitions of Mutulu
Shakur and Marilyn Buck Pursuant to 28 U.S.C. § 2255," undated, U.S. District
Court, Southern District of New York, Daniel Patrick Moynihan Courthouse, 17.

10. Ibid.

11. John Castellucci, *The Big Dance: The Untold Story of Weatherman Kathy
Boudin and the Terrorist Family That Committed the Brink's Robbery Murders*
(New York: Dodd, Mead & Company, 1986), 144.

12. "In the Matter of the Application of the United States of America for an Order
Authorizing the Interception of Wire Communications," 1987, 4, FBI Special
Agent David Mitchell (draft) (photocopy in author's possession).

13. *United States of America v. Julio Rosado, Andres Rosado, Ricardo Romero, Steven Guerra, and Maria Cueto*, Cr. 83-0025, "Sentence Memorandum of the
United States," U.S. District Court, Eastern District of New York, May 20, 1983,
Docplayer.net, https://docplayer.net/57118026-Name-title-supervisory-ar
chives-specialist-name-and-address-of-depository.html.

14. *United States of America v. Mutulu Shakur and Marilyn Buck*, SSS 82 Cr. 312 (CSH),
"Government's Memorandum of Law in Opposition to the Petitions of Mutulu
Shakur and Marilyn Buck Pursuant to 28 U.S.C. § 2255," undated, U.S. District
Court, Southern District of New York, Daniel Patrick Moynihan Courthouse, 35.

15. Ibid, 35.

16. "In the Matter of the Application of the United States of America for an Order
Authorizing the Interception of Wire Communications," 1987, 2, FBI Special
Agent David Mitchell (draft) (photocopy in author's possession).

17. Mychal Denzel Smith, "Assata Shakur Is Not a Terrorist," *Nation*, May 7, 2013, https://www.thenation.com/article/assata-shakur-not-terrorist/.

18. "Angela Davis and Assata Shakur's Lawyer Denounce FBI's Adding of Exiled Activist to Terrorists List," *Democracy Now!*, May 3, 2013, https://www.democracynow.org/2013/5/3/angela_davis_and_assata_shakurs_lawyer.

19. Eyder Peralta, "FBI Adds First Woman to Its Most Wanted Terrorists List," NPR, May 2, 2013, http://www.npr.org/sections/thetwo-way/2013/05/02/180658024/fbi-adds-first-woman-to-its-most-wanted-terrorist-list.

20. "In the Matter of the Application of the United States of America for an Order Authorizing the Interception of Wire Communications," 1987, 16, FBI Special Agent David Mitchell (draft) (photocopy in author's possession).

21. New York State Criminal Justice Institute, *Report of the Policy Study Group on Terrorism* (New York State: The Criminal Justice Institute, 1985), 100.

22. *United States of America v. Mutulu Shakur and Marilyn Buck*, SSS 82 Cr. 312 (CSH), attachment to "Exhibit D to Government's Memorandum of Law in Opposition to the Petitions of Mutulu Shakur and Marilyn Buck Pursuant to 28 U.S.C. § 225 (To Be Filed Under Seal)," undated, 35.

23. Ibid., 36–37.

24. "In the Matter of the Application of the United States of America for an Order Authorizing the Interception of Wire Communications," 1987, 16, FBI Special Agent David Mitchell (draft) (photocopy in author's possession), 16.

25. Author's interview with Kenneth Maxwell, Washington, DC, January 20, 2017.

26. Robert D. McFadden, "Police Raid Apartments to Gather Evidence on Killings in Rockland," *New York Times*, October 23, 1981, https://www.nytimes.com/1981/10/23/nyregion/police-raid-apartments-to-gather-evidence-on-killings-in-rockland.html.

27. Author's interview with Dr. James Wilson, Brooklyn, NY, December 28, 2016.

28. *United States of America v. Mutulu Shakur*, SSS 82 Cr. 312, U.S. District Court, Southern District of New York, March 12, 1987, exhibit 17–119, Jeff Weinstein, "Eating Around: Law and Your Order."

6. DEATH TO THE KLAN

1. Tom Robbins, "Judith Clark's Radical Transformation," *New York Times Magazine*, January 12, 2012, https://www.nytimes.com/2012/01/15/magazine/judith-clarks-radical-transformation.html.

2. Mary Patten, *Revolution as an Eternal Dream: The Exemplary Failure of the Madame Binh Graphics Collective* (Chicago: Half Letter Press, 2011), 45.

3. Letter to supporters, Moncada Library/Biblioteca Moncada, August 9, 1982, www.freedomarchives.org/Documents/Finder/Doc43_scans/43.correspon dence.moncadalibrary.8.9.1982.pdf.

4. Ibid.

5. Moncada Library, "Who's Behind the Police Vest Campaign?," Freedom archives.org, http://freedomarchives.org/Documents/Finder/DOC43_scans /43.flyer.who.behind.the.police.vest.campaign.pdf.

6. Bruce Vail, "Park Slope Radicals Keep Talking as Fed Grand Jury Probes Connections to Nyack Shootout," *Phoenix* (Brooklyn), March 18, 1982, Freedomarchives.org, http://freedomarchives.org/Documents/Finder/DOC 43_scans/43.article.phoenix.3.18.1982.pdf.

7. "Moncada Arrests in Dispute," *Phoenix* (Brooklyn), May 10, 1981.

8. "Community Bulletin from the Moncada Library," Freedomarchives.org, http://freedomarchives.org/Documents/Finder/DOC43_scans/43.Commu nityBulletin.flyer.pdf.

9. John Brown Anti-Klan Committee, "Amerika's Koncentration Kamps," *Death to the Klan!*, Fall 1984, 13.

10. Daniel Penny, "An Intimate History of Antifa," *New Yorker*, August 22, 2017, https://www.newyorker.com/books/page-turner/an-intimate-history-of -antifa.

11. Greensboro Truth & Reconciliation Commission, "Intelligence Gathering and Planning for the Anti-Klan Campaign," in *Greensboro Truth and Reconciliation Commission (GTRC) Final Report*, May 25, 2006.

12. Eric Hodge, Rebecca Martinez, and Phoebe Judge, "Criminal: Birth of a Massacre," WUNC, May 20, 2016, http://wunc.org/post/criminal-birth-massacre #stream/0.

13. Workers Viewpoint Organization, "Smash the Klan with the Correct Understanding and Armed Self-Defense," UNC Greensboro Digital Collections, http://libcdm1.uncg.edu/cdm/compoundobject/collection/CivilRights/id /411/rec/22.

14. Greensboro Truth & Reconciliation Commission, "Intelligence gathering."

15. Nelson N. Johnson, "An Open Letter to Joe Grady, Gorrell Pierce, and All KKK Members and Sympathizers," October 22, 1979, UNC Greensboro Digital Collections, http://libcdm1.uncg.edu/cdm/ref/collection/CivilRights/id/157.

16. Art Harris, "The Hardscrabble Heroes of Hatred," *Washington Post*, November 19, 1980, https://www.washingtonpost.com/archive/politics/1980/11

/19/the-hardscrabble-heroes-of-hatred/166c2260-54c4-4431-b07d-3ac22b
386278/?utm_term=.fdbe06c47a4b.

17. FBI, "May 19th Communist Organization: Domestic Security/Terrorism Investigation," New York Field Office, Oct 1, 1991, 16 (FBI FOIA release).

18. "Statement of Tim Blunk to the Parole Board," Lewisburg, Pennsylvania, February 1996, Susan Rosenberg Papers, Sophia Smith Collection, Smith College, 5.

19. Homer Bigart, "Newark Riot Deaths at 21 as Negro Sniping Widens; Hughes May Seek U.S. Aid; New Blazes Flare," *New York Times*, July 16, 1967, https://www.nytimes.com/1967/07/16/archives/newark-riot-deaths-at-21-as-negro-sniping-widens-hughes-may-seek-us.html.

20. Tom Kehoe and Beverly McCarron, "The Making of a Radical: From Bridgewater to Prison He Turns to Armed Struggle," *Courier-News* (Bridgewater, New Jersey), March 4, 1985, A-4.

21. Ibid.

22. Susan Rosenberg, *An American Radical: A Political Prisoner in My Own Country* (New York: Kensington Publishing Corp., 2011), 4.

23. "Statement of Tim Blunk to the Parole Board," 1996, Susan Rosenberg Papers, Sophia Smith Collection, Smith College, 5.

24. "Statement from Eve Rosahn in Solidarity with the Denver Conference," National Conference Against Repression and Fascism, May 26, 1982, Freedom archives.org,http://freedomarchives.org/Documents/Finder/DOC47_scans/47.statements.nationalconference.denver.may.1982.pdf.

25. *United States of America v. Mutulu Shakur and Marilyn Buck*, SSS 82 Cr. 312, "To: Family Re: Action to Stop Springboks," U.S. District Court, Southern District of New York, March 12, 1987 (document marked "Q10, 122 'F'").

26. Katherine Boo, "Tim Blunk's War," *Washington City Paper*, August 25–31, 1989, 18.

27. Dick Satran, "Blows at Apartheid Might Miss Their Target," *Phoenix* (Brooklyn), October 15, 1981.

28. FBI, "May 19th Communist Organization," airtel from acting director to all special agents in charge (SACs) and all legal attachés (LEGATs), September 24, 1987, 5 (FBI FOIA release).

29. "De Blasio Administration Unveils Plans for Borough-Based Jails to Replace Facilities on Rikers Island," NYC.gov, August 15, 2018, https://www1.nyc.gov/office-of-the-mayor/news/413-18/de-blasio-administration-plans-borough-based-jails-replace-facilities-rikers.

30. Patten, *Revolution as an Eternal Dream*, 51.

31. "Statement of Tim Blunk to the Parole Board," 1996, Susan Rosenberg Papers, Sophia Smith Collection, Smith College, 6.

32. "Opening Statement of Tim Blunk, Captured Resistance Fighter," March 7, 1985, Susan Rosenberg Papers, Sophia Smith Collection, Smith College, 3.

33. Quoted in Katherine Boo, "Tim Blunk's War," *Washington City Paper*, August 25–31, 1989, 18.

7. ELIZABETH FUCKED UP

1. FBI, Assistant Director in Charge, New York to Director, FBI, airtel, "Black Liberation Army (BLA) Domestic Terrorism," October 25, 1982, 2 (FBI FOIA release).

2. Arnold H. Lubasch, "Witness Says He Aided 2 Brink's Robbery Suspects," *New York Times*, June 19, 1983, https://www.nytimes.com/1983/06/19/nyregion/witness-says-he-aided-2-brink-s-robbery-suspects.html.

3. "In the Matter of the Application of the United States of America for an Order Authorizing the Interception of Wire Communications," 1987, FBI Special Agent David Mitchell, (draft) (photocopy in author's possession), 16.

4. Ibid., 16–17.

5. "In re Grand Jury Proceedings Involving Eve Rosahn, Appellant," decided January 21, 1982, OpenJurist, https://openjurist.org/671/f2d/690/in-re-grand-jury-proceedings-involving-eve-rosahn.

6. New York State Criminal Justice Institute, *Report of the Policy Study Group on Terrorism*, (New York: The Criminal Justice Institute, 1985), 34.

7. Frederick Zugibe and David L. Carroll, *Dissecting Death: Secrets of a Medical Examiner* (New York: Broadway Books, 2005), 115.

8. *People v. Boudin*, 114 Misc.2d 523 (1982), April 19, 1982, *Leagle*, https://www.leagle.com/decision/1982637114misc2d5231552.

9. Historical Society of the Nyacks, *Remembering the Brinks Robbery* (Nyack, NY: Historical Society of the Nyacks, 2017), 24.

10. FBI, Director FBI from SAC, Chicago, airtel, "May 19th Communist Organization," December 13, 1982, 27 (FBI FOIA release).

11. *Samuel Brown, Petitioner-appellant, v. John Doe, Warden, Respondent-appellee*, 2 F.3d 1236 (2d Cir. 1993), Justia, https://law.justia.com/cases/federal/appellate-courts/F3/2/1236/616074/.

12. Quoted in Kenneth Gribetz and H. Paul Jeffers, *Murder Along the Way: A Prosecutor's Personal Account of Fighting Violent Crime in the Suburbs* (New York: Pharos Books, 1989), 160.

13. "Brinks Case: Who Remains of the Major Players?" May 16, 2018, *The Journal News*, LoHud.com, https://www.lohud.com/story/news/local/rockland/2018/05/04/brinks-case-who-remains-major-players/580504002/.

14. Susan Rosenfeld, "NYROB: A Turning Point in Terrorism Investigations," Society of Former Special Agents of the FBI, September 2013, https://c.ymcdn.com/sites/socxfbi.site-ym.com/resource/resmgr/history_committee_articles/nyrob_(sept_2013).pdf.

15. Author's interview with Kenneth Maxwell, Washington, DC, January 20, 2017.

16. FBI, Special Agents in Charge, Chicago to Director, FBI, "May 19th Communist Organization (M19CO) December 13, 1982, 27.

17. Ibid, 27.

18. Ibid, 27.

19. *United States of America v. Mutulu Shakur*, SSS 82 Cr. 312-CSH, 656 F. Supp. 241 (1987), U.S. District Court, Southern District of New York, February 19, 1987, *Leagle*, https://www.leagle.com/decision/1987897656fsupp2411868.

20. John Castellucci, *The Big Dance: The Untold Story of Weatherman Kathy Boudin and the Terrorist Family That Committed the Brink's Robbery Murders* (New York: Dodd, Mead & Company, 1986), 40.

21. Judy Clark, "Remember the Fallen," *Urban Guerilla*, September 9, 2014.

22. *United States of America v. Mutulu Shakur*, SSS 82 Cr. 312-CSH, 656 F. Supp. 241 (1987), U.S. District Court, Southern District of New York, February 19, 1987, *Leagle*, https://www.leagle.com/decision/1987897656fsupp2411868.

8. WHAT THIS COUNTRY NEEDS IS A LITTLE MORE CHAOS

1. Letter from W. Donald Wier to District Court Judge, June 27, 1985, 2 (photocopy in author's possession).

2. FBI, "Elizabeth Anna Duke: FBI Identification Order #5086," New York, undated, 3 (photocopy in author's possession).

3. Quoted in William Sherman, "Beware! The FBI's Most Wanted Women," *Cosmopolitan*, March 1991, 230.

4. Letter from Mary A. Weir to United States District Court Judge, Eastern District of Pennsylvania, June 26, 1985, 1 (photocopy in author's possession).

5. Quoted in James Pinkerton, "Still on the Run: Now 54 and a Grandmother, '60s Radical from Austin Remains on FBI's Wanted List," *Houston Chronicle*, October 29, 1985, 1.

6. *Elizabeth Anna Duke v. North Texas State University*, no. 71-3198, United

States Court of Appeals, Fifth Circuit, January 10, 1973, *Casetext*, https://case text.com/case/duke-v-north-texas-state-university-2.

7. Ibid.

8. Ibid.

9. Letter from Daniel S. Brody to District Court Judge, June 26, 1985, 1, (photo-copy in author's possession).

10. "Unigel® Semi-Gelatin Nitroglycerin Dynamite Properties Density (g/cc) Avg Energya (cal/g) (cal/cc)," Dyno Nobel, *Industry Cortex*, http://www.industry cortex.com/datasheets/profile/254520738.

11. Ed Rampell, "The Unrepentant Radical," *Women's International Net Maga-zine*, part B, April 2001, University of Virginia, http://lists.village.virginia.edu /lists_archive/sixties-l/3062.html.

12. Ibid.

13. Ibid.

14. Quoted in Andrew Weist and Michael Doldge, *Triumph Revisited: Historians Battle for the Vietnam War* (New York: Routledge, 2010), 30.

15. Queers United in Support of Political Prisoners (QUISP), "Dykes and Fags Want to Know . . . : A Written Interview with Lesbian Political Prisoners Laura Whitehorn, Linda Evans and Susan Rosenberg," 1991, *Arm the Spirit— for Revolutionary Resistance* (blog), https://armthespiritforrevolutionary resistance.wordpress.com/2017/08/30/dykes-and-fags-want-to-know/.

16. *Conspiracy of Voices: Poetry, Writing and Art by the Women of the Resistance Conspiracy Case* (Washington, DC: Emergency Committee to Defend the Human and Legal Rights of Political Prisoners, 1990), 22.

17. Ibid., 23.

18. FBI, "Weatherman Underground Summary Dated 8/20/76, Part #2," https:// vault.fbi.gov/Weather%20Underground%20%28Weathermen%29/We ather%20Underground%20%28Weathermen%29%20Part%204%20of%206 /viewSummary.

19. Ibid.

20. Students for a Democratic Society (SDS), "Bring the War Home!," 1969, Uni-versity of Washington Libraries, Special Collections, http://digitalcollec tions.lib.washington.edu/cdm/ref/collection/protests/id/419.

21. "Linda Evans: Getting People to Like Us Isn't the Way to Win, Winning Is the Way to Win," *Berkeley Tribe*, April 24–May 1, 1970, 26.

22. District of Columbia Metropolitan Joint Terrorist Task Force (JTTF) to Her-bert Rutherford, memorandum, U.S. Marshal for the District of Columbia,

"Summary Background: *US v. Laura Whitehorn, et al.*," CR 88-0145, May 26, 1988, U.S. District Court, District of Columbia, E. Barrett Prettyman U.S. Courthouse, 5.

23. Staajabu, "A Visit with Political Prisoners Linda Evans and Marilyn Buck," *It's About Time . . .*, Winter 2001, *Issuu*, https://issuu.com/randalljaykay/docs /it_s_about_time_-_winter_2001.

24. Jennifer Ulrich, "Alan Berkman Papers Now Open," *Primary Sources* (blog), July 27, 2016, http://blogs.cuit.columbia.edu/hslarch/alan-berkman-papers -now-open/.

25. FBI, Special Agent [name redacted], New Orleans, Louisiana, FD-302 (REV 3-8-77), 5/21/85, 147 (FBI FOIA release).

26. *United States of America v. Laura Whitehorn, et al.*, Cr. 88-145-05, "Defendant Linda Evans' Memorandum in Aid of Sentencing," U.S. District Court for the District of Columbia, E. Barrett Prettyman U.S. Courthouse, November 30, 1990, 21.

27. "Sentencing Statement by Linda Evans, Resistance Conspiracy Case," December 4, 1990, Susan Rosenberg Papers, 1966–2002, Sophia Smith Collection, Smith College.

28. *United States of America v. Laura Whitehorn, et al.*, Cr. 88-145-05, "Memorandum of Points and Authorities in Support of Defendants' Motion to Dismiss the Indictment for Governmental Misconduct," U.S. District Court for the District of Columbia, E. Barrett Prettyman U.S. Courthouse, January 31, 1989, 10–11.

29. *United States of America, Plaintiff-appellee, v. Linda Sue Evans, Defendant-appellant*, 848 F.2d 1352 (5th Cir. 1988), June 23, 1988, Justia, https://law.justia .com/cases/federal/appellate-courts/F2/848/1352/292008/.

9. MORNING IN AMERICA

1. U.S. House of Representatives, Committee on Internal Security, *Terrorism: Part 2* (Washington, DC: U.S. Government Printing Office, 1974), *Babel*, https:// babel.hathitrust.org/cgi/pt?id=mdp.39015058386478;view=1up;seq=7.

2. Matthew Carr, *The Infernal Machine: A History of Terrorism* (New York and London: The New Press, 2006), 212.

3. "FBI Profiler Says Linguistic Work Was Pivotal in Capture of Unabomber," National Public Radio, August 22, 2017, https://www.npr.org/2017/08/22 /545122205/fbi-profiler-says-linguistic-work-was-pivotal-in-capture-of-una bomber.

4. Louis Harris, "Terrorism," Harris Survey, December 5, 1977, 1, Harris Poll, http://www.harrisinteractive.com/vault/Harris-Interactive-Poll-Research-TERRORISM-1977-12.pdf.

5. Ronald Reagan, "Remarks at the Annual Convention of the National Association of Evangelicals," Orlando, Florida, March 8, 1983, Ronald Reagan Presidential Foundation & Institute, https://www.reaganfoundation.org/media/50919/remarks_annual_convention_national_association_evangelicals_030883.pdf.

6. William Rosenau, "Murder and Mayhem in Suriname," *Foreign Policy*, February 24, 2014, http://foreignpolicy.com/2014/02/24/murder-and-mayhem-in-suriname/.

7. "Sundiata Convicted," Friends of Assata Shakur & Sundiata Acolie, undated leaflet, http://freedomarchives.org/Documents/Finder/DOC513_scans/Assata_Shakur/513.Assata.SundiataConvicted.pdf.

8. Jeremiah Denton, "The Role of the Senate Subcommittee on Security and Terrorism in the Development of U.S. Policy Against Terrorism," 13 *Ohio N.U.L. Rev.* 19 (1986), 21.

9. William Rosenau, "The 'First War on Terrorism?': U.S. Domestic Counterterrorism During the 1970s and Early 1980s," CNA Occasional Paper, October 2014, https://www.cna.org/cna_files/pdf/CRM-2014-U-008836.pdf.

10. Quoted in Todd Gitlin, *The Sixties: Years of Hope, Days of Rage* (New York: Bantam, 1993), 399.

11. SPLC, "Atomwaffen Division," undated, https://www.splcenter.org/fighting-hate/extremist-files/group/atomwaffen-division.

12. U.S. Senate, Committee on the Judiciary, *Terroristic Activity* (Washington, DC: U.S. Government Printing Office, 1974), 5.

13. U.S. House of Representatives, Committee on Public Works, *Security in Federal Buildings* (Washington, DC: U.S. Government Printing Office, 1971), 38.

14. Quoted in U.S. House of Representatives, *Domestic Intelligence Operations for Internal Security Purposes*, part I (Washington, DC: U.S. Government Printing Office, 1974), 3,489.

15. Thomas Stentz, "The Terrorist Organizational Profile: A Psychological Role Model," in Yonah Alexander and John M. Gleason, eds., *Behavioral and Quantitative Perspectives on Terrorism* (New York: Pergamon, 1981), 97.

16. Eileen MacDonald, *Shoot the Women First* (New York: Random House, 1991), xv.

17. H. H. A. Cooper, "Woman as Terrorist," in *The Criminology of Deviant Women*,

Freda Alder and Rita James Simon, eds. (Boston: Houghton Mifflin, 1979), 154.

18. Quoted in MacDonald, *Shoot the Women First*, xv.

19. Konrad Kellen, "On Terrorists and Terrorism," RAND Corporation, December 1982, https://www.rand.org/content/dam/rand/pubs/notes/2005/N1942.pdf.

20. Quoted in Bruce Hoffman, "Putting German Terrorism in Perspective: An American Response," *GHI Bulletin* 43 (Fall 2008), https://www.ghi-dc.org/file admin/user_upload/GHI_Washington/Publications/Bulletin43/59.pdf.

21. Philip Selznick, "The Organizational Weapon: A Study of Bolshevik Strategy and Tactics," R-201, RAND Corporation, January 1952, https://www.rand.org /content/dam/rand/pubs/reports/2006/R201.pdf.

22. Ivan Greenberg, *The Dangers of Dissent: The FBI and Civil Liberties Since 1965* (Lanham, MD: Lexington Books, 2010), 121.

23. U.S. Senate, Committee on the Judiciary, Subcommittee on Security and Terrorism, *Impact of Attorney General's Guidelines for Domestic Security Investigations (The Levi Guidelines)*, 1983, Hathi Trust Digital Library, https://catalog .hathitrust.org/Record/011342555.

24. Christopher Lydon, "J. Edgar Hoover Made the F.B.I. Formidable with Politics, Publicity, and Results," *New York Times*, May 3, 1974.

25. "Moments in U.S. Diplomatic History: The 'Lavender Scare': Homosexuals at the State Department," Association for Diplomatic Studies & Training, https:// adst.org/2015/09/the-lavender-scare-homosexuals-at-the-state-department/.

26. "Executive Order 10450: Security Requirements for Government Employment," National Archives, https://www.archives.gov/federal-register/codifi cation/executive-order/10450.html.

27. Quoted in U.S. Senate, *Intelligence Activities: Senate Resolution 21* [Church Committee hearings], vol. 2 (Washington, DC: U.S. Government Printing Office, 1976), 98.

28. William E. Dyson, Jr., interviewed by Stanley A. Pimentel, Society of Former Special Agents of the FBI, Inc., January 15, 2008, 37 (photocopy in author's possession).

29. W. Mark Felt, *The FBI Pyramid from the Inside* (New York: G. P. Putnam's Sons, 1979), 316.

30. U.S. Senate, Committee on the Judiciary, Subcommittee on Security and Terrorism, *Impact of Attorney General's Guidelines for Domestic Security Investigations (The Levi Guidelines)*, 1983, Hathi Trust Digital Library, https://catalog .hathitrust.org/Record/011342555.

31. Kenneth Maxwell, remarks at press conference, Albany, NY, January 9, 2017 (photocopy of transcript in author's collection).

32. Susan Rosenfeld, "NYROB—A Turning Point in Terrorism Investigations," Society of Former Special Agents of the FBI, September 2013, https://c.ymcdn.com/sites/socxfbi.site-ym.com/resource/resmgr/history_commit tee_articles/nyrob_(sept_2013).pdf.

33. William H. Webster, interviewed by William M. Baker, March 9 and 11, 2006, Society of Former Special Agents of the FBI, Inc. (photocopy of transcript in author's possession).

34. Robert D. McFadden, "Police Raid Apartments to Gather Evidence on Killings in Rockland," *New York Times*, October 23, 1981, https://www.nytimes.com/1981/10/23/nyregion/police-raid-apartments-to-gather-evidence-on-killings-in-rockland.html.

35. Claudia Wallis, "Heading for the Last Roundup," *Time*, November 9, 1981.

36. Kenneth Maxwell, email to author, February 20, 2019.

37. "In re Grand Jury Proceedings Involving Eve Rosahn, Appellant," 671 F.2d 690, United States Court of Appeals, Second Circuit, January 21, 1982, OpenJurist, https://openjurist.org/671/f2d/690/in-re-grand-jury-proceedings-involving-eve-rosahn.

38. FBI, "May 19th Communist Organization (M19CO); Domestic Security," November 23, 1983, 5, (FBI FOIA release).

10. IF NOT US, WHO?

1. Bruce Vail, "Park Slope Radicals Keep Talking as Fed Grand Jury Probes Connections to Nyack Shootout," *Phoenix* (Brooklyn), March 18, 1982, Freedom archives.org,http://freedomarchives.org/Documents/Finder/DOC43_scans/43 .article.phoenix.3.18.1982.pdf.

2. "Transcript of Interview by Clayton Riley WBAI of Donna Borup, Mary Patten and Denise Lewis on March 29, 1982," Susan Rosenberg Papers, Sophia Smith Collection, Smith College.

3. *Marilyn Buck, Petitioner v. United States of America*, No. 89-6316 in the Supreme Court of the United States, October Term, 1989, United States Department of Justice, https://www.justice.gov/sites/default/files/osg/briefs/1989/01/01/sg890230.txt.

4. Guy Hawtin, "May 19's Weird Sex Doctrines," *New York Post*, February 3, 1982.

5. *United States of America v. Mutulu Shakur and Marilyn Buck*, SSS 82 Cr. 312-CSH, "Transcript of a Conversation between Mutulu Shakur and Edward Jo-

seph on March 8, 1982, at Apartment 2L, 85 Barrow Street, New York, NY," U.S. District Court for the Southern District of New York, Daniel Patrick Moynihan Courthouse.

6. U.S. Secret Service (USSS), New York Field Office to Headquarters, "Subject: May 19th," File: ODN-00579, October 21, 1981, 8 (FBI FOIA release).

7. FBI, Director, FBI, from New York, airtel, "May 19th Communist Organization (M19CO)," December 13, 1982, 1 (FBI FOIA release).

8. U.S. Secret Service (USSS), New York Field Office to Headquarters, "Subject: May 19th," File: ODN-00579, October 21, 1981, 8 (FBI FOIA release).

9. FBI, Director, from New York, airtel, "May 19th Communist Organization; Domestic Security; New York," February 19, 1982, 4 (FBI FOIA release).

10. Jim Grossklag, "From Middletown, USA, to Holmesburg Prison: The Journey of Alan Berkman and The Life of the Movement," *Undergraduate Review* 1, no. 1 (1986): 47–58, Digital Commons at IWU, https://digitalcommons.iwu .edu/cgi/viewcontent.cgi?referer=https://www.google.com/&httpsredir =1&article=1006&context=rev.

11. "Chronology—Written by Alan," Alan Berkman Papers, Archives & Special Collections, Columbia University Health Sciences Library, undated, 1.

12. *United States v. Shakur*, SSS 82 Cr. 0312 (KTD), "Memorandum and Order," U.S. District Court, Southern District of New York, May 5, 1983, *Leagle*, https:// www.leagle.com/decision/19831426562fsupp86411272.

13. *United States of America v. Julio Rosado, Andres Rosado, Ricardo Romero, Steven Guerra, and Maria Cueto*, CR 83-0025, "Sentence Memorandum of the United States," U.S. District Court, Eastern District of New York, May 20, 1983, Doc player.net, https://docplayer.net/57118026-Name-title-supervisory-archives -specialist-name-and-address-of-depository.html.

14. "Information Memorandum and Victim Impact Statement: The Transfer of Silvia Baraldini," undated, Susan Rosenberg Papers, Sophia Smith Collection, Smith College.

15. FBI, "May 19th Communist Organization (M19CO); Domestic Security," November 23, 1983, 5 (FBI FOIA release).

16. *United States of America v. Laura Whitehorn, et al.*, Cr. 88-0145, untitled paper marked "Q10, 645Y, FBI Laboratory," U.S. District Court for the District of Columbia, E. Barrett Prettyman U.S. Courthouse.

17. Bommi Baumann, *How it All Began: The Personal Account of a West German Urban Guerrilla*, trans. Helene Ellenbogen and Wayne Parker (Vancouver: Arsenal Pulp Press, 2000), 46.

18. *United States of America v. Elizabeth Anna Duke*, Cr. 85-222-02, transcript of statement by Elizabeth Duke, undated, U.S. District Court, Eastern District of Pennsylvania, Philadelphia Federal Records Center, 6.

19. *United States of America v. Alan Berkman*, Cr. 85-0222, typewritten letter marked "Q10, 645Y, FBI Laboratory," U.S. District Court, Eastern District of Pennsylvania, National Archives at Philadelphia, undated, 5.

20. Author's telephone interview with David Mitchell, January 12, 2017.

21. *United States of America v. Mutulu Shakur and Marilyn Buck*, SSS 82 Cr. 312-CSH, affidavit of David Mitchell, U. S. District Court, Southern District of New York, 5 (photocopy in author's possession).

22. "Transcript of Susan Rosenberg Parole Hearing," Susan Rosenberg Papers, Sophia Smith Collection, Smith College, 6.

23. Arm the Spirit, *Enemies of the State: An Interview with Anti-imperialist Political Prisoners* (Montreal: Abraham Guillen Press, 2002), 9.

24. Terry Bisson, "Who Was John Brown?" in *Let Freedom Ring: A Collection of Documents from the Movements to Free U.S. Political Prisoners*, Matt Meyer, ed., (Oakland, CA: PM Press, 2008), 490.

25. *Out: The Making of a Revolutionary* (documentary), directed by Rhonda Collins and Sonja De Vries, Film Arts Foundation, 2000.

26. Ibid.

27. Bisson, "Who Was John Brown?" in *Let Freedom Ring*, 490.

28. *The Weather Underground* (documentary), directed by Sam Green and Bill Siegal, Free History Project, 2002.

29. Bill Ayers, *Fugitive Days: A Memoir* (Boston: Beacon Press, 2001), 242.

30. *The People, Plaintiff and Respondent, v. Timothy Francis Leary, Defendant and Appellant*, Court of Appeals of California, Second Appellate District, Division One, July 5, 1974, Justia, https://law.justia.com/cases/california/court-of-appeal/3d/40/527.html.

31. "Basic Information on Vietnam Women's Union," Vietnam Women's Union, April 20, 2005, http://hoilhpn.org.vn/newsdetail.asp?CatId=66&NewsId=819&lang=EN.

32. Laura Whitehorn, "The Seabirds Don't Lie," *Feminist Wire*, November 26, 2014, http://www.thefeministwire.com/2014/11/toni-cade-bambara-and-vietnam/.

33. Frantz Fanon, *The Wretched of the Earth*, trans. Constance Farrington (New York: Grove Press, 1963), 94.

34. U.S. Department of the Army, *Unconventional Warfare Devices and Techniques—References*, April 1966, Internet Archive, https://archive.org

/stream/milmanual-tm-31-200-1-unconventional-warfare-devices-and-tech niques—-/tm_31-200-1_unconventional_warfare_devices_and_techniques _-_references_djvu.txt.

35. Brian Burrough, "Meet the Weather Underground's Bomb Guru," *Vanity Fair*, March 29, 2015, https://www.vanityfair.com/culture/2015/03/weather -underground-bomb-guru-burrough-excerpt.

11. WE ARE THE REVOLUTIONARY FIGHTING GROUP

1. Stephen Kinzer, "Federal Office Building on Staten Island Damaged by a Bomb," *New York Times*, January 30, 1983, http://www.nytimes.com /1983/01/30/nyregion/federal-office-building-on-staten-island-damaged-by -a-bomb.html.

2. *United States of America v. Laura Whitehorn, et al.*, Cr. 88-0145, "Defendants' Reply to Government's Response to Defendant's Motion to Dismiss for Pros-ecutorial Misconduct," undated, U.S. District Court for the District of Colum-bia, E. Barrett Prettyman U.S. Courthouse, 6.

3. Jon B. Jansen and Stefan Weyl, *The Silent War: The Underground Movement in Germany* (Philadelphia and New York: J. B. Lippincott, 1943), 152.

4. FBI, "May 19th Communist Organization: Domestic Security/Terrorism Investigation: Office of Origin, New York," October 1, 1991, 2 (FBI FOIA release).

5. Cathy Wilkerson, *Flying Close to the Sun: My Life and Times as a Weatherman* (New York: Seven Stories Press, 2007), 379.

6. "Thoughts on the Surrender of Kathy Power," Urban Guerilla, http://ur banguerilla.org/wp-content/uploads/United-States/6-Political-Prisoners /4-Secondary-Sources/1993/Thoughts-on-the-Surrender-of-Kathy-Power -December-1993.pdf.

7. Photocopy of untitled, undated, M19th document in author's possession.

8. Susan Rosenberg, *An American Radical: A Political Prisoner in My Own Coun-try* (New York: Kensington Publishing Corp., 2011), 10.

9. *United States of America v. Laura Whitehorn, et al.*, Cr. 88-0145, government exhibit T, U.S. District Court for the District of Columbia, E. Barrett Pretty-man U.S. Courthouse.

10. *United States of America v. Laura Whitehorn, et al.*, Cr. 88-0145, government exhibit P, "Rules of Security and Operations," U.S. District Court for the Dis-trict of Columbia, E. Barrett Prettyman U.S. Courthouse, 1.

11. "Resistance Conspiracy Case," *off our backs*, Vol. 19, No. 5, May 1989, JSTOR, https://www.jstor.org/stable/i25796799.

12. U.S. Department of Justice, press release, May 11, 1988, Montgomery Blair Sibley website, http://www.montgomeryblairsibley.com/library/Duke6.pdf.

13. "Giorgio," *Memoirs of an Italian Terrorist* (New York: Carroll & Graf, 2003), 156.

14. "Washington Navy Yard, Alan's Duty Station, Aug 1964–Oct 1966," *The World This Week* (blog), September 16, 2013, http://alansviews.blogspot.com /2013/09/washington-navy-yard-alans-duty-station.html.

15. "Navy Regional Data Automation Center, Washington, D.C. Procurement of Automatic Data Processing Equipment," August 24, 1990, Defense Technical Information Center, http://www.dtic.mil/docs/citations/ADA380993.

16. "Informal Interorganizational Glossary of EOD Terminology," March 2017, Explosive Ordnance Disposal Centre of Excellence, https://www.eodcoe.org /files/en/standardization/concept-doctrine-standardization/terminology /new-eod-terminology.pdf.

17. "Washington Navy Yard Feels Bomb Blast in Computer Area," *New York Times*, August 18, 1983, http://www.nytimes.com/1983/08/18/us/washing ton-navy-yard-feels-bomb-blast-in-computer-area.html.

18. *United States v. Laura Whitehorn, et al.*, Cr. 88-145, "Government's Memorandum in Aid of Sentencing," United States District Court for the District of Columbia, E. Barrett Prettyman U.S. Courthouse, November 13, 1990, 3.

19. "Armed Resistance Unit: Communiqué No. 2," August 17, 1983, in Committee to Fight Repression, *"Build a Revolutionary Resistance Movement": Communiqués from the North American Armed Clandestine Movement, 1982–1985* (New York: Committee to Fight Repression, 1985), 9.

20. U.S. Department of Justice, press release, May 11, 1988, America's Survival, http://www.usasurvival.org/home/docs/buck_indictment.pdf.

21. Ibid.

22. Alan Berkman, unpublished memoir/manuscript, undated, "Chapter 2—in the garbage. Underground," undated, Alan Berkman Papers, Archives & Special Collections, Columbia University Health Sciences Library, 2.

23. "Thoughts on the Surrender of Kathy Power."

24. Kelley Ellsworth, "Resistance Conspiracy Case," *off our backs*, May 31, 1989, 20–21.

25. Quoted in Alison Jamieson, *The Heart Attacked: Terrorism and Conflict in the Italian State* (London and New York: Marion Boyars, 1989), 267–68.

26. Susan Rosenberg, *An American Radical: A Political Prisoner in My Own Country* (New York: Kensington Publishing Corp., 2011), 9.

27. "Resistance Conspiracy Case," *off our backs*, Vol. 19, No. 5, May 1989, JSTOR, https://www.jstor.org/stable/i25796799.

28. Quoted in Alison Jamieson, "Entry, Discipline and Exit in the Italian Red Brigades," *Terrorism and Political Violence* 2, no. 1 (1990): 5.

29. Photocopy of untitled, undated M19th document in author's possession.

30. Sarah Schulman, *The Sophie Horowitz Story* (Tallahassee, FL: Naiad Press, 1984), 17.

31. Photocopy of untitled, undated M19th document in author's possession.

12. TONIGHT WE BOMBED THE U.S. CAPITOL

1. FBI, FD-302, November 10, 1983, 1 (FBI FOIA release).

2. U.S. Senate, "Bomb Explodes in Capitol," November 7, 1983, United States Senate, https://www.senate.gov/artandhistory/history/minute/bomb_ex plodes_in_capitol.htm.

3. Robert Pear, "Bomb Explodes in Senate's Wing of Capitol; No Injuries Reported," *New York Times*, November 8, 1983, http://www.nytimes.com /1983/11/08/us/bomb-explodes-in-senate-s-wing-of-capitol-no-injuries-re ported.html.

4. Quoted in A. Sexton, "In Dubious Battle," *Pacific Historical Review* 73, no. 2 (May 2004), JSTOR, https://www.jstor.org/stable/10.1525/phr.2004.73.2.249 ?seq=1#page_scan_tab_contents.

5. Armed Resistance Unit, "Communiqué No. 3: The U.S. Capitol Bombing, November 7, 1983," in Committee to Fight Repression, *"Build a Revolutionary Resistance Movement": Communiqués from the North American Armed Clandestine Movement, 1982–1985* (New York: Committee to Fight Repression, 1985), 13.

6. Ibid., 14.

7. "Armed Resistance Movement—Capitol Bombing—November 7, 1984," *Arm the Spirit—For Revolutionary Resistance*, December 5, 2017, https://armthe spiritforrevolutionaryresistance.wordpress.com/2017/12/05/armed-resist ance-unit-capitol-bombing-november-7-1983/.

8. Ibid.

9. FBI, FD-302, November 9, 1983, 1 (FBI FOIA release).

10. FBI, FD-302, November 10, 1983, 1 (FBI FOIA release).

11. Ibid., 1.

12. FBI, FD-302, November 14, 1983, unpaginated.

13. U.S. Senate Select Committee on Intelligence, *The FBI Investigation of the Committee in Solidarity with the People of El Salvador (CISPES)* (Washington, DC: U.S. Government Printing Office, 1989), 52–53.

14. *USA v. Laura Whitehorn, et al.*, Cr. 88-145-01, "Government's Supplemental Response to Defendant Whitehorn's Motion for Reconsideration of Bond," U.S. District Court for the District of Columbia, E. Barrett Prettyman U.S. Courthouse, May 26, 1989, attachment marked "C61-2-70."

15. *USA v. Laura Whitehorn, et al.*, Cr. 88-145-01, U.S. District Court for the District of Columbia, E. Barrett Prettyman U.S. Courthouse, attachment marked "Q10, 645X, FBI Laboratory."

16. "Red Guerrilla Resistance, April 4, 1984," in Committee to Fight Repression, *"Build a Revolutionary Resistance Movement,"* 34.

17. Richard Halloran, "Large Exercise with Honduras to Start April 1," *New York Times*, March 24, 1984, https://www.nytimes.com/1984/03/24/world/large-exercise-with-honduras-to-start-april-1.html.

18. Vincent Del Giudice, "A Bomb Exploded at the Officer's Club," UPI, April 20, 1984, https://www.upi.com/Archives/1984/04/20/A-bomb-exploded-at-the-officers-club-at-the/1056451285200/.

19. Ibid.

20. "Red Guerrilla Resistance, April 20, 1984," in Committee to Fight Repression, *"Build a Revolutionary Resistance Movement,"* 36.

21. *United States of America v. Linda Sue Evans*, Cr. N-85-36 PD, transcript of testimony of J. Kenneth Moore, Jr., United States District Court, District of Connecticut, National Archives at Boston, 140.

13. THIS WILL BLOW A HOLE IN YOU

1. U.S. Drug Enforcement Administration (DEA), DEA headquarters, Washington, DC, from DEA Hartford RO, "Impersonation of Federal Agents," September 17, 1984, 1 (FBI FOIA release).

2. FBI, Director, FBI, from New Haven, airtel, "Attn: Criminal Investigative Division/Fugitive Unit," January 23, 1985, 5 (FBI FOIA release).

3. Vincent Del Giudice, "FBI Looks for Possible Link in Latest Bombing," UPI, April 20, 1984, https://www.upi.com/Archives/1984/04/20/FBI-looks-for-possible-link-in-latest-bombing/4420451285200/.

4. FBI, "May 19th Communist Organization: Domestic Security/Terrorism Investigation: Office of Origin, New York," October 1, 1991, 9 (FBI FOIA release).

5. "Armed Resistance Unit/Revolutionary Fighting Group/Red Guerrilla Resistance Communiqués," *Arm the Spirit*, December 12, 2017, https://armthespir itforrevolutionaryresistance.wordpress.com/2017/12/12/armed-resistance -unit-revolutionary-fighting-group-red-guerrilla-resistance-Communiqués/.

14. PUT OUT THE FUCKING CIGARETTE

1. Photocopy of undated May 19th letter, "Greetings comrades," in author's possession.
2. *United States of America v. Susan Lisa Rosenberg and Timothy Blunk*, Cr. 84-360, grand jury indictment, United States District Court for the District of New Jersey, Martin Luther King, Jr. Federal Building and Courthouse, Newark, NJ, December 6, 1984, 1.
3. *United States of America v. Susan Lisa Rosenberg and Timothy Blunk*, Cr. 84-360, "Findings of Fact," United States District Court for the District of New Jersey, Martin Luther King, Jr. Federal Building and Courthouse, Newark, NJ, December 21, 1984, 11.
4. Ibid.
5. Quoted in Henry Hurt, "The Capture of Susan Lisa Rosenberg," *Reader's Digest*, April 1985, 72.
6. "Prints of Fugitive Tied to Chesimard," *Newark Star-Ledger*, March 16, 1985.
7. *United States v. Susan Lisa Rosenberg and Timothy Blunk*, Cr. 84-360, superseded indictment, filed February 28, 1985, 10–11, U.S. District Court for the District of New Jersey, Martin Luther King Federal Building and Courthouse.
8. *United States v. Susan Lisa Rosenberg and Timothy Blunk*, Cr. 84-360, "Findings of Fact and Conclusions of Law," December 17, 1984, 8, U.S. District Court for the District of New Jersey, Martin Luther King Federal Building and Courthouse.
9. "Susan Rosenberg and Tim Blunk," *Breakthrough: Political Journal of Prairie Fire Organizing Committee*, IX, no. 1 (Spring/Summer 1985), 50.
10. Quoted in Hurt, "The Capture of Susan Lisa Rosenberg," 74.
11. Susan Rosenberg, *An American Radical: A Political Prisoner in My Own Country* (New York: Kensington Publishing Corp., 2011), 17.
12. *United States of America v. Laura Whitehorn, et al.*, Cr. 88-0145, "Self-criticism," government exhibit B, U.S. District Court for the District of Columbia, E. Barrett Prettyman U.S. Courthouse, undated.
13. Ibid., 8.
14. Author's interview with Donald R. Wofford, Wilmington, NC, February 27, 2017.

15. *U.S. v. Whitehorn*, 652 F. Supp. 395 (S.D.N.Y., 1987), https://casetext.com /case/us-v-whitehorn-2.

16. *United States of America v. Laura Whitehorn, et al.*, Cr. 88-0145, "Dear Friends," government exhibit A, U.S. District Court for the District of Columbia, E. Barrett Prettyman U.S. Courthouse, January 23, 1989, 2.

17. Ibid.

18. Quoted in Katherine Boo, "Tim Blunk's War," *Washington City Paper*, August 25–31, 1989, 20.

19. *United States of America v. Susan Lisa Rosenberg and Timothy Blunk*, Cr. 84-360, "Transcript of Proceedings (Sentence)," United States District Court for the District of New Jersey, Martin Luther King, Jr. Federal Building and Courthouse, May 20, 1985, 31.

20. *United States of America v. Susan Lisa Rosenberg and Timothy Blunk*, Cr. 84-360, "Excerpt of Transcript of Proceedings," December 21, 1984, United States District Court for the District of New Jersey, Martin Luther King, Jr. Federal Building and Courthouse, 1.

21. Quoted in Katie Zezima, "Cruz Calls Trump's Sister a 'Radical Pro-Abortion Extremist' Judge," *Washington Post*, February 15, 2016, https://www .washingtonpost.com/news/post-politics/wp/2016/02/15/cruz-calls -trumps-sister-a-radical-pro-abortion-extremist-judge/?utm_term=.2b 9515ddcbe9.

15. *REALITÄTSVERLUST*

1. Carlos Marighella, *Mini-Manual of the Urban Guerrilla* (Toronto: Arm the Spirit, 2002), 28.

2. Mark Kram, "A Wink at a Homely Girl," *Sports Illustrated*, October 10, 1966, https://www.si.com/vault/1966/10/10/612169/a-wink-at-a-homely-girl.

3. *United States of America v. Alan Berkman*, Cr. 85-0222, "Government's Proposed Findings of Fact and Conclusions of Law Re: Search of the Alameda Apartment on May 11, 1985," January 14, 1987, U.S. District Court, Eastern District of Pennsylvania, Philadelphia Federal Records Center, 2.

4. FBI wanted poster, June 13, 1982 (original in author's possession).

5. Ibid.

6. *United States of America v. Linda Sue Evans*, "Government's Sentencing Memorandum," Cr. 85-337, U.S. District Court, Eastern District of Louisiana (photocopy in author's possession), undated, 6.

7. Konrad Kellen, "On Terrorists and Terrorism," RAND Corporation, December

1982, https://www.rand.org/content/dam/rand/pubs/notes/2005/N1942 .pdf.

8. Gilda Zwerman, Patricia Steinhoff, and Donatella Porta, "Disappearing Social Movements: Clandestinity in the Cycle of New Left Protest in the U.S., Japan, Germany, and Italy," *Mobilization: An International Quarterly* 5, no. 1 (2000): 97, http://mobilizationjournal.org/doi/abs/10.17813/maiq.5.1 .0w068105721660n0.

9. *United States of America v. Laura Whitehorn, et al.*, Cr. 88-0145, government exhibit T, U.S. District Court for the District of Columbia, E. Barrett Pretty-man U.S. Courthouse.

10. Dennis Tourish, "How Cults Can Produce Killers," *Irish Times*, July 16, 2005, https://www.irishtimes.com/opinion/how-cults-can-produce-killers-1.469140.

11. Bruce Vail, "Park Slope Radicals Keep Talking as Fed Grand Jury Probes Con-nections to Nyack Shootout," *Phoenix* (Brooklyn), March 18, 1982, Freedom archives.org, http://freedomarchives.org/Documents/Finder/DOC43_scans /43.article.phoenix.3.18.1982.pdf

12. *United States of America v. Laura Whitehorn, et al.*, Cr. 88-0145, "Government's Memorandum in Aid of Sentencing," U.S. District Court for the District of Columbia, E. Barrett Prettyman U.S. Courthouse, 16.

13. *United States of America v. Laura Whitehorn, et al.*, Cr. 88-0145, "Opinion," U.S. District Court for the District of Columbia, E. Barrett Prettyman U.S. Court-house, 54.

14. Erik Nielson, "'It Could Have Been Me': The 1983 Death of a NYC Graffiti Artist," *Code Switch*, NPR, September 16, 2013, http://www.npr.org/sections /codeswitch/2013/09/16/221821224/it-could-have-been-me-the-1983-death -of-a-nyc-graffiti-artist.

15. Selwyn Raab, "Autopsy Finds Bumpurs Was Hit by Two Blasts," *New York Times*, November 27, 1984, http://www.nytimes.com/1984/11/27/nyregion /autopsy-finds-bumpurs-was-hit-by-two-blasts.html.

16. Committee to Fight Repression, *"Build a Revolutionary Resistance Move-ment": Communiqués from the North American Armed Clandestine Movement, 1982–1985* (New York: Committee to Fight Repression, 1985), 50.

17. "Statements of Susan Rosenberg and Tim Blunk, Anti-imperialist Resistance Fighters," May 20, 1985, Freedomarchives.org, https://freedomarchives.org /Documents/Finder/DOC511_scans/RCC/511.RCC.StatementsOfSusan RosenbergAndTimBlunk.5.20.85.pdf.

18. "Clifford Glover Contingent: Stop Killer Cops" (Coloring book), Freedomar

chives.org, http://www.freedomarchives.org/Documents/Finder/DOC37 _scans/37.Clifford.Glover.Coloring.Book.Web.pdf.

19. Ibid.

20. Committee to Fight Repression, *"Build a Revolutionary Resistance Movement,"* 53.

21. *United States v. Laura Whitehorn, et al.*, Cr. 88-145, "Government's Memorandum in Aid of Sentencing," U.S. District Court for the District of Columbia, E. Barrett Prettyman U.S. Courthouse, November 13, 1990, 16.

22. Committee to Fight Repression, *"Build a Revolutionary Resistance Movement,"* 50.

23. *Out: The Making of a Revolutionary* (documentary), directed by Rhonda Collins and Sonja De Vries, Film Arts Foundation, 2000.

24. *United States of America v. Rosado, et al.*, Cr. 83-0025, "Sentence Memorandum of the United States," U.S. District Court, Eastern District of New York, 52.

25. *United States of America v. Elizabeth Anna Duke*, Cr. 85-222-02, U.S. District Court, Eastern District of Pennsylvania, undated, Philadelphia Federal Records Center, 48.

26. *United States v. Laura Whitehorn, et al.*, Cr. 88-0145, government exhibit D, U.S. District Court for the District of Columbia, E. Barrett Prettyman U.S. Courthouse, undated, 3.

27. Albert Bandura, "Mechanisms of Moral Disengagement in Terrorism," in Walter Reich (ed.), *Origins of Terrorism: Psychologies, Ideologies, Theologies, States of Mind* (Washington, DC: Woodrow Wilson Center Press, 1998), 176.

28. *United States of America v. Alan Berkman*, Cr. 85-222, "Government's Sentencing Memorandum," U.S. District Court, Eastern District of Pennsylvania, National Archives at Philadelphia, 1.

16. NONCONSENSUAL ENTRY

1. *United States v. Laura Whitehorn, et al.*, Cr. 88-0145, government exhibit Q, U.S. District Court for the District of Columbia, E. Barrett Prettyman U.S. Courthouse, undated, 1.

2. *United States v. Laura Whitehorn, et al.*, Cr. 88-0145, "Affadavit of Raymond Jechorek, Jr.," U.S. District Court for the District of Columbia, E. Barrett Prettyman U.S. Courthouse, January 23, 1989, 2.

3. *United States of America v. Marilyn Buck*, 84 Cr. 220 (CSH), "Government's Memorandum of Law in Opposition to Buck's Motion to Suppress Evidence Seized from Apartment D, Building 5714, The Alameda, Baltimore, Maryland,"

U.S. District Court, Southern District of New York, Daniel Patrick Moynihan Courthouse, September 8, 1987, 6.

4. "In Re: John Doe, testimony of John Mandrafina," Grand Jury Proceedings, May 16, 1985, Boston Federal Records Center.

5. *United States of America v. Marilyn Buck*, September 8, 1987; *US v. Shakur*, 82 Cr. 312, "Government's Memorandum in Opposition."

6. Jane Gross, "Brink's Suspect Held Without Bail After She Refuses to Enter Plea," *New York Times*, May 14, 1985.

7. *United States of America v. Linda Sue Evans*, Cr. 85-337, U.S. District Court, Southern District of New York, Government's Sentencing Memorandum, November 14, 1985, 8.

8. *United States of America v. Linda Sue Evans*, Cr. N-85-36 (PCD), FBI FD-302, "SA Donald William Gavin and SA William J. Rhodes," May 16, 1985, U.S. District Court, District of Connecticut, Boston Federal Records Center, 1.

9. *U.S. v. Whitehorn*, 652 F. Supp. 395 (S.D.N.Y. 1987), https://casetext.com/case /us-v-whitehorn-2.

10. *United States of America v. Alan Berkman*, Cr. 85-222, "Findings of Fact," January 14, 1987, U.S. District Court, Eastern District of Pennsylvania, Philadelphia Federal Records Center, 8.

11. Ibid.

12. District of Columbia Metropolitan Joint Terrorist Task Force (JTTF) to Hebert Rutherford, memorandum, U.S. Marshal for the District of Columbia, "Summary Background: *US v. Laura Whitehorn, et al.*," CR 88-145, May 26, 1988, U.S. District Court, District of Columbia, E. Barrett Prettyman U.S. Courthouse, 4.

13. State of New York Department of Correctional Services, "Inmate Misbehavior Report," 83G-313, September 4, 1985, 1 (photocopy in author's possession).

14. *United States of America v. Alan Berkman*, Cr. 85-222, "Findings of Fact," January 14, 1987, U.S. District Court, Eastern District of Pennsylvania, Philadelphia Federal Records Center, 11.

15. U.S. Department of Justice, Federal Bureau of Investigation, "Baltimore Division: June 21, 1985," June 21, 1985, 1 (FBI FOIA release).

16. *United States of America v. Alan Berkman*, Cr. 85-222, testimony of Special Agent William A. Scobie, U.S. District Court, Eastern District of Pennsylvania, Philadelphia Federal Records Center, 132.

17. "U.S. Special Grand Jury Proceedings in re: Laura Jane Whitehorn," June 7, 1985, 8, U.S. District Court for the District of Maryland, in *United States of*

America v. Laura Whitehorn, et al., Cr. No. 88-145-05, "Memorandum of Points and Authorities in Support of Defendants' Motion to Dismiss the Indictment for Governmental Misconduct," U.S. District Court for the District of Columbia, E. Barrett Prettyman U.S. Courthouse, January 31, 1989, 10–11.

17. PUT YOUR GODDAMN HANDS UP WHERE WE CAN SEE THEM

1. *United States of America v. Alan Berkman*, Cr. 85-222, "Statement of the Facts," undated, U.S. District Court, Eastern District of Pennsylvania, Philadelphia Federal Records Center, 1.
2. Alan Berkman, unpublished memoir/manuscript, "1. The Bust," undated, 1, Alan Berkman Papers, Archives & Special Collections, Columbia University Health Sciences Library, 1.
3. Ibid., 2.
4. *United States of America v. Alan Berkman*, Criminal No. 85-222, Letter from Morales to Berkman, marked "A1-9-E p. 6," U.S. District Court, Eastern District of Pennsylvania, Philadelphia Federal Records Center, 1.
5. Berkman, "1. The Bust," 2.
6. Ibid., 3.
7. Selwyn Raab, "New York Doctor Held as Fugitive in Brink's Case," *New York Times*, May 25, 1985, http://www.nytimes.com/1985/05/25/nyregion/new-york-doctor-held-as-fugitive-in-brink-s-case.html.
8. *United States of America v. Alan Berkman*, Cr. 85-222, "Government's Sentencing Memorandum," April 29, 1987, U.S. District Court, Eastern District of Pennsylvania, Philadelphia Federal Records Center, 11.
9. *U.S. v. Berkman*, Cr. 85-222, testimony of Michael Macys, U.S. District Court, Eastern District of Pennsylvania, Philadelphia Federal Records Center, 29.
10. Ibid., 30.
11. *U.S. v. Berkman*, Cr. 85-222, statement of Elizabeth Duke, U.S. District Court, Eastern District of Pennsylvania, Philadelphia Federal Records Center, 10.
12. Ibid., 6.
13. Ibid., 20.
14. *United States of America v. Elizabeth Anna Duke*, CR. 85-222-02, "Government's Memorandum in Opposition to Defendant's Motion for Revocation of Detention Order," U.S. District Court, Eastern District of Pennsylvania, Philadelphia Federal Records Center, 4.

AFTERMATH

1. *United States of America v. Laura Whitehorn, et al.*, 710 F. Supp. 803 (D.D.C. 1989), April 11, 1989, https://casetext.com/case/us-v-whitehorn.

2. *United States of America v. Laura Whitehorn, et al.*, grand jury indictment (June 3, 1987), U.S. District Court for the District of Columbia, America's Survival website, https://www.usasurvival.org/home/docs/buck_indict ment.pdf.

3. *United States of America v. Laura Whitehorn*, 710 F. Supp. 803 (D.D.C. 1989), April 11, 1989.

4. FBI, Acting Director [name redacted], from Los Angeles, undated, 3; and FBI, "May 19th Communist Organization: Domestic Security/Terrorism Investigation/Office of Origin: New York, October 1, 1991, 28 (FBI FOIA releases).

5. Diana Block, *Arm the Spirit: A Woman's Journey Underground and Back* (Oakland, CA: AK Press, 2009), 166.

6. John Kifner, "Neighbors Anyone Would Want, and Most Wanted by F.B.I., Too," *New York Times*, December 9, 1994, https://www.nytimes.com/1994/12/09/us/neighbors-anyone-would-want-and-most-wanted-by-fbi-too.html.

7. "Statements of Susan Rosenberg and Tim Blunk, Anti-imperialist Resistance Fighters," Freedomarchives.org, https://freedomarchives.org/Documents/Finder/DOC511_scans/RCC/511.RCC.StatementsOfSusanRosenbergAndTimBlunk.5.20.85.pdf.

8. "When Your Husband Has AIDS; The Victims Within; America's Toughest Prison," ABC News, April 10, 1982.

9. Quoted in Jeffrey Mervis, "Researcher Loses Job at NSF After Government Questions Her Role as 1980s Activist," *Science*, September 10, 2014, https://www.sciencemag.org/news/2014/09/researcher-loses-job-nsf-after-government-questions-her-role-1980s-activist.

10. Letter from J. Michael Quinlan to Ian Martin [Amnesty International], U.S. Department of Justice, Bureau of Prisons, June 12, 1987, 1, (photocopy in author's possession).

11. Amnesty International, "United States of America: The High Security Unit, Lexington Federal Prison, Kentucky," AMR 51/34/88, August 1988, Freedom archives.org, https://freedomarchives.org/Documents/Finder/DOC510_scans/Lexington/510.amnesty.international.lexington.report.1988.pdf.

12. Quoted in Charles Mitchell, "The Soviet Union Launched A Counterattack Friday on President Reagan," UPI, May 27, 1988, https://www.upi.com/Ar

chives/1988/05/27/The-Soviet-Union-launched-a-counterattack-Friday-on -President/5419580708800/.

13. Quoted in Mary McGrory, "Awaiting a Daughter's Return," *Washington Post*, October 2, 1990, https://www.washingtonpost.com/archive/politics/1990 /10/02/awaiting-a-daughters-return/0265e90e-77b6-4ebc-a11b-58e72c7cd 087/?utm_term=.a7480e72ef5c.

14. U.S. Department of Justice, "Department of Justice Statement Regarding the Transfer of Silvia Baraldini," August 24, 1999, United States Department of Justice, https://www.justice.gov/archive/opa/pr/1999/August/375crm.htm.

15. Gian Marco Chiocci and Massimo Malpica, "Baraldini Does Not Change Her Hair: Rally With Former US Terrorists," *Il Giornale* (Milan), April 11, 2008.

16. Benjamin Weiser, "Former Terrorist Now Fights for Parole," *New York Times*, November 5, 1999, https://www.nytimes.com/1999/11/05/nyregion/former -terrorist-now-fights-for-parole.html.

17. U.S. Senate, Committee on the Judiciary, "President Clinton's Eleventh Hour Pardons," February 14, 2001, https://www.govinfo.gov/content/pkg/CHRG -107shrg76344/html/CHRG-107shrg76344.htm.

18. *Conspiracy of Voices: Poetry, Writing and Art by the Women of the Resistance Conspiracy Case* (Washington, DC: Emergency Committee to Defend the Human and Legal Rights of Political Prisoners, 1990), 2.

19. Dan Berger, "Marilyn Buck's Playlist," *Polygraph* 23–24 (2013), 112.

20. Quoted in Polman, "Tempo: Story Behind the Mystery Man of the Brinks Job," *Chicago Tribune*, January 2, 1986, D1.

21. Transcript of Dick Polman interview with Berkman, August 1985, Berkman Papers, Archives & Special Collections, Columbia University Health Sciences Library.

22. Ibid.

23. FBI, "PH 183G-1915 SUC C (SQ10)" (FBI FOIA release).

24. Russell Rickford, " 'Liberated Territories' and Black Radical Praxis," *Black Perspectives*, March 24, 2016, https://www.aaihs.org/liberated-territories/.

25. Jan Hoffman, "Healing on Parole; Doctor and Ex-prisoner, He Treats Others on Probation," *New York Times*, January 10, 1994, https://www.nytimes .com/1994/01/10/nyregion/healing-on-parole-doctor-and-ex-prisoner-he -treats-others-on-probation.html.

26. Greg Donaldson, *Zebratown: The True Story of a Black Ex-con and a White Single Mother in Small-Town America* (New York: Simon & Schuster, 2010), 209.

27. Rachel Nolan, "Behind the Cover Story: Tom Robbins on Judith Clark," *New*

York Times, January 17, 2012, https://6thfloor.blogs.nytimes.com/2012/01/17 /behind-the-cover-story-tom-robbins-on-judith-clark/.

28. *People of the State of New York v. Judith Clark*, indictment nos. 81-285, 82-6, affidavit of Judith Clark, December 2002, Parole for Judy Clark website, https:// judithclark.org/17/wp-content/uploads/2016/12/judy_clark_2002_affida vit.pdf.

29. Jim Dwyer, "She Faced Cuomo and Got Clemency: He Got 'a Sense of Her Soul,'" *New York Times*, January 3, 2017, https://www.nytimes.com/2017/01 /03/nyregion/new-york-judith-clark-gov-andrew-cuomo-clemency.html.

30. Ibid.

31. Quoted in Thomas Tracy, "Sergeant's Union Boss Livid after Gov. Cuomo Commutes Sentence of Judith Clark, Driver in Deadly Brinks Robbery," *Daily News* (New York), December 31, 2016, https://www.nydailynews.com/new-york/sba -boss-blasts-cuomo-cutting-judith-clark-sentence-short-article-1.2929809.

32. Quoted in "Rockland County Executive Ed Day's Statement on Commutation of Brinks Robbery Criminal's Sentence," *Rockland County Times*, December 30, 2016, https://www.rocklandtimes.com/2016/12/30/rockland-county -executive-ed-days-statement-on-commutation-of-brinks-robbery-crimi nals-sentence/.

33. New York State Department of Corrections and Community Supervision, "Parole Board Hearing of Judith Clark," April 20, 2017, 196.

34. Carl Campanile, "Parole Board Rejects Cuomo's Request to Release Brinks Robbery Driver," *New York Post*, April 21, 2017, https://nypost.com/2017 /04/21/parole-board-rejects-cuomos-request-to-release-weather-under ground-driver/.

35. Glenn Blain, "Parole Denied for Judith Clark Who Was Granted Clemency by Cuomo for Her Role in Fatal Weather Underground Heist," *Daily News* (New York), April 21, 2017, https://www.nydailynews.com/news/crime/judith -clark-denied-parole-cuomo-granted-clemency-heist-article-1.3087241.

36. Quoted in Denis Slattery and Larry McShane, "One-Time Radical Judith Clark Paroled 38 Years After Notorious Triple Homicide in 1981 Brinks Armored Car Robbery," *Daily News* (New York), April 17, 2019, https://www.nydailynews .com/new-york/ny-judith-clark-paroled-20190417-xihs5hhcz5c7rfbgd4n fh324gq-story.html.

37. Police Benevolent Association, "NYC PBA Statement on Parole of Judith Clark," April 17, 2019, https://www.nycpba.org/press-releases/2019/pba-on -judith-clark-parole/.

38. Byron A. Sage, Mack Wallace, and Carolyn Wier, "The Central Texas Counterterrorism Working Group," *FBI Law Enforcement Bulletin* 64, no. 3 (March 1995): 9, National Criminal Justice Reference Service, https://www.ncjrs.gov/pdffiles1/Digitization/154478NCJRS.pdf.

39. Martha Trowbridge, "Terrible Truth," March 21, 2014, http://terribletruth.marthatrowbridgeradio.org/blog/2014/05/21/america-held-hostage/.

40. Jeremy Tanner and Mary Murphy, "FBI May Be Close to Catching 'Thelma and Louise' Fugitives: $50,000 Reward," PIX11, September 27, 2013, https://pix11.com/2013/09/27/fbi-hunting-for-thelma-and-louise-criminals-in-81-killing-acid-attack-on-a-cop/.

41. "Interpol's Most Wanted Americans," CBS News, https://www.cbsnews.com/pictures/interpols-most-wanted-americans/8.

42. Quoted in Roz Hamlett with Joseph Pentangelo, "PAPD: Bringing a Fugitive to Justice," *Portfolio*, September 6, 2016, https://portfolio.panynj.gov/2016/09/06/papd-bringing-a-fugitive-to-justice/.

43. Mary Patten, *Revolution as an Eternal Dream: The Exemplary Failure of the Madame Binh Graphics Collective* (Chicago: Half Letter Press, 2011), 11.

44. Daniel Oppenheimer, *Exit Right: The People Who Left the Left and Reshaped the American Century* (New York: Simon & Schuster, 2016), 59.

45. "Open Letter: Standing with Palestine in the Spirit of 'Sumud,'" *openDemocracy*, April 28, 2016, https://www.opendemocracy.net/us-prisoner-labor-and-academic-solidarity-delegation-to-palestine/open-letter-standing-with-palestine.

46. Ned Ryun, "Antifa Is a Domestic Terrorist Organization and Must Be Denounced By Democrats," Fox News, September 18, 2017, https://www.foxnews.com/opinion/antifa-is-a-domestic-terrorist-organization-and-must-be-denounced-by-democrats.

47. Kathleen Belew, *Bring the War Home: The White Power Movement and Paramilitary America* (Cambridge, MA, and London: Harvard University Press, 2018).

48. David M. Perry, "How White American Terrorists Are Radicalized," *Pacific Standard*, March 26, 2018, https://psmag.com/social-justice/how-white-american-terrorists-are-radicalized.

49. George W. Bush, "President Discusses War on Terrorism," U.S. Department of State, November 8, 2001, https://2001-2009.state.gov/s/ct/rls/rm/2001/5998.htm.

INDEX

Page numbers in *italics* refer to picture captions.

295

ABOUT THE AUTHOR

WILLIAM ROSENAU, Ph.D., is a senior research scientist at CNA, a nonprofit research and analysis organization, and a fellow in the International Security program at New America. He has also worked as a political scientist at RAND, as a counterterrorism adviser at the State Department, as a special assistant in the Pentagon's special operations office, and as a staffer on a U.S. Senate terrorism subcommittee. His articles have been published in the *New York Times*, the *Wall Street Journal*, *Foreign Policy*, the *National Interest*, and the *Atlantic*. He has appeared on CNN, *BBC World News*, *CBS Evening News*, and elsewhere, and currently lives in Washington, DC.